INDUSTRIAL LAW

INDUSTRIAL LAW

Volume I

ARUN KUMAR

ATLANTIC
PUBLISHERS & DISTRIBUTORS

Published by
ATLANTIC PUBLISHERS AND DISTRIBUTORS
B-2, Vishal Enclave, Opp. Rajouri Garden, New Delhi-27
Phones : 5413460, 5429987, 5466842

Sales Office
4215/1, Ansari Road, Darya Ganj, New Delhi-110 002
Phones : 3273880, 3285873, 3280451
Fax : 91-11-3285873
e-mail : info@atlantibooks.com
web : www.atlanticbooks.com

ISBN 81-269-0209-4 Vol. I
ISBN 81-269-0210-8 Vol. II
ISBN 81-269-0199-3 Set

Typeset at
APD Computer Graphics, Delhi
Printed in India at
Nice Printing Press, Delhi

PREFACE

This ideal textbook deals with the study of Industrial Law in details to meet the specific requirements of the students, teachers and laymen.

Most of the books written on the subject are just compilation of the various Acts passed by the Indian Government relating to industry laws, rules and regulations. As this textbook is meant for the students, I have taken special pains to help the readers in the memorization of the subject. Thus, while the subject of the book has been sub-divided into many chapters, each chapter has been sub-divided into topics given in central headings. Each topic in the central heading has been further sub-divided into side headings. Then, each side heading has been further sub-divided into a number of running headings. These have been numbered as 1, 2, 3, etc. Each such numbers have been further divided into (i), (ii), (iii), etc. Each of these have been further sub-divided into (a), (b), (c), etc.

Thus, each Act mentioned in this book carries central headings, side headings and running headings numbered as described above. Where the Act does not have headings, I have inserted my own headings for clarification. Where numbers are not marked in the Act itself I have marked them in the above order.

This pedagogical method of presentation of the latest matter drawn from authentic sources shall make the book particularly valuable to the students. Thus, facilitation of memorization of the subject is a unique feature of the book. Besides, simple and lucid language, practical problems, questions for exercise are challenging features that require students to assimilate what they have learned.

Suggestions, if any, for the improvement of the book in the next edition are very cordially invited.

ARUN KUMAR

CONTENTS

VOLUME 2

PART FIVE

SOCIAL SECURITY

PART ONE
INTRODUCTORY

1
Industrial Legislations in India

LEGISLATION PERTAINING TO WAGES

Payment of Wages Act, 1936

Payment of wages is governed by payment of Wages Act, 1936 and Minimum Wages Act, 1948 as amended from time to time, both of which extend to the whole of India. The payment of Wages Act, 1936, applies to persons employed under the Factories Act, 1948 in any railway and industrial establishment such as tramway or motor transport service, air transport service, docks, inland vessels, mines, quarries or oil fields, plantations, workshops in which articles are produced and establishments in which any work relating to construction, development or maintenance of buildings, roads, bridges or canals, etc., is being carried on. It applies only to those employees who are in receipt of wages the average of which falls below Rs. 1600 per month. The Government is considering revision of the wage ceiling of Rs. 1,600 per month.

Employers cannot withhold wages earned by workers nor can they make any unauthorised deductions Payment, much be made before expiry of a specified day after the last day of the wage period. Fines can be imposed for only those acts or omissions which have been approved by an appropriate authority and must not exceed an amount equal to three per cent of wages payable. If payment of wages is delayed or if wrongful deductions are made, workers, or their trade union can file a claim. Payment or overtime in schedule employments is governed by Minimum Wages Act, 1948.

Minimum Wages Act, 1948

The Minimum Wages Act, 1948 empowers the Government to fix minimum wages for employees working in specified employments. It provides for review and revision of minimum wages already fixed after suitable intervals not exceeding five years. The Central Government is the appropriate agency in relation to any scheduled employment carried on by or under its authority agency in railway administration or in relation to mines, oilfields or major ports or any corporation established under the Central Act. The State Governments are the appropriate agencies in relation to other scheduled employments. The central Government is concerned to a limited extent with building and construction activities mostly carried on by Central Public Works Department, Ministry of Defence, etc. and agricultural farms under the Ministry of Labour, Defence and Agriculture. The bulk of such employments fall in the state spheres and state governments are required to fix/revise wages and ensure their implementation to respect of scheduled employment within their spheres. Enforcement of Minimum Wages Act in Central sphere is secured through the Central Industrial Relations Machinery (CIRM). Minimum wages under the Minimum Wages Act, 1948 have been fixed for 1,135 scheduled employment including 40 scheduled employments under the Central sector. Proposals to made amendments in the Minimum Wages Act are under active consideration of the Government.

LEGISLATION PERTAINING TO WORKING CONDITIONS

Payment of Bonus Act, 1965

The Payment of Bonous Act, 1965 provides for payment of bonous to employees as defined under the Act. "According to the employees" means any person (other than an apprentice) employed on a salary or wage not exceeding Rs. 2,500 per mensem in any industry to do any skilled or unskilled, manual, supervisory, managerial, administrative, technical or clerical work for hire or reward for hire or reward. However, according to section 12 of the Act, the bonus is payable to employees whose salary or wage exceeds Rs. 1,600 per mensem. The Central Government on receipt or representations from trade unions/individuals/associations for enhancement or removal of the above ceilings, decided to enhance the eligibility limit for payment of bonus from Rs. 2,500 to Rs. 3,500 per month. An radiance was promulgated on 9 July 1995 to give effect to the aforesaid amendments. Later on the ordinance was promulgated on 9 July 1995 to give effect to the Payment of Bonus Act, 1965 which received the assent of the Present on 30 August 1995. The Government is again considering proposals fore review/abolition of wage ceilings prescribed under Payment of Bonus Act.

Working Journalists Act, 1955

The Working Journalists and Other Newspaper Employees (Conditions of Service) and Miscellaneous Provisions Act, 1995 regulates conditions of service of working journalists and other persons employed in newspaper establishments. The Act provides for the setting up of Wage Boards for fixation and revision of rates of wages in respect of working journalists, newspaper/news agency employees. In the past, the wage Boards for such employees were set up in the years 1956, 1963 and 1985. The Wage Boards set up in 1985 under the Chairmanship of Justice U.N Bachawat submitted its final report in May 1989. The Government accepted the main recommendations of Bachawat Wage Boards and the state governments we requested to implement the recommendations and were also advised to establish tripartite committees/ special cells at the state level in this regard. As per information received from the state government as on 1 January 1988 out of 1,710 newspaper establishments 622 have fully, and 28 partially implemented the recommendations of Bachawat Wage Boards. Efforts are continuing to pursue the state governments for effective implementation.

On persistent demands form the working journalists and other newspaper employees for the setting up of Wage Boards to consider wage revisions, the Government, in September 1994, constituted two Wage Boards - One for the working journalists and the other for non-journalist newspaper and news-agency employees under the common Chairmanship of retired Chief Justice Rajkumar Singh. The Wages Boards submitted an Interim Report on the Interim Rate of Wages recommending enhancement by 15 per cent of the basic wages with effect from 20 April 1995. The Government examined this recommendation of the Boards and decided to grant interim enhancement of wages at the rate of 20 per cent of basic wage and an additional amount of Rs. 100 per months, with effect from 20 April 1995.

After the setting up of the Wage Boards on 2 September 1994 there were also demands from newspaper employees and employer's organization for increasing the number of representatives on the Boards. The Government agreeing to provide a wider representation on these Boards introduced a Bill in Parliament for increasing one representative in each category of representations, namely, employer's /employees/ independent members. The Bill was passed by both Houses of Parliament as Working Journalists and Other Newspaper Employees (Conditions of Service) and Miscellaneous Provisions (Amendment) Act, 1996 on 28 September 1996.

Contract Labour (Regulation and Abolition) Act, 1970

The Contract Labour (Regulation and Abolition) Act, 1970 has been enacted to regulate the employment of contract labour in certain establishments and for matter connected therewith. The Act provides for the constitution of Central and State Advisory Boards to advise the concerned governments on matters arising out of the administration of the Act.

The Central Government has issued a number of notification prohibiting employment of Contract Labour in different categories of works, jobs and processes as in mines, railways, Food Corporation of India's godowns, port trust, etc. The Central Advisory Contract Labour Board has also constituted a number of committees to enquire into the question of prohibition of contract labour system in different establishments.

Child Labour (Prohibition and Regulation) Act, 1986

India has all along followed a operative policy in the matter of tackling the problem of child labour, and always stood for constitutional, statutory and developmental measures that are required to eliminate child labour. India has ratified six ILO conventions relating to child labour and three of them as early as in the first quarter of the twenty century. Legislative provisions have been made in various laws to protect children from exploitation at work and to improve their working conditions. In addition, a comprehensive law namely the Child Labour (Prohibition and Regulation) Act, 1986 prohibits employment of children hazardous occupations and processes and regulates their employment in some other areas.

The National Policy on Child Labour was formulated in 1987 which apart from requiring enforcement of legal provisions to protect the interests of children, envisages focussing of general development programmes for the benefit of child labour and project-based plan of action in areas of high concentration of child labour. Under the project action plan of the policy, National Child Labour Projects (NCLP) have been set up in different areas to rehabilitate child labour. A major activity undertaken under the NCLP is the establishment of special schools to provide non-formal education., vocational training, supplementary nutrition, etc., to children withdrawn from employment. The programme for the elimination of child labour received further inpetus after the announcement of the new programme for the rehabilitation of children working in hazardous employments. Under the programme, 76 projects have been sanctioned to cover around 1.5 lakh working children in Andhra Pradesh, Madhya Pradesh, Gujarat,

Orissa, West Bengal, Bihar, Rajasthan, Uttar Pradesh, Maharashtra, Karnataka and Tamil Nadu where child labour in endemic.

The number of working children who have been covered by special schools is a miniscule of the total number of working children waiting to be released and rehabilitated. Considering the magnitude of the problem and paucity of resources human, material and financial, a sequential, gradual but integrated approach has been adopted. The ultimate objective of the National Child Labour Projects is to convert working children into productive and participative members of society.

The Government commitment of addressing the problem of child labour is reflected in the announcement made in the National Agenda for Government (1998). The agenda states that the aim is to ensure that no child remains illiterate, hungary or lacks medical care and that measures are taken to eliminate child labour. The need for time-bound action has also been emphasise by the Hon'be Supreme Court. The Supreme Court in India in its judgement dated 10 December 1996 in Writ Petition (Civil) No. 465/1986 has given certain directions regarding the manner in which children working in hazardous occupations are to be regulated and improved upon. The important directions given in this judgement include payment of compensation amounting to Rs. 20,000 by the offending employers for every child employed in hazardous occupation, constitution of the Child Labour Rehabilitation-cum-Welfare Fund giving alternative employment to an adult member of the family in place of the child withdrawn from the hazardous occupation or payment of an amount of Rs. 5,000 for each child employed in hazardous employment by the appropriate Government, completion of the survey of working children within a period of six months (*i.e.*, by 10 June, 1997), payment of interest on the corpus of Rs. 25,000 (Rs. 20,000 to be paid by the employer and Rs. 5,000 to the contributed by the appropriate government) to the family of the child withdrawn from work, provision of education in a suitable institution for the child withdrawn from work, etc. The Government has already initiated steps for giving effect to the directions of the Supreme Court.

Equal Remuneration Act, 1976

Women Constitute a significant part of the work-force of India but they lag being men in terms of level and quality of employment. The Census of India has registered 22.73 per cent of female population as workers, 90 million persons in absolute terms out of a total female population of 403 million. The majority of women workers are employed in the rural areas. Amongst rural woman workers, 870 per cent are employed in unorganised sectors like household industries, petty trades and services, building and construction, etc. The employment of women in the orgainsed sector (both public and private sectors) as on 31 March 1996 was about 4.43 million. This constitutes 15.8 per cent of the total orgainsed sector employment in the country. The distribution of women employees in major industries reveals that community, social and personal services sectors continued to absorb the majority of women employees. The lowest employment of women was noticed in electricity, gas and water sectors. In factory, mine and plantation establishments woman workers constitute 11.7 per cent and 36 per cent of the total workers.

The main focus of the policies of the Government with regard to women labour has been to remove the handicaps under which they work, to strengthen their bargaining capacity, to improve their wages and working conditions to enhance their skills and to open up better employment opportunities for them. A Separate cell, namely, Women Labour Cell is functioning in the Ministry of Labour to address these problems. The Maternity Benefit Act, 1961 and Equal Remuneration Act, 1976 are the protective and anti-exploitative legislations which have been enacted to protect and safeguard the interests of women workers at the workplace. The Equal Remuneration Act stipulates payment of equal remuneration to men and women workers for same and similar nature of work. The Act also prohibits any gender discrimination in recruitment and service conditions. Under the Act a committe has been set up at the Centre to advise the Government on providing increasing employment opportunities for women and generally reviewing the steps taken for effective implementation of the Act. Similar committees have also been set up by the state government and Union Territory Administrations. The Central Advisory Committee at the National Level and the Advisory Committee at the State Level along with competent authorities oversee the process of implementation of the Equal Remuneration Act.

The National Vocational Training Institute (NVTI), Noida (UP) and the 10 Regional Vocational Training Institutes (RVTIs) for women in different parts of India impart basic and advanced levels of vocational training to women in areas with high employment/self employment potential. Special attention has also been given to the modernisation and establishment of women's Industrial Training Institutes (ITIs) under the World Bank-aided Vocational Training Project. A Women's Cell under the Directorate General of Employment and Training (DGE&T) coordinates with states in the matter of vocational training of women. The employment exchange took special care to cater to the job needs of women registered with them. During January-September 1997, 1,46,001 women secured employment through employment exchanges.

To improve the working conditions and increase the employment potential of women, financial assistance is being given to voluntary organisations for taking up action-oriented projects.

Bonded Labour System (Abolition) Act, 1976

Bonded Labour System stands abolished in the country from 1975 through the Bonded Labour System (Abolition) Act, 1976. The Act envisages release of all bonded labourers, liquidation of their debts their rehabilitation. Incidence of bonded labour system has been reported from 12 states, *viz.*, Andhra Pradesh, Bihar, Gujarat, Haryana, Karnataka, Kerala, Madhya Pradesh, Maharashtra, Orrisa, Rajasthan, Tamil Nadu and Uttar Pradesh.

Under the Bonded Labour System (Abolition) Act 1976, identification and release of bonded labourers is the direct responsibility of the state government concerned. For the purpose of implementing the provisions of the Act, state governments may confer necessary powers on the District Magistrates. With a view to supplementing efforts of state government a Centrally Sponsored Scheme has been in existence since 1978-79 under which state government are provided Central Financial Assistance for rehabilitation of released bonded labourers. The scheme envisages provision of rehabilitation grant up to a ceiling limit of Rs 10,000 per bonded labourer, half of which is given as Central share. The pattern of assistance under this scheme can be either land-based, non-land based or skill-craft based. A sum Rs. 4,34,148 lakh has been released under this scheme since 1978-79 till 31 March 1988. The state governments have also been advised to suitably integrate/dovetail the Centrally-Sponsored Scheme for rehabilitation of bonded labourers with other on-going anti-poverty so as to pool the resources for effective rehabilitation of bonded labour.

SAFETY, HEALTH AND WELFARE OF WORKERS IN FACTORIES

The Factories Act, 1948

The Factories Act, 1948 is the principal legislation for regulating various aspects relating to safety, health and welfare of workers employed in factories. This Act is a Central enactment with aims at protecting workers employed in factories from industrial and occupational hazards. State Governments and Union Terriorty Administrations frame rules under the Act and enforce provisions of the Act rules through their factory inspectorship. The Directorate General, Factory Advice Service and Labour Institute (DGFASLI) Mumbai, an attached office of the Ministry of Labour, renders technical advice to the State/ Unions Territories in regard to administration and enforcement, of the Factories Act. With four regional labour institutes at Mumbai, Calcutta, Kanpur and Chennai under its control, the DGFASLI also undertakes support research facilities and carries out promotional activities through education and training in matters concerning occupational safety and health. The Directorate General also concerning occupational safety and health. The Directorate General also reviews the position regarding implementation and enforcement of the Act.

Prescribing a 48 hour week for adult workers, the Factories Act forbids, employment of children under 14 years of age in any factory. Minimum standards of lighting, ventilation, safety and welfare services which employers must provide in their factories have also been laid down. Factories employing over 30 women workers are required to provide a creche for their children. Shelters, rest-rooms and lunchrooms are required to be provided by factories employing over 150 workers. Factories with 250 workers or more have to appoint welfare officers. The factories Act was amended in 1987 in order to impose a general duty on occupiers to ensure health and safety of workers and on designers, manufacturers, importers and suppliers to ensure that articles designed, manufactured, etc. are without risk to health and safety of workers. A new chapter for regulating safety and health aspect in hazardous industries was incorporated in the Act.

Dock Workers (Safety, Health and Welfare) Act, 1986

Provisions relating to safety, health and welfare of workers employed in docks are contained in the Dock Workers (Safety, Health and Welfare) Act, 1986 and rules and regulations framed thereunder. The Act came into force on 15 April 1987. Enforcement of this Act in all the major ports is the responsibility of the Ministry of Labour and this responsibility is discharged through the DGFASLI, Mumbai the DSFASLI being the Chief Inspector of Docks is also entrusted with the responsibility of enforcing in major ports the Manufacture, Storage and Import of Hazardous Chemical Rules, 1989 framed under the Environment (Protection) Act, 1986.

Mines Act, 1952

Provisions for safety, health and welfare of workers employed in mines are contained in the Mine Act, 1952 and rules and regulation framed thereunder. These provisions are enforced by the Ministry of Labour through the Directorate General of Mines safety. The Directorate General with its headquarters at Dhanbad and its zonal, regional and sub-regional officers spread all over the mining areas in the country has for its functions inspection of mines, investigation of all fatal accidents, grant of statutory permission, approval of mines safety equipment, appliances and material conduct examinations for grant of statutory competency certificate, safety promotional incentives including organisation of national award and national safety conferences, etc.

The Emigration Act, 1983

The Emigration Act, 1983, which came into force with effect from 30 December 1983, regulates emigration of citizens of India for employment in other countries on contractual basis and seeks to ensue welfare and self-regard the interest of workers. As on 30 December, 1992, number of Indian workers who had gone abroad for employment, in terms of the provisions of the Emigration Act, 1983, was about 3.80 lakhs compared to 2.00 lakh in 1991. Under the provisions of the Act, an employer can recruit any citizens of India for employment in any country or place outside India either through a recruiting agent competent under the Act to make such recruitment or directly in accordance with valid permit issued by the Central Government under the Act. The competent authorities to grant permit for deployment of Indians abroad are Protector General of Emigrants (PGE) And Heads of Indian Missions abroad. The Act also provides that anyone intending to recruit Indians for employment abroad can do so after obtaining a Registration Certificate Form to PGE under the provisions of the Act.

Certain categories of persons are not required to obtain emigration clearance for seeking employment abroad. They are entitled to get the Stamp of "Emigration Check Not Required" (ECNR) on their passports from the passport officers by showing proof of their eligibility. Such individuals are : (i) persons going abroad in managerial capacity in hotels, restaurants, tea-houses or other places of public resort, etc., possessing specialised degrees in these fields; (ii) all gazetted government servants; (iii) all income - tax payers (including agricultural income-tax payers) in respect of their individual capacity. Proof of assessment to income-tax and actual payment of income-tax for last three years (act merely payments advance tax); (iv) all professional degree holders, such as doctors holding MBBS degree or degrees Ayurveda of Homeopathy, accredited journalists, engineers, chartered accountants, costs etc., (v) spouses and dependent children of category of persons listed from (ii) to (iv); (vi) all persons who have been staying abroad for more than three years (the period of three years could be either in one stretch or broken) and spouse and children of such person; (vii) seamen in possession of CDC and sea cadets; (viii) all diplomatic/official passports holders; (ix) dependent children of parents whose passports are classified as ECNR below 24; (x) persons holding permanent immigration visas such as in UK, USA and Australia; (xi) Persons holding graduation or higher degree; (xii) Persons holding diplomas from recognised institutions like polytechnics;

(xiii) nurse possessing qualifications recognised under the Indian Nursing Council Act, 1947; (xiv) all persons above the age of 60 years; (xv) all visitors to Pakistan and Bangladesh; (xvi) all persons going to any country in Europe or North; (xvii) persons possessing certificates of vocational training from government recognised institution.

SOCIAL SECURITY

Workmen's Compensation Act, 1923

A beginning was made in social security with the passing of the Workmen's Compensation Act in 1923. The Act provides for payment of compensation to workmen and their dependents in case of injury and accident (including certain occupational disease) arising out of and in the course of employment and resulting in disablement or death. The Act applies to railway servants and persons employed in any such capacity as is specified in Schedule II of the Act. Schedule II includes persons employed in factories, mines, plantations, mechanically propelled vehicles, construction works and certain other hazardous occupations. Minimum rates of compensation for permanent total disablement and death have been fixed at Rs 60,000 and Rs 50,000 respectively. Maximum amount for death and permanent total disablement can go up to Rs 2.28 lakh and Rs 3.74 respectively depending on age and wages of workmen.

Maternity Benefits Act, 1961

The Maternity Benefit Act, 1961 regulates employment of women in certain establishments for a certain period before and after childbirth and provides for maternity and other benefits. The Act applies to mines, factories, circus, industry, plantation, shops and establishments employing ten or more persons, except employees covered under the Employees State Insurance Act, 1948. It can be extended to other establishments by the State Governments. There is no wage limit for coverage under the Act.

Employees' State Insurance Act

The Employees' State Insurance Act is applicable in the first instance, to non-seasonal factories using power and employing 10 or more persons and non-power using factories employing 20 or more persons. Under the enabling provisions contained in the Act, the Act is being extended by the State Governments to new classes of establishments, namely, shops, hotels, restaurants, cinemas, including preview theatres, road motor transport undertakings and newspaper establishments employing 20 or more persons. It covers employees drawing wages not exceeding Rs 6,500 with effect from 1 January 1997. The Act provides medical care in kind and cash benefits in the contingency of sickness, maternity and employment injury and pension for dependents in the event of the death of a worker because of employment injury. Full medical care including hospitalisation is also being progressively made available to members of the family of the insured persons. As on 31 March 1999 there were 129 ESI hospitals and 42 annexes with 28,266 beds and 1,503 dispensaries under the scheme. The total number of employees covered were about 85.24 lakh.

Employees' Pension Scheme, 1995

This scheme was introduced for the industrial workers with effect from 16 November 1995. Under the Scheme, pension at the rate of 50 per cent pay is payable to the employees on retirement/superannuation on completion of 33 years' contributory service. A minimum 10 years' service is required for entitlement to pension. Depending upon the salary and service of the employee at the time of death the scheme also provides for grant of family pension ranging from Rs 450 per month to Rs 2,500 per month. In addition, children-pension at the rate of 25 per cent of widow pension subject to a minimum of Rs 115 per child is also payable up to two children. The scheme is financed by diverting employer's share of provident fund representing 8.33 per cent of the monthly wage to the pension fund. In addition, the Central Government also contributes to the scheme at the rate of 1.16 per cent of the wage.

The Employees' Provident Funds and Miscellaneous Provisions (Amendment) Act, 1998 (10 of 1998). The Employees' Provident Funds and Miscellaneous Provisions Act, 1952 provides for the institution of compulsory provident fund, pension fund and deposit-linked insurance for the benefit of employees in factories and establishments. While examining the Demands for Grants for the Ministry of Labour, the Standing Committee of Parliament on Labour and Welfare had made certain suggestions for amendment of the Act. The Employee's Provident Funds and Miscellaneous Provisions (Amendment) Bill, 1997 was introduced in Rajya Sabha, *inter alia*, to provide for the following : (i) to raise the minimum rate of provident fund contribution from 8.33 per cent to 10 per cent and the maximum rate from 10 per cent to 12 per cent of the monthly wages in order to promote saving and ensure availability of higher retiral benefits; (ii) to make a provision that a person who is, or has been, or is qualified to be a judge of a High Court or a District Judge shall be eligible for appointment as the Presiding Officer of the Appellate Tribunal; (iii) to abolish the provision of three years' infancy period so as to bring the factories / establishments within the scope of the Act from the date of their establishment/ registration.

The Bill was introduced but could not be passed by the Parliament as both Houses were not in session. To achieve the purposes of the aforesaid Bill, the Employees' Provident Funds and Miscellaneous Provisions (Amendment) Ordinance, 1997 (Ord. 17 of 1997) was promulgated by the President on 22 September 1997. The Eleventh Lok Sabha was dissolved on 4 December 1997. Therefore, to give continued effect to the provisions of the said Oridnance, the Employees' Provident Funds and Miscellaneous Provisions (Amendment) Second Ordinance, 1997. (Ord. 25 of 1997) was promulgated by the President on 25 December 1997 As the Bill to replace the aforesaid Ordinance could not be passed during the Twelfth Lok Sabha in February 1998, the Ordinance was repromulgated for the third time on 23 April 1998, as the Employees' Provident Funds and Miscellaneous Provisions (Amendment) Ordinance, 1998 (Ord. 8 of 1998).

The Employees' Provident Funds and Miscellaneous Provisions (Amendment) Bill, 1998 has been passed by the Parliament and received the assent of the President on 23 June 1998 replacing the aforesaid Ordinance.

The Payment of Gratuity (Amendment) Act, 1998 (11 of 1998). The Payment of Gratuity Act, 1972 provides for payment of gratuity to employees engaged in factories, mines, oilfields, plantations, ports, railway companies, shops and other establishments. On receipt of representations from trade unions, the Payment of Gratuity (Amendment) Bill, 1997 was introduced in Parliament to enhance the amount of gratuity from rupees one lakh to rupees two lakh and fifty thousand. As the Bill could not be passed, the President promulgated on 24 September 1997, the payment of Gratuity (Amendment) Ordinance, 1997 (Ord. 18 of 1997) to give effect to the provisions of the said Bill. As the Eleventh Lok Sabha was dissolved, the President Promulgated, on 25 December 1997, the Payment of Gratuity (Amendment) Second Ordinance, 1997 (Ord. 26 of 1997) to give continued effect to the provisions of the said Ordinance. As the Bill could not be passed by Parliament immediately after the constitution of the Twelfth Lok Sabha, the President repromulgated, on 23 April 1998, the Payment of Gratuity (Amendment) Ordinance, 1998 (Ord. 10 of 1998) to give continued effect to the provisions of the earlier Ordinance.

The Payment of Gratuity (Amendment) Act, 1998 was passed by Parliament and assented to by the President on 22 June 1998. This Act enhances the amount of gratuity from rupees one lakh to rupees three lakh and fifty thousand (instead of rupees two lakh and fifty thousand as provided in the Ordinance) keeping in view the Fifth Pay

Commission's Recommendations and consequent increase in the amount of gratuity payable to Government employees.

QUESTIONS FOR EXERCISE

1. Explain Labour Legislations in India pertaining to Wages?
2. Describe the Labour Legislation in India pertaining to working conditions?
3. Describe Labour Legislation about Factories and Mines?
4. State the latest developments in Employees P.F. Act.
5. What amendments have been made in Gratuity Acts?

2

The Collection of Statistics Act, 1953

The Collection of Statistics Act 1953 replaces the Industrial Statistics Act, 1942. It came into force on 10th November 1956. It extends to the whole of India [Section 1 (2)].

Object

The object of the Act is to facilitate the collection of statistics of certain kinds relating to industries, trade and commerce.

DEFINITIONS

1. Appropriate Government [Section 2 (a)]. It is —

(i) the Central Government, in relation to the collection of statistics under a direction issued by the Central Government under Section 3 and

(ii) the State Government, in relation to the collection of statistics under a direction issued by the State Government under Section 3.

2. Commercial concern [Section 2 (b)]. It is a public limited company or a co-operative society or a firm or any other person or body of persons engaged in trade or commerce and includes —

(i) a concern engaged in banking or insurance;

(ii) a financial corporation;

(iii) a concern engaged in shipping and navigation;

(iv) a concern engaged in the business of brokers dealing in shares, stocks and securities and commodities;

(v) a concern engaged in the business of advertising consultants;

(vi) a light railway;

(vii) a concern engaged in road transport service;

(viii) a concern engaged in air transport service;

(ix) a rubber, tea, coffee or cinchona plantation;

(x) a concern engaged in the business of forwarding and clearing agents;

(xi) any other concern which, in the opinion of the Central Government, is a commercial concern and is declared to be such by that Government by notification in the Official Gazette, but does bot include an industrial concern.

3. Factory [Section 2 (c)]. It is as defined in Section 2 (m) of the Factories Act, 1948.

4. Industrial Concern [Section 2 (d)]. It is a public limited company or a co-operative society or a firm or any other person or body of persons engaged in the manufacture, assembling, packing, preservation or processing of goods or in mining or in the generation or distribution of electricity or any other form of power.

5. Owner [Section (2) (e)]. In relation to a commercial or an industrial concern. Owner is the person who, or the authority which, has the ultimate control over the affairs of the concern. Where the said affairs are entrusted to a manager or managing director, such manager or managing director shall be deemed to be the owner of the concern.

COLLECTION OF STATISTICS (SECTION 3)

By notification in the Official Gazette, the appropriate Government may direct that statistics shall be collected relating to any of the following matters :

1. any matter relating to any industry or class of industries;

2. any matter relating to any commercial or industrial concern or class of commercial or industrial concerns, and in particular, any matter relating to factories;

3. any of the following matters so far as they relate to welfare of labour and conditions of labour, namely,

(i) prices of commodities,

(ii) attendance,

(iii) living conditions including housing, water supply and sanitation,

(iv) indebtedness,

(v) rents of dwelling houses,

(vi) wages and other earnings,

(vii) provident and other funds provided for labour,

(viii) benefits and amenities provided for labour,

(ix) hours of work,

(x) employment and unemployment,

(xi) industrial and labour disputes,

(xii) labour turnover,

(xiii) trade unions.

When by notification in the Official Gazette, the appropriate Government directs, that statistics shall be collected relating to any of the above matters, the provisions of the Act shall apply in relation to those statistics.

Limitations

1. A State Government is not authorised to issue any direction under the Act with respect to the collection of statistics relating to any matter falling under any of the entries specified in List 1 in the Seventh Schedule to the Constitution.

2. Where the Central Government has issued any direction for the collection of statistics relating to any matter, no State Government shall, except with the previous approval of the Central Government, issue any similar direction for so long as the collection of statistics by the Central Government remains to be completed.

3. Likewise, where a State Government has issued a direction for the collection of statistics relating to any matter, the Central Government shall not issue any similar direction for so long as the collection of statistics by the State Government remains to be completed. But where statistics have to be collected with reference to 2 or more States, the Central Government may issue a direction.

STATISTICS AUTHORITY

1. Appointment. The appropriate Government may appoint an officer to be the statistics authority for the purpose of collecting any statistics directed by it to be collected (Section 4).

2. Powers of Statistics Authority to call for Information (Section 5). The statistics authority may serve on the owner of an industrial or commercial concern or any other person a notice requiring him to furnish the prescribed information or returns relating to any matter in respect of which statistics are to be collected. The notice may be served by post. The form in which and the person to whom or the authorities to which, such information or returns should be furnished, the particulars which they should contain and the intervals within which such information or returns should be furnished shall be such as may be prescribed.

3. Right of Access to Records or Documents (Sections 6). The statistics authority or any person authorised by him shall, for the purpose of the collection of any statistics under the Act, have access to any relevant record or document in the possession of any person required to furnish any information or returns under the Act. At reasonable times he may enter any premises where he believes such records or documents are kept. He may inspect or take copies of relevant records or documents or ask any question necessary for obtaining any information required to be furnished under the Act.

4. Restriction on the Publication of Information and Returns (Section 7). No information, no individual return and no part of an individual return with respect to any particular industrial or commercial concern shall be published in a manner as would enable any particulars to be identified as referring to a particular concern without the prior consent of the owner of that concern in writing.

5. Confidential. Except for the purpose of a prosecution under the Act or under the Indian Penal Code, 1860, no person who is not engaged in the collection of statistics under the Act shall be permitted to see any information or individual return referred to above [Section 7 (2)].

PENALTIES (Section 8)

1. Penaties for Violation of Norms. If any person;

(a) required to furnish any information or return :

(i) wilfully refuses or without lawful excuse neglects or furnish the required information or return; or

(ii) wilfully furnishes or causes to be furnished any information or return which he knows to be false; or

(iii) refuses to answer, or wilfully gives a false answer to, any question necessary for obtaining any information required to be furnished under the Act; or

(b) impedes the right of access to relevant records or documents or the right of entry conferred by Section 6;

he shall for each such offence be punishable with fine which may extend to Rs. 500 and in the case of a continuing offence to a further fine which may extend to Rs. 200 for each day after the first during which the offence continues.

2. Penalty for Improper Disclosure of Information or Returns (Section 10). If any person engaged in connection with the collection of statistics under the Act wilfully discloses any information or the contents of any return given or made under the Act, he shall be punishable for such offence with imprisonment for a term which extend to 6 months, or with fine which may extend to Rs. 1,000, or with both.

OFFENCES

1. Offences by Companies (Section 9). If the person guilty of an offence under Section 8 is a company, every person who at the time the offence was committed was in charge of and was responsible to the company for the conduct of the business of the company, as well as the company, shall be deemed to be guilty of the offence and shall be liable to be proceeded against and punished accordingly. But if a person proves that the offence was committed without his knowledge or that he exercised all due diligence to prevent the commission of such offence, he shall not be liable to punishment.

Where it is proved that the offence has been committed with the consent or connivance of or is attributable to any neglect on the part of any director, manager, secretary or other officer of the company, such director, manager, secretary or other officer shall also be deemed to be guilty of that offence and shall be liable to be proceeded against and punished accordingly.

'Company' here means any body corporate and includes a firm or other association of individuals, and 'director' in relation to a firm means a partner in the firm.

2. Cognizance of Offences (Section 11). No prosecution for an offence under Section 8 shall be instituted except by or with the sanction of the statistics authority. Again, no prosecution for an offence under Section 10 shall be instituted except by or with the consent of the appropriate Government.

POWERS

1. Power of Central Government to give Directions (Section 12). The Central Government may give directions to a State Government as to the carrying into execution of the Act in the State.

2. Protection of Action taken in Good Faith (Section 13). No suit or other legal proceeding shall lie against (1) the appropriate Government, (2) the statistics authority, (3) any other person acting under the authority of the appropriate Government or of the statistics authority, in respect of anything which is in good faith done or intended to be done in pursuance of the Act or of any rules or directions issued thereunder.

3. Power to make Rules (Section 14). The appropriate Government may, subject to the condition of previous publication, by notification in the Official Gazette, make rules for the purpose of carrying out the purposes of the Act. All rules made under Section 14 shall be laid, as soon as may be, before Parliament or, as the case may be, before appropriate State Legislature.

Section 15 repeals the Industrial Statistics Act, 1942.

QUESTIONS FOR EXERCISE

1. What is the object of the Collection of Statistics Act, 1953?
2. Define the following terms according to the Collection of Statistics Act, 1953 :
   (a) Appropriate Government; (b) Commercial concern; (c) Industrial concern; (d) Owner.
3. What are the matters in relation to which statistics may be collected under the Collection of Statistics Act, 1953?
4. Who is the statistics authority appointed under the Collection of Statistics Act, 1953? Mention his powers?
5. What are various offences punishable under the Collection of Statistics Act, 1953? Mention the penalties for these offences.

3

The Employment Exchanges (Compulsory Notification of Vacancies) Act, 1959

Objectives

(a) To assess the employment potential in various categories of establishments and to have a better appreciation of the labour market,

(b) To enable the Government to formulate its policy of training in technical education and

(c) To help the unemployed persons, both skilled and semi-skilled, to seek an appropriate employment.

APPLICATION AND SCOPE OF THE ACT

1. The Act extends to the whole of India [Section 1 (2)].

2. It shall come into force in a State on such date as the Central Government may, by notification in the Official Gazette, appoint in this behalf for such State and different dates may be appointed for different States or for different areas of the State [Section 1 (3)].

Where the Act does not apply (Section 3).

The Act shall not apply in relation to vacancies —

(1) in any employment in agriculture (including horticulture) in any establishment in private sector other than employment as agricultural or farm machinery operatives;

(2) in any employment in domestic service;

(3) in any employment the total duration of which is less than 3 months;

(4) in any employment to do unskilled office work;

(5) in any employment connected with the staff of Parliament [Section 3 (1)].

(6) Unless the Central Government otherwise directs by notification in the Official Gazette in this behalf, the Act shall also not apply in relation to —

(a) vacancies which are proposed to be filled through promotion or by absorption of surplus staff of any examination conducted or interview held by, or on the recommendation of, any independent agency, such as the Union or a State Public Service Commission and the like;

(b) vacancies in an employment which carries a remuneration of less than Rs. 60 in a month [Section 3 (2)].

DEFINITIONS

1. Appropriate Government [Section 2 (a)]. It is 'Central Government' in relation to —

(a) any establishment of any railway, major port, mine or oilfield, or

(b) any establishment owned, controlled or managed by (i) the Central Government or a department of the Central Government, (ii) a company in which not less than 51 per cent of the share capital is held by the Central Government or partly by the Central Government and partly by one or more State Governments, (iii) a corporation (including a co-operative society) established by or under a Central Act which is owned, controlled or managed by the Central Government.

In relation to any other establishment, the appropriate Government means the Government of the State in which the establishment is situate.

2. Employee [Section 2 (b)]. 'Employee' is any person who is employed in an establishment to do any work for remuneration.

3. Employer [Section 2 (c)]. 'Employer' is any person who employs one or more other persons to do any work in an establishment for remuneration and includes any person entrusted with the supervision and control of employees in such establishment.

4. Employment Exchange [Section 2 (d)]. It is any office or place established and maintained by the Government for the collection and furnishing of information, either by the keeping of registers or otherwise respecting —

(i) persons who seek to engage employees,

(ii) persons who seek employment and

(iii) vacancies to which persons seeking employment may be appointed.

5. Establishment [Section 2 (e)]. It is —

(a) any office, or

(b) any place where any industry, trade, business or occupation is carried on.

Establishment in Public Sector [Section 2 (f)]. It is an establishment owned, controlled or managed by

(1) the Government or a department of the Government;

(2) a Government company as defined in Section 617 of the Companies Act, 1956;

(3) a corporation (including a co-operative society) established by or under a Central, Provincial, or State Act, which is owned, controlled or managed by the Government;

(4) a local authority.

Establishment in Private Sector [Section 2 (g)]. It is an establishment which is not an establishment in public sector and where ordinarily 25 or more persons are employed to work for remuneration.

6. Unskilled Office Work [Section 2 (i)]. It is work done in an establishment by any of the following categories of employees, namely,

(1) Daftri; (2) Jamadar, orderly and peon;(3) dusting man or farash; (4) process server; (5) watchmen; (6) sweeper; (7) any other employees doing any routine or unskilled work which the Central Government may, by notification in the Official Gazette, declare to be unskilled office work.

NOTIFICATION OF VACANCIES

1. Notification of Vacancies to Employment Exchanges (Section 4)

(i) *In public sector* : After the commencement of this Act in any State or area thereof, the employer in every establishment in public sector in that State or area shall, before filling up any vacancy in any employment in that establishment, notify that vacancy to such employment exchanges as may be prescribed [Section 4 (1)].

(ii) *In private sector* : The appropriate Government may, by notification in the Official Gazette, require that from such date as may be specified in the notification, the employer in every establishment in private sector or every establishment pertaining to any class or category of establishments in private sector shall, before filling up any vacancy in any employment in that establishment, notify that vacancy to such employment exchanges as may be prescribed.

The employer shall thereupon comply with such requisition [Section 4 (2)].

The manner in which the vacancies to in Section 4 (1) or 4 (2) shall be notified to the employment exchanges and the particulars of employments in which such vacancies have occurred or are about to occur shall be such as may be prescribed [Section 4 (3)].

There is no provision in the Act rendering invalid any appointments made by the employer, when he makes those appointments without complying with the requirements of Section 4 (1) and 4 (2).

Vacancies should be notified to the local employment exchanges having jurisdiction over the area where office in which the vacancies occur is situated. The mere fact that the head of the department who makes the appointment has his headquarters at a different place would not be an excuse for not notifying the local employment exchange concerned of such vacancies [Narsimhamurthi (M.C.) *Vs.* Director of Collegiate Education, (1967) 2 L.L.J. 606].

Nothing in Section 4 (1) and 4 (2) shall be deemed to impose any obligation upon any employer to recruit any person through the employment exchange to fill any vacancy merely because that vacancy has been notified under Section 4 (1) or 4 (2) [Section 4 (4)].

2. Employer to furnish Information and Returns (Section 5)

After the commencement of this Act in any State or area thereof, the employer in every establishment in public sector in that State or area shall furnish such information or return as may be prescribed in relation to vacancies that have occurred or are about to occur in that establishment, to such employment exchanges as may be prescribed.

The appropriate Government may, by notification in the Official Gazette, require that from such date as may be specified in the notification the employer in every establishment in private sector or every establishment pertaining to any class or category of establishments in private sector shall furnish such information or return as may be prescribed in relation to vacancies that have occurred or are about to occur in that establishment to such employment exchanges as may be prescribed. The employer shall thereupon comply with such requisition.

The form in which, and the intervals of time at which, such information or return shall be furnished and the particulars which they shall contain shall be such as may be prescribed.

3. Right of Access to Records or Documents (Section 6)

Such officer of Government as may be prescribed in this behalf, or any person authorised by him in writing, shall have access to any relevant record or document in the possession of any employer required to furnish any information or return under Section 5. The officer may enter at any reasonable time any premises where he believes such records or documents to be and inspect or take copies of relevant record or documents or ask any question necessary for obtaining any information required under Section 5.

PENALTIES

1. If any employer fails to notify to the employment exchanges prescribed for the purpose any vacancy in contravention of Section 4 (1) or 4 (2) he shall be punishable for the first offence with fine which may extend to Rs. 500 and for every subsequent offence with fine which may extend to Rs. 1,000 [Section 7 (1)].

2. If any person —

(a) required to furnish any information or returns —

(i) refuses or neglects to furnish such information or

(ii) furnishes or causes to be furnished any information or returns which he knows to be false; or

(iii) refuses to answer, or gives a false answer to, any question necessary for obtaining any information required to be furnished under Section 5; or

(b) impedes the right of access to relevant records or documents or the right of entry conferred by Section 6;

he shall be punishable for the first offence with fine which may extend to Rs. 250 and for every subsequent offence with fine which may extend to Rs. 500 [Section 7 (2)].

MISCELLANEOUS

1. Cogizance of Offences (Section 8). No prosecution for an offence under the Act shall be instituted except by, or with the sanction, of such officer of Government as may be prescribed in this behalf or any person authorised by that officer in writing.

2. Protection of Action taken in Good Faith (Section 9). No suit, prosecution or other legal proceeding shall lie against any person for anything which is in good faith done, or intended to be done, under the Act.

3. Power to make Rules (Section 10). The Central Government may, by notification in the Official Gazette, and subject to the condition of previous publication, make rules for carrying out the purposes of the Act [Section 10 (1)]. All rules made under the Act shall be laid before each House of Parliament as soon as may be after they are made and shall be subject to such modification as Parliament may make during the session in which they are so laid or the session immediately following [Section 10 (3)].

QUESTIONS FOR EXERCISE

1. Define the following terms as used in the Employment Exchanges (Compulsory Notification of Vacancies) Act, 1959 :

   (a) Appropriate Government, (b) Employer, (c) Employee, (d) Establishment, (e) Unskilled office work.

2. What is the object of Employment Exchanges (Compulsory Notification of Vacancies) Act, 1959? To which the Act (a) applies, (b) does not apply?

3. Describe the statutory provisions regarding notification of vacancies in public sector and private sector to Employment Exchanges.

4. Describe the penalties if an establishment fails to notify any vacancies to an Employment Exchange.

4

The Apprentices Act, 1961

The model Standing Orders framed under the Industrial Employment (Standing Orders) Act, 1946, contained some statutory provisions relating to apprentices. With the passage of time, these provisions were found to be inadequate. A need was felt for the regulation by law of the training and employment conditions of the apprentices. The apprentices Act, 1961 was enacted to meet this need to provide for the regulation and control of training of apprentices and for certain other matters connected therewith. Under the Act, employers in specified industries are obliged to train a certain number of apprentices for designated trades according to prescribed national standards.

The Apprentices Act 1961 came into force on 1st March 1962. The latest amendment to the Act was made in 1986.

SCOPE AND COVERAGE OF THE ACT

The Act extends to the whole of India [Section 1 (2)]. It applies to any area or any industry in any area if the Central Government by notification in the Official Gazette specifies that area or industry to which it shall apply [Section 1 (4)]. The trade or occupation or any subject field in engineering or technology or vocational course to which the Act is made applicable by the Central Government is called 'designated trade' [Section 2 (e)].

The Central Government has by different notifications specified different groups of industries in different areas in which the provisions of the Act have been brought into force with effect from the dates mentioned therein [Section 1 (3)]. Provision has been made in the Act for the reservation of training places in every designated trade by the employer for the Scheduled Castes and Scheduled Tribes.

Areas not Covered in the Act. Section 1 (4) specifically provides that the provisions of the Act shall not apply to —

(1) any area or any industry in any area unless the Central Government by notification in the Official Gazette specifies that the provisions of the Act shall apply to it with effect from the date as may be mentioned in the notification;

(2) any special apprenticeship scheme for imparting training to apprentices as may be notified by the Central Government in the Official Gazette [Section 1 (4)].

DEFINITION OF APPRENTICE

1. The term 'apprentice' is derived from the French word *apprendre* which means "to learn".

2. Section 2 (aa) of the Act defines 'apprentice' as "a person who is undergoing apprenticeship training in pursuance of a contract of apprenticeship."

3. According to Oxford Dictionary 'apprentice' is defined as "a learner of a craft : one who is bound by legal agreement to serve an employer for a period of years, with a view to learn some handicraft, trade, etc., in which the employer is reciprocally bound to instruct him."

4. According to James *Vs.* Le Ray. Johns (N.Y.) 274 an apprentice is bound to obey his master in all his lawful commands, take care of his property, and promote his interest, endeavour to learn his trade or business, and perform all the conditions of his contract not contrary to law. He must not leave his master's service during the term of his apprenticeship.

NATURE OF APPRENTICESHIP CONTRACT

Essence of Contract

The essence of a contract of apprenticeship between a master on the one hand and an apprentice on the other is that the master should teach and the apprentice should serve and learn. This contract to teach and to learn distinguishes it from an ordinary contract of hiring and service.

MEANING OF RELATIONSHIP

While dealing with the nature of the relationship of masters and servants in comparison with other relationships in Halsbury's Laws of England, third edition, Volume 25, the following passage appears at Para 877, pages 451. 452 :

> "By a contract of apprenticeship a person is bound to another for the purpose of learning a trade or calling, the apprentice undertaking to serve the master for the purpose of being taught, and the master undertaking to teach the apprentice. Where teaching on the part of the master or learning on the part of the other person is not the primary but only an incidental object, the contract is one of service rather than of apprenticeship; but, if the right of receiving instruction exists, a contract does not become one of service because, to some extent, the person to

whom it refers does the kind of work that is done by a servant, or because he receives pecuniary remuneration for his work."

Section 18 of the Act provides :

"Save as otherwise provided in this Act —

(a) every apprentice undergoing apprenticeship training in a designed trade in an establishment shall be a trainee and not a worker and

(b) the provisions of any law with respect to labour shall not apply to or in relation to such apprentice."

Thus, Apprentices are mere trainees and not employees or workers. They are not employed for wages. After the period of apprenticeship is over the employer is not bound to employ them.

DEFINITIONS

1. All India Council [Section 2 (a)]. It is the All India Council of Technical Education established by the resolution of the Government of India in the former Ministry of Education (No. F.F 16-10/44-E. III dated the 30th November 1945).

2. Apprentice [Section 2 (aa)].

3. Apprenticeship Adviser [Section 2 (b)]. 'Apprenticeship Adviser' is the Central Apprenticeship Adviser appointed under Section 26 (1) or the State Apprenticeship Adviser appointed under Section 26 (2).

4. Apprenticeship Council [Section 2 (c)]. 'Apprenticeship Council' is the Central Apprenticeship Council or the State Apprenticeship Council established under Section 24 (1).

5. Apprenticeship training [Section 2 (aaa)]. It is a course of training in any industry or establishment undergone in pursuance of a contract of apprenticeship and under prescribed terms and conditions which may be different for different categories of apprentices.

6. Appropriate Government [Section 2 (d)]. It is the Central Government in relation to :

(a) the Central Apprenticeship Council, or

(b) the practical training of graduate or technician apprentices, or of technician (vocational) apprentices; or

(c) any establishment of any railway, major port, mine or oilfield; or

(d) any establishment owned, controlled or managed by (i) the Central Government or a department of the Central Government, (ii) a company in which not less than 51 per cent of the share capital is held by the Central Government or partly by that Government and partly by one or more State Government, (iii) a corporation (including a co-operative society) established by or under a Central Act which is owned, controlled or managed by the Central Government.

But in relation to (a) a State Apprenticeship Council, or (b) any establishment other than an establishment specified above, the appropriate Government means the State Government.

7. Board or State Council of Technical Education [Section 2 (dd)]. Board of State Council of Technical Education is the Board or State Council of Technical Education established by the State Government.

8. Designated trade [Section 2 (e)]. It is any trade or occupation or any subject field in engineering or technology or any vocational course which the Central Government, after consultation with the Central Apprenticeship Council, may, by notification in the Official Gazette, specify as a designated trade for the purposes of the Act.

In exercise of the powers conferred by Section 2 (e) of the Apprenticeship Act. 1961, and after consultation with the Central Apprenticeship Council, the Central Government has specified the following subject fields for vocational courses as designated trades, for the purposes of the Act, namely :

(1) Accountancy and Auditing; (2) Banking; (3) Marketing and Salesmanship; (4) Office Secretaryship/Stenography. (5) Food Preservation; (6) Poultry farming; (7) Fisheries/Fish Processing; (8) Dairying; (9) Medical Laboratory / Technology/Assistants; (10) Health worker; (11) Nursing; (12) Child Care and Nutrition; (13) Crop Cultivation/Production; (14) Sericulture; (15) Apiculture; (16) Floriculture; (17) Plant Protection; (18) Textile Designing; (19) Civil Construction/Maintenance; (20) Mechanical Servicing.

9. Employer [Section 2 (f)]. 'Employer' is any person who employs one or more other persons to do any work in an establishment for remuneration and includes any person entrusted with the supervision and control of employees in such establishment.

10. Establishment [Section 2 (g)]. It includes any place where any industry is carried on.

Establishment in Private Sector [Section 2 (h)]. It is an establishment which is not an establishment in public sector.

Establishment in Public Sector [Section 2 (i)]. It is an establishment owned, controlled or managed by (1) the Government or a department of the Government; (2) a Government company as defined in Section 617 of the Companies Act, 1956; (3) a corporation (including a co-operative society) establishment by or under a Central, Provincial or State Act, which is owned, controlled or managed by the Government; (4) a local authority.

11. Graduate or Technician Apprentice [Section 2 (f)]. 'Graduate or technician apprentice' is an apprentice who holds, or is undergoing training in order that he may hold, a degree or diploma in engineering or technology or equivalent qualification granted by any institution recognised by the Government and undergoes apprenticeship training in any such subject field in engineering or technology as may be prescribed.

12. Industry [Section 2 (h)]. It is any industry or business in which any trade, occupation or subject field in engineering, or technology or any vocational course may be specified as a designated trade. The words 'or any vocational course' have been added by the Amendment Act of 1986.

13. National Council [Section 2 (l)]. 'National Council' is the National Council for Training in Vocational Trades established by the resolution of the Government of India in the Ministry of Labour (Directorate-General of Resettlement and Employment) (No. TR/E.P.-24/56, dated the 21st August 1956), and renamed as the National Council for Vocational Training by the resolution of the Government of India in the Ministry of Labour (Directorate-General of Employment and Training) (No. DGET / 12 / 21 / 80-TC dated the 30th September, 1981). The renaming part of this clause has been added by the Amendment Act of 1986.

14. Regional Board [Section 2 (mm)]. 'Regional Board' is any Board of Apprenticeship Training registered under the Societies Registration Act, 1860 at Bombay, Calcutta, Madras or Kanpur.

15. State [Section 2 (n)]. 'State' includes a Union Territory.

16. State Council [Section 2 (o)]. 'State Council' is a State Council for Training in Vocational Trades established by a State Government.

17. State Government in Relation to a Union Territory [Section 2 (p)]. It means the administrator of the Union Territory.

18. Technician (Vocational) Apprentice [Section 2 (pp)]. 'Technician (vocational) apprentice' is an apprentice who holds or is undergoing training in order that he may hold a certificate in vocational course involving 2 years of study after the completion of the secondary stage of school education recognised by the all India Council of Technical Education and undergoes apprenticeship training in any such subject field in any vocational course as may be prescribed [Section 2 (pp) has been added by the Apprentices (Amendment) Act, 1986].

19. Trade apprentice [Section 2 (q)]. 'Trade apprentice' is an apprentice who undergoes apprenticeship training in any such trade or occupation as may be prescribed.

APPRENTICES AND THEIR TRAINING

1. Qualifications (Section 3)

An apprentice is a person who is undergoing apprenticeship training in a designated trade in pursuance of a contract of apprenticeship [Section 2 (aa)].

A person shall not be qualified for being engaged as an apprentice to undergo apprenticeship training in any designated trade, unless he :

(1) is 14 years of age or above and

(2) satisfies the standards of education and physical fitness as may be prescribed for apprenticeship training.

Different standards may be prescribed by the Central Government in relation to apprenticeship training in different designated trades and for different categories of apprentices.

2. Eligibility

In pursuance of the power given to the Central Government under Section 37 (1) to make rules, it has been laid down in the Apprenticeship Rules, 1962 that a person shall be eligible for being engaged as :

(1) a trade apprentice, if he satisfies the minimum educational qualifications specified in Schedule 1 to the Apprenticeship Rules, 1962;

(2) a graduate or technician or technician (vocational) apprentice, if he satisfies one of the minimum educational qualifications specified in Schedule I-A to the Apprenticeship Rules, 1962 (Rule 3) and

(3) an apprentice if he satisfies the minimum standards of physical fitness specified in Schedule 2 to the Apprenticeship Rules, 1962 (Rule 4).

3. Reservation of Training Places (Section 3-A)

(i) In every designated trade, training places shall be reserved by the employer for the Scheduled Castes and Scheduled Tribes. *Where there is more than one designated trade in an establishment, such training places shall be reserved also on the basis of the total number of apprentices in all the designated trades in that establishment* [Section 3-A (1)]. The italicised words have been added by the Apprentices (Amendment) Act, 1986.

(ii) The number of training places to be reserved for the Scheduled Castes and Scheduled Tribes shall be such as may be prescribed, having regard to that population of the Scheduled Castes and the Scheduled Tribes in the State concerned [Section 3-A (2)].

4. Contract of Apprenticeship (Section 4)

(i) *Conditions* : For engaging any person as an apprentice to undergo apprenticeship training in a designed trade, two conditions have to be satisfied :

(a) A contract of apprenticeship must be entered into between the apprentice (or with his guardian if he is a minor) and the employer [Section 4 (1)].

(b) The contract of apprenticeship must be sent by the employer to the Apprenticeship Adviser for registration [Section 4 (4)]. The Apprenticeship Adviser shall not register the contract unless he is satisfied that the person described as an apprentice in the contract is qualified under the Act for being engaged as an apprentice to undergo apprenticeship training in the designated trade specified in the contract [Section 4 (5)].

(ii) *Commencement of Apprenticeship Training* : The apprenticeship training shall be deemed to have commenced on the date on which the contract of apprenticeship has been entered into [Section 4 (2)].

(iii) *Terms and Conditions in Contract of Apprenticeship Training* : The contract of apprenticeship may contain such terms and conditions as may be agreed to by the parties to the contract. But such terms or conditions must not be inconsistent with any provision of the Act and rules made thereunder [Section 4 (3)].

(iv) *Modification of the Terms and Conditions* : Where the Central Government, after consulting the Central Apprenticeship Council, makes any rule varying the terms and conditions of apprenticeship training of any category of apprentices undergoing such training, then, the terms and conditions of every contract of apprenticeship relating to that category of apprentices and subsisting immediately before the making of such rule shall be deemed to have modified accordingly [Section 4 (6)].

5. Minor as an Apprentice

(i) *Meaning of Minor* : A minor is a person who have not attained 18 years of age (Section 3 of the Indian Majority Act, 1875). An agreement entered into by or with a minor is void [*Mohiri Bibi* v. *Dharmodas Ghose*, (1903) 30 Cal. 359; Section 11 of the Indian Contract Act, 1872]. His estate is however liable for necessaries supplied to him or his dependents (Section 68 of the Indian Contract Act, 1872). Necessaries include not only necessary goods but also necessary services like education, instruction, and training [Roberts *Vs.* Gray (1913) 1 K.B. 520].

(ii) *Conditions for Contract* : A contract of apprenticeship of a minor would fall in the category of necessary services, as it is for the benefit of the minor. A minor can, therefore, enter into a legal binding contract of apprenticeship if he satisfies the conditions laid down in the Act [R. *Vs*. Petrox, 4 T.R. 1961], *i.e.*,

(a) he has attained the age of 14 years;

(b) he satisfies the prescribed standards of education and physical fitness (Section 3) and

(c) his guardian has entered into a contract of apprenticeship with the employer [Section 4 (1)].

6. Novation of Contract of Apprenticeship (Section 5)

The requirements of Section 5 are follows :

(i) The employer with whom the contract of apprenticeship has been entered into is for any reason unable to fulfil his obligations under the contract.

(ii) It is agreed, with the approval of the Apprenticeship Adviser, between the employer, the apprentices or his guardian and any other employer that the apprentice shall be engaged as an apprentice under the other employer for the unexpired portion of the period of apprenticeship training.

(iii) The Apprenticeship Adviser approves the agreement.

(iv) The agreement is registered with the apprenticeship Adviser.

On registration with the Apprenticeship Adviser, the agreement shall be deemed to be the contract of apprenticeship between the apprentice or his guardian and the other employer. The contract of apprenticeship with the first employer shall terminate on and from the date of such registration. No obligation under that contract shall be enforceable at the instance of any party to the contract against the other party thereto.

7. Period of Apprenticeship Training (Section 6)

(i) In the case of trade apprentices who, having undergone institutional training in a school or other institution recognised by the National Council for Vocational Training have passed the trade tests or examinations conducted by that Council, the period of apprenticeship training shall be such as may be determined by that Council or by an institution recognised by the Council [Section 6 (a)].

(ii) In the case of trade apprentices who, having undergone institutional training in a school or other institution affiliated to or recognised by a Board or State Council of Technical Education or any other authority which the Central Government may, by notification in the Official Gazette, specify in this behalf, passed the trade tests or examinations conducted by that Board or State Council or authority, the period of apprenticeship training shall be such as may be prescribed [Section 6 (aa)].

The words or examination after trade tests contemplated in Section 6 (a) and Section 6 (aa) have added by the Apprentices (Amendment) Act, 1986.

(iii) In the case of other trade or graduate or technician apprentices or technician (vocational) apprentices, the period of apprenticeship training shall be such as may be prescribed [Section 6 (b) and (c)].

8. Number of Apprentices for a Designated Trade (Section 8)

(i) *Power of Central Government* : Power is given to the Central Government to determine for each designated trade the ratio of trade apprentices to workers other than unskilled workers in that trade. The Central Government shall do so after consulting the Central Apprenticeship Council and by order in the Official Gazette. But there is nothing to prevent any employer from engaging a number of trade apprentices in excess of the ratio determined by the Central Government [Section 8 (1)]. In determining the ratio, the Central Government shall have regard to —

(a) the facilities available for apprenticeship training under the Act in the designated trade concerned and

(b) the facilities that may have to be made available by the employer for the training of graduate or technician apprentices or technician (vocational) apprentices, if any, in pursuance of any notice issued to him under Section 8 (3-A) [Section 8 (2)].

(ii) *Power of Apprenticeship Advisor* : The Apprenticeship Adviser may, by notice in writing, require an employer to engage the required number of trade apprentices (*i.e.*, within the ratio determined by the Central Government for any designated trade in his establishment), to undergo apprenticeship training in that trade. The employer shall comply with such requisition by the Apprenticeship Adviser [Section 8 (3)].

The Central Apprenticeship Adviser or any other person not below the rank of an Assistant Apprenticeship Advisor authorised by the Central Apprenticeship Adviser in writing in this behalf shall, having regard to —

(a) the number of managerial persons (including technical and supervisory persons) employed in a designated trade;

(b) the number of management trainees engaged in the establishment;

(c) the totality of the training facilities available in a designated trade;

(d) such other factors as he may consider fit in the circumstances of the case;

by notice in writing, require an employer to impart training to such number of graduate or technician apprentices, technician (vocational) apprentices, in such trade in his establishment as may be specified in such notice and the employer shall comply with such requisition [Section 8 (3-A)].

Several employers may join together for the purpose of providing practical training to the apprentices under them by moving them between their respective establishments [Section 8 (4)].

(iii) *Powers of Appropriate Government* : Where, having regard to the public interest, a number of apprentices in excess of the ratio determined by the Central Government or in excess of the number specified in a notice issued under Section 8 (3-A) should in the opinion of the appropriate Government be trained, the appropriate Government may require employers to train the additional number of apprentices [Section 8 (5)]. Every employer shall comply with the requisition if the Government concerned makes available such additional facilities and such additional financial assistance as are considered necessary by the Apprenticeship Adviser for the training of the additional number of apprentices [Section 8 (6)]. If an employer is not satisfied with the decision of the Apprenticeship Adviser as regards additional facilities and financial assistance for the training of the additional number of apprentices, he may make a reference to the Central Apprenticeship Council. Such reference shall be decided by a Committee appointed by the Central Apprenticeship Council for the purpose and the decision of that Committee shall be final [Section 8 (7)].

9. Termination of Apprenticeship Contract (Section 7)

The contract of apprenticeship shall terminate —

1. On the Expiry of the Period of Apprenticeship Training [Section 7 (1)].

2. By Order in Writing terminating the Contract by the Apprenticeship Adviser. On an application by either party to terminate the contract of apprenticeship [Section 7 (3)]. The procedure in this case is as follows :

Either party to a contract of apprenticeship may make an application to the Apprenticeship Adviser for the termination of the contract. When any such application is made, the Apprenticeship Adviser shall send by post a copy thereof to the other party to the contract [Section 7 (2)]. After considering the contents of the application and objections, if any, filed by the other party, the Apprenticeship Adviser may terminate the contract.

Conditions for Termination

Before terminating the contract, the Apprenticeship Adviser must be satisfied that —

(a) the parties to the contract or any of them have or has failed to carry out the terms and conditions of the contract and

(b) it is desirable in the interests of the parties or any of them to terminate the same [Section 7 (3)].

Where a contract of apprenticeship is terminated for failure on the part of the employer to carry out the terms and conditions of the contract, the employer shall pay to the apprentice such compensation as may be prescribed. Where a contact of apprenticeship is terminated for failure on the part of the apprentice to carry out the terms and conditions of the contract, the apprentice or his guardian shall refund to the employer as cost of training such amount as may be determined by the Apprenticeship Adviser [Proviso to Section 7 (3)].

3. On Novation of Contract of Apprenticeship (Section 5). A contract of apprenticeship may also terminate on its novation. This happens when an apprentice under one employer is transferred to some other employer for the remaining term of the apprenticeship contract.

10. Practical and Basic Training of Apprentices and Related Instruction (Sections 9 and 10)

(i) **Meaning**. According to Section 18 (a), every apprentice undergoing apprenticeship training in a designated trade in a establishment is a trainee and not a worker. As such an obligation has been imposed on employers for imparting training to every apprentice engaged by them. Sections 9 and 10 deal with this and the important provisions of these Sections are as follows :

(ii) **Practical and basic training of apprentices (Section 9).** (1) Every employer shall make suitable arrangements in his workshop for imparting a course of practical training to every apprentice engaged by him in accordance with the programme approved by the Apprenticeship Adviser [Section 9 (1)].

(2) The Central Apprenticeship Adviser or any other person (not below the rank of an Assistant Apprenticeship Adviser) authorised by the Central Apprenticeship Adviser in writing shall be given all reasonable facilities for access to each apprentice. This provision has been made with a view to test the work of the apprentices and to ensure that the Practical training is being imparted in accordance with the approved programme [Section 9 (2)].

The State Apprenticeship Adviser or any other person (not below the rank of an Assistant Apprenticeship Adviser) authorised by the State Apprenticeship Adviser in writing shall also be given such facilities in relation to which the appropriate Government is the State Government [Proviso to Section 9 (2)].

(3) Apprentices who have not undergone institutional training in a school or other institution recognised by the National Council for Vocational Training or any other institution affiliated to or recognised by a Board or State Council of Technical Education or any other authority which the Central Government may, by notification in the Official Gazette, specify in this behalf, shall, before admission in the workshop for practical training, undergo a course of basic training [Section 9 (3)].

(4) Where an employer employs in his establishment 500 or more workers, the basic training shall be imparted to the apprentices either in separate parts of the workshop building or in a separate building which shall be set up by the employer himself. The appropriate Government may grant loans to the employer on easy terms and repayable by easy instalments to meet the cost of the land, construction and equipment for such separate building [Section 9 (4)].

If an employer has more than one factories at different places, each having less than 500 workers but the total strength of workers of all the factories exceeds 500, all the factories will be treated as one unit for the purposes of the applicability of the Act [Shaw Wallace & Co. Ltd., Madras *Vs*. Director of Employment & Training, Madras, (1977) 51 F.J.R. 208].

(5) If the number of apprentices to be trained at any time in any establishment in which 500 or more workers are employed is less than 12, the employers in relation to such establishment may depute all or any of such apprentices to any Basic Training Centre or Industrial Training Institute for basic training in any designated trade, in either case, run by the Government [Section 9 (4-A)]. Where the employer so deputes any apprentice he shall pay to the Government the expenses incurred by the Government on such training, at such rate as may be specified by the Central Government [Section 9 (4-B)].

(6) Where an employer employs in his establishment less than 500 workers, the basic training shall be imparted to the trade apprentices in training institutes set up by the Government [Section 9 (5)].

(7) In any such training institute, which shall be located within the premises of the most suitable establishment in the locality or at any other convenient place, the trade apprentices engaged by 2 or more employers may be imparted basic training [Section 9 (6)].

(8) The syllabus of and the equipment to be utilised for practical training, including basic training, shall be such as may be approved by the Central Government in consultation with the Central Apprenticeship Council [Section 9 (7) and (7-A)].

(9) Recurring costs (including the cost of stipends), if any, incurred by an employer in connection with practical training including basic training imparted to trade apprentices shall be borne by the employer if the number of workers employed by him is 500 or more. But if the number is less than 500 the recurring cost shall be borne by the employer and the Government in equal shares up to such limit as may be laid down by the Central Government and beyond that limit, by the employer alone [Section 9 (8) (a)]. The trade apprentices referred to here are other than those who have undergone institutional training in a school or other institution recognised by the National Council for Vocational Training or a Board or State Council of Technical Education (referred to in Section 6).

Recurring costs (including the cost of stipends, if any) in case of trade apprentices who have undergone training (referred to above) incurred by an employer in connection with practical training, including basic training, shall, in every case, be borne by employer [Section 9 (8) (b)].

Recurring costs (excluding the cost of stipends) incurred by an employer in connection with practical training imparted to graduate or technician apprentices or technician (vocational) apprentices shall be borne by the employer. The cost of stipends shall be borne by the Central Government and the employer in equal shares up to such limit as may be laid down by the Central Government and beyond that limit, by the employer alone [Section 9 (8) (c)].

11. Related Instruction of Apprentices (Section 10)

(1) A trade apprentice who is undergoing practical training in an establishment shall, during the period of practical training, be given a course of related instruction (which shall be appropriate to the trade). This course shall be approved by the Central Government in consultation with the Central Apprenticeship Council, with a view to giving the trade apprentice such theoretical knowledge as he needs in order to become fully qualified as a skilled craftsman [Section 10 (1)].

(2) Related instruction shall be imparted at the cost of the appropriate Government but the employer shall, when so required, afford all facilities for imparting such instruction [Section 10 (2)].

(3) Any time spent by a trade apprentice in attending classes on related instruction shall be treated as part of his paid period of work [Section 10 (3)].

(4) In the case of trade apprentices who, after having undergone a course of institutional training, have passed the trade tests conducted by the National Council for Vocational Training or have passed the trade tests and examinations conducted by a Board or State Council of Technical Education or any other authority which the Central Government may, by notification in the Official Gazette, specify in this behalf, the related instruction may be given on such reduced or modified scale as may be prescribed [Section 10 (4)].

(5) Where any person has, during his course in a technical institution, become a graduate or technician apprentice or technician (vocational) apprentice and during his apprenticeship training he has to receive related instruction, then the employer shall release such person from practical training to receive the related instruction in such institution. The period of release shall be specified by the Central Apprenticeship Adviser or by any other person not below the rank of an Assistant Apprenticeship Adviser authorised by the Central Apprenticeship Adviser in writing in this behalf [Section 10 (5)].

12. Health, Safety and Welfare of Apprentices (Section 14)

Where any apprentices are undergoing training in a factory, the provisions of Chapters III, IV and V of the Factories Act, 1948 shall apply in relation to the health, safety and welfare of the apprentices as if they were workers within the meaning of that Act. When any apprentices are undergoing training in a mine, the provisions of Chapter V of the Mines Act, 1952 shall apply in relation to the health and safety of the apprentices as if they were persons employed in the mine.

13. Hours of Work, Overtime, Leave and Holidays (Section 15)

A. Hours of work. The weekly and daily hours of work of an apprentice while undergoing practical training in a workshop shall be such as may be prescribed [Section 15 (1)].

The weekly hours of work of trade apprentice whole undergoing practical training shall be as follows :

(i) The total number of hours per week shall be 42 to 48 (including the time spent on related instruction).

(ii) Trade apprentices undergoing basic training shall ordinarily work for 42 hours per week (including the time spent on related instruction).

(iii) Trade apprentices during the second year of apprenticeship shall work for 42 to 45 hours per week (including the time spent on related instruction).

(iv) Trade apprentices during the third and subsequent years of apprenticeship shall work for the same hours of work per week as other workers in the establishment [Rule 8 (1) of the Apprenticeship Rules, 1962].

Further, the hours of training of the trade apprentice shall not be between 10 P.M. and 6 P.M. except with the prior approval of the Apprenticeship Adviser [Rule 8 (2) of the Apprenticeship Rules, 1962].

Graduate or technician apprentices or technician (vocational) apprentices shall work according to the normal hours of the department in the establishment to which they are attached for training [Rule 8 (3) of the Apprenticeship Rules, 1962].

B. Overtime. An apprentice shall not be required or allowed to work overtime except with the approval of the Apprenticeship Adviser. The Apprenticeship Adviser shall not grant such approval unless he is satisfied that such overtime is in the interest of the training of the apprentice or in the public interest [Section 15 (2)].

C. Leave and Holidays. An apprentice shall be entitled to such leave as may be prescribed and to such holidays as are observed in the establishment in which he is undergoing training [Section 15 (3)].

As per Rule 9 of the Apprenticeship Rules, 1962, an apprentice is entitled, in case of establishments where proper leave rules do not exist or the total of different types admissible to the workers is less than 37 days in a year, to the following leave :

(i) *Casual Leave* : It shall be admissible for a maximum period of 12 days in a year. Any holidays intervening during the period of casual leave shall not be counted for the purpose of the limit of 12 days. Casual leave not utilised during any year shall stand lapsed at the end of the year. It shall not be combined with medical leave.

(ii) *Medical Leave* : Medical leave up to 15 days for each year of training may be granted to the apprentice. The unused leave shall be allowed to accumulate up to a maximum of 40 days. Any holiday intervening the period of medical leave shall be treated as medical leave. The employer may call upon the apprentice to produce a medical certificate from a registered medical practitioner in support of his medical leave. The employer may also arrange a special examination of an apprentice.

(iii) *Extraordinary Leave* : Extraordinary leave up to a maximum of 10 days in a year may be granted to the apprentice, after he has exhausted his casual and medical leave.

14. Holding of Test and Grant of Certificate (Section 21)

(i) *Test* : Every trade apprentice who has completed the period of training shall appear for a test to be conducted by the National

Council for Vocational Training to determine his proficiency in the designated trade in which he has undergone his apprenticeship training [Section 21 (1)]. The trade apprentice who passes the test shall be granted a certificate of proficiency in the trade by the National Council [Section 21 (2)].

(ii) *Assessment* : The progress in apprenticeship training of every graduate or technician apprentice or technician (vocational) apprentice shall be assessed by the employer from time to time [Section 21 (3)]. Every graduate or technician apprentice or technician (vocational) apprentice who completes his apprenticeship traiing to the satisfaction of the concerned Regional Board shall be granted a certificate of proficiency by that Board [Section 21 (4) as amended by the Amendment Act of 1986].

15. Offer and Acceptance of Employment (Section 22)

(i) *Obligations* : It is not obligatory on the part of the employer to offer any employment to any apprentice who has completed the period of his apprenticeship training in his establishment. Likewise, it is not obligatory on the part of the apprentice to accept any employment under the employer [Section 22 (1)]. But a contract of apprenticeship may contain a condition that the apprentice shall, after the successful completion of the apprenticeship training, serve the employer. In such a case, the employer shall, on the completion of training by the apprentice, be bound to offer suitable employment to the apprentice. The apprentice shall also be bound to serve the employer in that capacity for such period and on such remuneration as may be specified in the contract [Section 22 (2)].

(ii) *Revisions* : If the period of apprenticeship or remuneration is not, in the opinion of the Apprenticeship Adviser, reasonable, he may revise such period on remuneration so as to make it reasonable. The period or remuneration so revised shall be deemed to be the period or remuneration agreed to between the apprentice and the employer [Proviso to Section 22 (2)].

16. Records and Returns (Section 19)

(i) Every employer shall maintain records of the progress of training of each apprentice undergoing apprenticeship training in his establishment in the prescribed form [Section 19 (1)]. He shall also furnish such information and returns in such form, to such authorities and at such intervals, as may be prescribed [Section 19 (2)].

(ii) Rule 10 of the Apprenticeship Rules, 1962 deals with the records and returns to be maintained by the employer in respect of apprentices.

17. Settlement of Disputes (Section 22)

(i) *Dispute to be referred to Apprenticeship Adviser for decision* : Any disagreement or dispute between an employer and an apprentice arising out of the contract of apprenticeship shall be referred to the Apprenticeship Adviser for decision [Section 20 (1)]. The expression 'dispute arising out of the contract of apprenticeship' will include not only disputes directly touching the contract of apprenticeship but all incidental and consequential matters in relation to contract. Such disputes could easily arise in matters of training, discipline, treatment of an apprentice, nature of his work, health and safety (Sections 14, 15 and 17).

(ii) *Appeal to Apprenticeship Council* : Any party aggrieved by the decision of the Apprenticeship Adviser may within 30 days from the date of communication to him of such decision, prefer an appeal against the decision to the Apprenticeship Council. Such appeal shall be heard and determined by a Committee of that Council Appointed for the purpose [Section 20 (2)]. An appeal is maintainable under Section 20 (2) only against the decision of the Apprenticeship Adviser made under Section 20 (1). If an order is made under Section 7 (3) (b) and not under Section 20 (1), appeal against the order is not maintainable under Section 20 (2) [Jai Prakash Singh *Vs.* Central Apprenticeship Council, (1979) Lab. I.C. 482].

(iii) The decision of the Committee under Section 20 (2) and subject only to such decision, the decision of the Apprenticeship Adviser under Section 20 (1) shall be final [Section 20 (3)]. But this finality cannot affect the writ jurisdiction of the High Courts under Arts. 226 and 227 of the Constitution to correct errors apparent on the face of the record and set aside *ultra vires* orders.

OBLIGATIONS OF EMPLOYERS AND APPRENTICES

1. Obligations of Employers (Section 11, 13, 16 and 19)

(i) *Obligations under Section 11* : Every employer shall have the following obligations in relation to an apprentice, namely,

(a) to provide the apprentice with the training in his trade in accordance with the provisions of the Act, and the rules made thereunder;

(b) if the employer is not himself qualified in the trade, to ensure that a person who possesses the prescribed qualifications is placed in charge of the training of the apprentice;

(c) to carry out his obligations under the contract of apprenticeship.

(ii) *Obligation of Payment under Section 13* : (a) The employer shall pay to every apprentice during the period of apprenticeship training a stipend at a rate not less than the prescribed minimum rate or the rate which was being paid by the employer on 1st January, 1970, to the category of apprentices under which such apprentice falls whichever is higher, as may be specified in the contract of apprenticeship. The stipend so specified shall be paid at such intervals and subject to such conditions as may be prescribed [Section 13 (1)].

(b) The employer shall not pay any apprentice on the basis of piece work or require any apprentice to take part in any output bonus or other incentive scheme [Section 13 (2)].

(iii) *Employer's Liability for Compensation for Injury* (Section 16) : If personal injury is caused to an apprentice by accident arising out of and in the course of his training as an apprentice, the employer shall be liable to pay compensation. The amount of compensation shall be determined and paid, so far as may be, in accordance with the provisions of the Workmen's Compensation Act, 1923, subject to the modifications specified in the Schedule to the Apprentice Act.

(iv) *Modifications* : These modifications are as follows : In the Workmen's Compensation Act, 1923, for the definitions of 'employer', 'wages' and 'workman', the following definitions shall be substituted :

(a) 'Employer' means an employer as defined in the Apprentices Act, 1961, who has engaged on or more apprentices.

(b) 'Wages' means the stipend payable to an apprentice under Section 13 (1) of the Apprentices Act, 1961.

(c) 'Workman' means any person who is engaged as an apprentice as defined in the Apprentices Act, 1961, and who in the course of his apprenticeship training is employed in any such capacity as is specified in Schedule II to the Workmen's Compensation Act.

The special provisions relating to masters and seamen as contained in the Workmen's Compensation Act and those relating to contracting do not apply to apprentices. Further, a registered trade union cannot appear before a Labour Commissioner on behalf of an apprentice.

(v) *Obligation to maintain Records and to furnish Returns* (Section 19) : Every employer shall maintain records of the progress of training of each apprentice undergoing apprenticeship training in his establishment and to furnish such information and returns in such form, to such authorities and at such intervals, as may be prescribed.

2. Obligations of Apprentices (Sections 12, 13 and 17)

(i) *Obligations of Trade Apprentices under Section* 12 (1) : Every trade apprentice undergoing apprenticeship training shall have the following obligations, namely :

(a) to learn his trade conscientiously and diligently and endeavour to qualify himself as a skilled craftsman before the expiry of the period of training;

(b) to attend practical and instructional classes regularly;

(c) to carry out all lawful orders of his employer and superiors in the establishment and

(d) to carry out his obligations under the contract of apprenticeship.

(ii) *Conduct and Discipline* (Section 17) : In all matters of conduct and discipline, the apprentice shall be governed by the rules and regulations in all matters of conduct and discipline, applicable to employees of the corresponding category in the establishment in which the apprentice is undergoing training.

(iii) *Payment of Apprentices* [Section 13 (2)] : An apprentice shall not receive from the employer any payment on the basis of piece-work or take part in any output bonus or other incentive scheme.

(iv) *Obligations of Graduate or Technician Apprentices or Technician (Vocational) Apprentices* : According to Section 12 (2), every graduate or technician apprentice or technician (vocational) apprentice undergoing apprenticeship training shall have the following obligations, namely :

(a) to learn his subject field in engineering or technology or vocational course conscientiously and diligently at his place of training;

(b) to attend the practical and instructional classes regularly;

(c) to carry out all lawful orders of his employer and superiors in the establishment;

(d) to carry out his obligations under the contract of apprenticeship which shall include the maintenance of such records of his work as may be prescribed.

AUTHORITIES UNDER THE ACT

(1) The National Council for Vocational Training (or the National Council) established by the Government of India,

(2) The Central Apprenticeship Council.

(3) The State Council for Training in Vocational Trades (or the State Council) established by a State Government.

(4) The All-India Council of Technical Education.

(5) The Regional Boards of Apprenticeship Training.

(6) The Boards or State Councils of Technical Education.

(7) The State Apprenticeship Council.

(8) The Central Apprenticeship Adviser.

(9) The State Apprenticeship Adviser [Section 23 (1)].

FUNCTIONS OF AUTHORITIES

1. The authorities shall, in relation to apprenticeship training under the Act, perform such functions as are assigned to them by or under this Act or by the Government [Section 23 (3)].

2. Every State Council for Training in Vocational Trades shall be affiliated to the National Council for Vocational Training [Section 23 (2)]. It shall, in addition to its other functions, also perform such functions as are assigned to it by the National Council for Vocational Training [Proviso to Section 23 (3)].

3. Every Board or State Council of Technical Education and every Regional Board of Apprenticeship Training shall be affiliated to the Central Apprenticeship Council [Section 23 (2-A)].

1. Central Apprentice ship Council. The Central Government shall, by notification in the Official Gazette, establish the Central Apprenticeship Council [Section 24 (1)].

Constitution of Central Apprenticeship Council. The Central Apprenticeship Council shall consist of a Chairman and a Vice-Chairman and such number of other members as the Central Government may think expedient to be appointed. The appointment shall be made by the Government by notification in the Official Gazette from among the following categories of persons, namely :

(a) representatives of employers in establishments in the public and private sectors;

(b) representatives of the Central Government and of the State Governments;

(c) persons having special knowledge and experience on matters relating to industry, labour and technical education and

(d) representatives of the All-India Council of Technical Education and of the Regional Boards of Apprenticeship Training [Section 24 (2)].

The number of persons to be appointed as members of the Central Apprenticeship Council from each of these categories, the term of office of, the procedure to be followed in the discharge of their functions by, and the manner of filling vacancies among, the members of this Council, shall be such as may be prescribed [Section 24 (3)].

The fees and allowances, if any, to be paid to the Chairman and the Vice-Chairman and the other members of the Central Apprenticeship Council, shall be determined by the Central Government [Section 24 (6)].

2. State Apprenticeship Council. The State Government shall, by notification in the Official Gazette, establish the State Apprenticeship

Council [Section 24 (1)]. Every State Apprenticeship Council shall be affiliated to the Central Apprenticeship Council [Section 23 (2)]. In addition to its other functions [Section 23 (3)], it shall also perform such other functions as are assigned to it by the Central Apprenticeship Council [Proviso to Section 23 (3)].

Constitution of State Apprenticeship Council. The State Apprenticeship Council shall consist of a Chairman and a Vice-Chairman and such number of other members as the State Government may think expedient to be appointed. The appointment shall be made by the State Government by notification in the Official Gazette from among the following categories of persons, namely :

(a) representatives of employers in establishments in the public and private sectors;

(b) representatives of the Central Government and of the State Government;

(c) persons having special knowledge and experience of matters relating to industry, labour and technical education and

(d) representatives of the Board or the State Council of Technical Education [Section 24 (4)].

The number of persons to be appointed as members of the State Apprenticeship Council from each of these categories, the term of office of, the procedure to be followed in the discharge of their functions by, and the manner of filling vacancies among, the members of this Council, shall be such as the State Government may, by notification in the Official Gazette, determine [Section 24 (5)].

The fees and allowances, if any, to be paid to the Chairman and Vice-Chairman and the other members of the State Apprenticeship Council shall be determined by the State Government [Section 24 (6)].

3. Central Apprenticeship Adviser. The Central Government shall, by notification in the Official Gazette, appoint a suitable person as the Central Apprenticeship Adviser [Section 26 (1)]. He shall be the Secretary to the Central Apprenticeship Council [Section 26 (3)].

Powers of Central Apprenticeship Adviser (Section 29). Subject to any rules made in this behalf, the Central Apprenticeship Adviser or such other person (not below the rank of an Assistant Apprenticeship Adviser) as may be authorised by the Central Apprenticeship Adviser in writing may :

(a) with such assistants, if any, as he thinks fit, enter, inspect and examine any establishment or part thereof at any reasonable time;

(b) examine any apprentice employed therein or require the production of any register, record or other documents maintained in pursuance of the Act and take on the spot or otherwise statements of any person which he may consider necessary for carrying out the purposes of the Act;

(c) make such examination and inquiry as he thinks fit in order to ascertain whether the provisions of the Act and the rules made thereunder are being observed in the establishment;

(d) exercise such other powers as may be prescribed [Section 29 (1)].

But no person shall be compelled under Section 29 to answer any question or make any statement which may tend directly or indirectly to incriminate him [Section 29 (2)].

4. State Apprenticeship Adviser. The State Government shall, by notification in the Official Gazette, appoint a suitable person as the State Apprenticeship Adviser [Section 26 (2)]. He shall be the Secretary to the State Apprenticeship Council [Section 26 (3)]. He may also exercise any of the powers specified in Clauses (a), (b), (c) or (d) of Section 29 (1) (discussed earlier in connection with the powers of the Central Apprenticeship Adviser) in relation to establishments for which the appropriate Government is the State Government [Proviso to Section 29 (1)].

5. Deputy and Assistant Apprenticeship Advisers. The Government may appoint suitable persons as Additional, Joint, Regional, Deputy and Assistant Apprenticeship Advisers to assist the Apprenticeship Adviser in the performance of his functions [Section 27 (1)]. These persons shall, subject to the control of the Apprenticeship Adviser, perform such functions as may be assigned to them by the Apprenticeship Adviser [Section 27 (2)].

QUALIFICATION OF ADVISERS (Section 28).

Every Apprenticeship Adviser and every Additional, Joint, Regional, Deputy or an Assistant Apprenticeship Adviser appointed under the Act shall be deemed to be a public servant within the meaning of Section 21 of the Indian Penal Code, 1860.

VACANCIES NOT TO INVALIDATE ACTS AND PROCEEDINGS (Section 25)

No act done or proceedings taken by the National Council for Vocational Training, the Central Apprenticeship Council, the State Council for Training in Vocational Trades, or the State Apprenticeship Council under the Act shall be questioned on the ground merely of the existence of any vacancy in, or defect in the constitution of, such Council.

PENALTIES AND OFFENCES

1. Penalties (Section 30). An employer shall be punishable with imprisonment for a term which may extend to 6 months or with fine or with both if he :

(a) engages as an apprentice a person who is not qualified for being so engaged, or

(b) fails to carry out the terms and conditions of a contract of apprenticeship, or

(c) contravenes the provisions of the Act relating to the number of apprentices which he is required to engage under those provisions [Section 30 (1)].

Further an employer or any other person shall be punishable with imprisonment for a term which may extend to 6 months or with fine or with both, if he :

(a) is required to furnish any information or return but he

(i) refuses or neglects to furnish such information or return, or

(ii) furnishes or causes to be furnished any information or return which is false and which he either knows or believes to be false or does not believe to be true, or

(iii) refuses to answer, or gives a false answer to, any question necessary of obtaining any information required to be furnished by him, or

(b) refuses or wilfully neglects to afford the Central or the State Apprenticeship Adviser or any other person authorised by the Central or State Apprenticeship Adviser in writing any reasonable facility for making any entry, inspection, examination or inquiry authorised by or under the Act, or

(c) requires an apprentice to work overtime without the approval of the Apprenticeship Adviser, or

(d) employs an apprentice on any work which is not connected with his training, or

(e) makes payment to an apprentice on the basis of piece-work, or

(f) requires an apprentice to take part in any output bonus or incentive scheme [Section 30 (2)].

2. Penalty where no Specific Remedy is provided [Section 31]. If any employer or any other person contravenes any provision of the Act for which no punishment is provided in Section 30, he shall be punishable with fine which may extend to Rs. 500.

3. Offences by Companies (Section 32). If the person committing an offence under the Act is a company, every person who, at the time the offence was committed, was in charge of, and was responsible to the company for the conduct of business of the company, as well as the company, shall be deemed to be guilty of the offence and shall be liable to be proceeded against and punished accordingly. But if any such person liable to punishment proves that the offence was committed without his knowledge or that he exercised all due diligence to prevent the commission of such offence, he shall not be liable [Section 32 (1)].

Where an offence under the Act has been committed by a company and it is proved that the offence has been committed with the consent or connivance of, or is attributable to any negligence on the part of, any director, manager, secretary or other officer of the company, such director, manager, secretary or other officer shall also be deemed to be guilty of that offence and shall be liable to be proceeded against and punished accordingly [Sec. 32 (2)].

'Company' in Section 32 means a body corporate and includes a firm or other association of individuals and

'Director' in relation to a firm means a partner in the firm (Explanation to Section 32).

4. Cognizance of Offences (Section 33). Every complaint for offences under the Act or the rules made thereunder shall be made in writing to the Apprenticeship Adviser within 6 months from the date on which the offence is alleged to have been committed, otherwise the Court shall not take cognizance of any such offence.

5. Protection of Action taken in Good Faith (Section 36). No suit, prosecution or other legal proceedings shall lie against any person for anything which is in good faith done under the Act.

POWERS AND RULES

1. Power to make Rules (Section 37). The Central Government may, after consulting the Central Apprenticeship Council, by notification in the Official Gazette, make rules for carrying out the purposes of the Act [Section 37 (1)]. These rules may provide that a contravention of any such rule shall be punishable with fine which may extend to Rs. 50 [Section 37 (2)].

2. Rules to be laid before Parliament. Every rule made under Section 37 shall be laid as soon as amy be after it is made before each House of Parliament while it is in session for a period of 30 days. This period of 30 days may be comprised in one session or in 2 or more successive sessions. If both the Houses agree in making any modification in the rule, the rule shall thereafter have effect only in such modified form. If both the Houses agree that the rule should not be made, the rule shall thereafter be of no effect. But any such modification or annulment shall be without prejudice to the validity of anything previously done under that rule [Section 37 (3)].

3. Delegation of Powers (Section 34). The Central Government may, by notification in the Official Gazette, delegate any power exercisable by it under the Act or the rules made thereunder subject to certain conditions and directions, to such officer or authority as may be specified in the notification. Likewise, the State Government may also delegate its powers to such officer or authority as may be specified in the notification.

QUESTIONS FOR EXERCISE

1. Define the following terms as used in the Apprentices Act, 1961 :
   (a) Apprentice; (b) Appropriate Government; (c) Designated trade; (d) Employer; (e) Industry; (f) Health, safety and welfare of apprentices.
2. Explain the object of the Apprentices act, 1961.
3. Who is an 'apprentice?' Is he a workman under the Apprentices Act, 1961? State the qualification for being engaged as an apprentice.
4. Can a person be engaged to undergo apprenticeship training in a designated trade without entering into a contract apprenticeship?
5. What are the terms and conditions contained in a contract of apprenticeship? Must such a contract be registered?
6. State the number of apprentices in a designated trade.
7. When does a contract of apprenticeship terminate? What should an employer do to terminate the contract of apprenticeship with an apprentice?
8. State the obligations of apprentices and employers under a contract of apprenticeship?
9. State the provisions of the Apprentices Act, 1961 as regards practical and basic training of apprentices and related instruction of apprentices.
10. State the Provisions of the Apprentices Act, 1961 as regards hours of work, overtime, leave and holidays, of an apprentice?
11. Describe the various authorities under the Apprentices Act, 1961. What are their functions?
12. State the various offences under the Apprentices Act, 1961. What are the penalties provided for such offences?

PART TWO
PAYMENT OF WAGES

5

Wage and Salary Administration

DEFINITION OF WAGES

1. *Benham* — "Wage means the amount paid to the labour for his services by the employer."

2. *Yoder and Heneman* — "Wages are the compensation of wage earners, the numerous employees who use the tools and equipment for their employers to produce goods and services that are sold by their employers."

3. *P. M. Stank* — "Wages is that labour's remuneration which creates the utility."

TYPES OF WAGES

1. Money Wages. Money Wages refer to the monetary form of wage payment. Normally the wages earned by employees are expressed in terms of money. Money wages, however, do not express real or intrinsic price of any work unless we know what the wages can buy. Thus, they do not express the real worth of job. They only express the amount in terms of currency. The real wages give the actual worth of the amount.

2. Real Wages. Real Wages refer to the purchasing power of money wages. It represents the actual exchange value of wage rates. It reflects an adjustment to changes in the price level based on price indices.

3. Minimum Wages. The concept of minimum wage has developed due to different standards in different countries. In Indian reference minimum wages means the minimum amount which an employer thinks necessary for the sustenance of life and preservation of the efficiency of the worker. According to Fair Wage Committee, the minimum wages must also provide for some measure of education — medical requirements and amenities.

4. The Living Wages. According to the Committee on Fair Wages, the living wages represent the highest level of the wages and include all amenities which a citizen living in a modern civilized society is to expect when the economy of the country is sufficiently advanced and the employer is able to meet the expanding aspirations of his workers. Traditionally, the living wage is "a will-of-the wisp" which floats a little further ahead, an arm's length out of reach. It belongs to the same category as "squaring the circle". After considering various observations made by Indian and Foreign authorities, the Committee observed that "the living wage should enable the male earner to provide for himself and his family not merely the basic essential of food, clothing and shelter but a measure of frugal comfort including education for the children, protection against ill-health, requirements of essential social needs, and a measure of insurance against the more important misfortunes including old age." It was felt that when such a wage is to be determined, the considerations of national income and capacity to pay of industry concerned has to be taken into account. The committee was of the opinion that although living wage standard should be made the ultimate goal, "it is generally recognized that the present level of our national income does not permit the payment of a living wage on standards prevalent in more advanced countries."

5. Fair Wages. In order to bring about improved relations between labour and management an effort has been made in modern times that the labour gets a fair deal at the hands of owners and managers of industries. Various proposals were undertaken at the Industries Conference in 1947 and a resolution known as the Industrial Truce Resolution was passed. It provided for the payment of fair wages to labour. The Government of India appointed a Fair Wages Committee in 1948 to determine the principles on which fair wages should be based and to suggest the lines on which those principles should be applied. According to the report of this Committee, Fair Wages is that wages which the labourer gets for his work just near to minimum wages and living wages. Generally, the current rate of wages being paid in the enterprise are known as fair wages.

TYPES OF WAGE VARIATION

1. Time Variations. According to the economic conditions of the country wages may vary from time to time. In slump period, the wage rates may be cut whereas the inflationary pressures may hike wage rates. Price and wage indices are prepared for the two periods to measure the variations in prices and wages and adjust accordingly.

2. Regional Variations. There are different wage rates in different regions for the same work in the same industry. For example, Cotton textile mills in U.P. pay lower wages to their workers in comparison to the wages paid in cotton textile mills in Maharashtra or Gujarat. This may be due to the several reasons such as economic development of the region, demand and supply of the workers, cost of living index and standard of living etc.

3. Industrial Variations. Wage rates differ from industry to industry. An industry may pay more to its workers in the same region for similar work. Various factors influence the wage rates such as demand and supply of skilled labour, nature of work and working conditions in the industry, place of industry in the national economy etc.

FACTORS AFFECTING WAGE RATES

1. Demand and Supply. The wage rates are fixed by the demand and supply position of the workers in the labour market. If labour is in short supply, the workers will offer their services only if they are paid well. If their supply is in plenty labour will be available at cheaper rates.

2. Bargaining Power. To a considerable extent wages also depend on the relative bargaining power of the labour unions and the employers. If the labour unions are strong enough to force the employers, the wages are determined at a higher level in comparison to other units where unions are weak.

3. Cost of Living. Progressive employers do not work with the blind forces of demand and supply. They take due notice of the cost of living for the workers at a place and try to fix the wages to ensure a decent living wage to the workers. Cost of living various under inflationary and deflationary pressures. Labour unions come out with a demand of wage adjustment according to the cost of living index number.

4. Conditions of Product Market. The wage levels are influenced by the degree of competition prevailing in the market for the product of the industry. If it is a keen competitive market the wage level may be at par with the value of the net additions made by the workers to the total output. But if imperfect competition exists in the product market wages may not reach this level.

5. Comparative Wages. Wage rates must be consistent with the wage paid by other firms in the same industry. The comparative wages will increase the job satisfaction among the workers.

6. Ability to pay. Wages rates are influenced by the ability of industry or a firm to pay its workers. Firms earning huge profits may naturally afford much better wage rates and more facilities to its workers in comparison to those firms which are earning only marginal profits.

7. Productivity of Labour. Productivity is the main basis of wage determination. Higher wages are paid in firms, where productivity of labour is high, as compared to other firms where it is low.

8. Job Requirements. If a job requires higher skill, greater responsibility and risk, the worker placed on that job will naturally get higher wages in comparison to other jobs which do not require the same degree of skill, responsibility or risk.

9. Government Policy. As the bargaining powers of the worker is not enough to ensure fair wages in all industries, the Government has to interfere in regulating wage rates to guarantee minimum wage rates in order to cover the essentials of a decent living.

10. Good will of the Company. Employers who want to establish themselves as good employees in the society fix higher wages for their workers. It also attracts qualified employees.

OBJECTIVES OF A SOUND WAGE AND SALARY POLICY

An essential ingredient of wage and salary administration in an organisation a sound wage policy should be carefully developed to safeguard the interests of (a) management, (b) the employees, (c) the consumers and (d) the community. Following objectives must be borne in mind while formulating the wage policy.

1. To link with Productivity. In some way or the other wage plan must be linked with the productivity of the workers otherwise it will not be fair for either the management or the workers or both.

2. To link with Job Requirement and Skill. A satisfactory wage plan should correlate the job classification and skill in terms of job requirements. Due consideration should be given to factors such as skill, length of time required in learning, versatility required and working conditions.

3. To lower Cost of Production. To cater the interest of the plan should usually result in the reduction of per unit of production. It makes possible lowered prices and higher profits so that a share of higher efficiency should be passed on to the society by way of lower price. Thus, a good wage and salary plan ensures the gains of higher productivity to the workers, management and consumers :

(i) Workers by way of higher wages and incentives;

(ii) Management by way of lower and higher profits and

(iii) Consumers by way of better quality and lower price.

4. To provide Incentive System. A satisfactory wage plan must include in incentive system of wage payment to the efficient workers to produce more and to increase the efficiency of the low efficiency of the low efficient work.

5. To provide Proper Wage Differentials. The wage plan should have proper wage differentials based on proper 'Job Evaluation' so that wages earned by different categories of workers have a proper relation to the content and its worth. Moreover, difference in wage rates at different jobs must be justified.

6. To guarantee Minimum Wage. The wage plan must guarantee a minimum wage to protect the interest of the workers against conditions over which they have no control. It should take care of the minimum essential needs of the workers in a given environment to maintain his working efficiency.

7. To provide Flexibility. Wage plan should be flexible enough to meet the changing conditions without involving much administrative cost.

8. To evolve Good industrial Relations. Wage is the centre of all disputes. It should be fair so that good industrial relations be maintained and improved. For this purpose, it is necessary that the employees and the Union must be informed about the procedure used to establish the wage rates. Every employee should be informed of his position in the wage structure.

9. To provide Rationale. The wages should be comparable to the wages being paid in other firms in the same locality and of the same industry. It will reduce the labour turnover.

10. To give Sound Selection and Placement. A wage plan should attract able persons to the organisations. It should reduce the recruitment training and development cost. Introduction of performance appraisal studies as a regular feature will help the management in transfers, promotions etc.

11. To hedge Against Inflation. Inflation is today a regular feature of economy. A sound wage system must have a provision to prevent erosion of real wages by binding it with the cost of living index. Workers must be paid dearness allowance for the increased cost of living. It is necessary for the present though it is not a permanent solution of the eroded money value.

QUESTIONS FOR EXERCISE

1. Define Wages and explain its types.
2. What are various types of wage variations? Describe factors affecting wage rates.
3. What are the objectives of a sound wage and salary policy?

6

The Payment of Wages Act, 1936

ESSENTIALS OF SATISFACTORY WAGE SYSTEM

1. Simple. The wage system should be simple to understand as otherwise the workers look at it with suspicion. A complex wage system leads to strikes and agitations which may be hindrances in having harmonious employer employee relationship.

2. Satisfaction. The wage system should be satisfactory from the point of view of both employees and employers. The rewards to the employee should be fair and must give low per unit cost to the employer. The system should have the approval of the trade union.

3. Incentive to Work. The wage system should provide a sufficient incentive to workers to work hard and with great care. It should enable an efficient worker to earn more.

4. Guaranteed Minimum Wage. The system should guarantee a minimum wage to every worker.

5. Certain. The wage system should not have any element of ambiguity or uncertainty.

6. Quality Output. The wage system should encourage the worker not only to increase quantum of output but also to improve the quality of output.

7. Flexible. The wage system must be adaptable to necessary changes.

8. Common. The wage system should be common in the some locality or industry.

9. Economical. The wage system should be economical in operation. It should increase the overall efficiency of worker.

10. Distinction between Skilled and Unskilled Worker. The wage system should distinguish between skilled and unskilled worker. Skilled workers should be rewarded for the efforts made by them for acquiring skill.

11. Practical. The wage system adopted by an organisation should be practical. Some premium or bonus plans are theoretically quite attractive but they are not fit for practical use.

WAGE VARIATION

Wage variations means differences in wages at different places times and in different concerns for different persons. Wage variations are found to exist in different employments, occupation and localities.

TYPE OF WAGE VARIATIONS

1. On the Basis of Period. At time wages differ due to economic circumstances. Deflation leads to the reduction in wage rates while inflation increases the wages and other allowances. Price and wage index is prepared on this basis for mutual comparison. Change in income are measured and compensated.

2. On the Basis of Region. Wage rates differ at different places at different regions. For example, cloth mills at Maharashtra and Gujarat pay more than the mills in U.P. This may be due to economic development of the region labour demand and supply, expenses and living standards.

3. On the Basis of Industries. Wage rates differ according to industries. Iron and Steel industry pay more than the cloth mill. Again this is influenced by different elements like skilled workers, demand and supply position, nature and conditions of work place and industry in national development.

FACTORS INFLUENCING WAGE VARIATION

The factors which create wage differences may be the existence of non-competing group in the labour market, market imperfections and different labour qualities.

Wage also vary due to the personnel qualifications of lobour — educational qualifications, training and experience. Hence, there is difference of wages among worker from enterprise and place to place.

1. Demand and Supply of Labour. Like other things the value of labour is assessed on its demand and supply. Wages rates will rise if the demand of labour is more than the supply. If demand is less than the supply the wages will fall down.

2. Industry's Ability to pay. Industry's ability to pay also count much the determination of wages. If the industry have more profit, it can pay more as compared to other industries.

3. Comparative Wages. The local labour market and the wages of other industries is noted while assessing the wage rates. Wages in other units of the same nature should be noted. This develops labour satisfaction and checks labour migration.

4. Living Standard. Living standard of a place determines the wages. Labour need the maximum amount that they satisfy needs of their dependants.

5. Job Requirements. Jobs requiring more labour efficiency responsibilities and risk have rates of wages. Worker in mining get more than ordinary labour.

6. Productivity. Labours production ability influences the wage rates. If a worker does more and better work in comparison to others, he will get more wages while those producing less and below average good will get less wages.

7. Bargaining Power. Where labour union are effective and solid, it influences the wage rates. Rates of wages will be more in such enterprises as here collective bargaining is effective.

8. Government Policy. Government tries to build the wage rates and rate policies. It fixes the minimum wage rates and declares the rules for bonus, dearness allowance.

9. Name of Good Employer. Some companies wish to have a name as a good employer in the society. Naturally, they give higher wages and attract better workers which increase production and profit.

10. Incentives. Industries providing many fringe benefits and more chances of promotion, keep wage rates at lower level. The wage rates are high where such benefits are lacking.

In a country where even living wages are not paid to workers, the need to protect the wages earned by them can hardly be over-emphasised. Before the Payment of Wages Act, 1936 was passed, evils of withholding wages, delays in paying wages and making unreasonable deductions out of wages were quite prevalent.

The Payment of Wages Act, 1936 was to regulate the payment wages to certain classes of persons employed in industry [D'Costa, A.V.G.I.P. Rly. *Vs*. B.C. Patel, A.I.R. (1955) S.C. 412].

1. Chief Characteristics. The Act extends to the whole of India [Section 1 (2)]. It was extended to Jammu and Kashmir by the Central Labour Laws [Extension to Jammu and Kashmir] Act, 1970. The latest amendment to the Act was made in 1982. The Amending Act came into force with effect from 15th October 1982. Essentially meant for the benefit of industrial employees not getting very high salaries the provisions of the Act were enacted to safeguard their interest [Milkhi Ram *Vs*. State of Punjab, A.I.R. (1964) Punj. 513].

2. The Act does not apply to Persons Whose Wages exceed Rs. 1,600 Per Month [Sec. 1 (6)]. This limit was raised from Rs. 1,000 to Rs. 1,6000 by the Payment of Wages (Amendment) Act, 1982. It provides against irregularities in payment of wages and unauthorised deductions therefrom by the employers [Arvind Mills Ltd. *Vs*. Gadgil, A.I.R. (1941) Bom. 26; Armugham *Vs*. Jawahar Mills, A.I.R. (!956) Mad. 79].

3. It ensures payment of wages in a particular form and at regular intervals without unauthorised deductions.

Application of the Act

1. The act applies to the payment of wages to persons employed in any factory, to persons employed (otherwise than in a factory) upon any railway by a railway administration and to an industrial or other establishment specified in Clauses (a) to (g) of Section 2 (ii) (which defines industrial or other establishment). The persons employed upon a railway by a railway administration may have been employed either directly or through a sub-contractor by a person fulfilling a contract with a railway administration [Section 1 (4)].

2. The State Government may after giving 3 months' notice extend the provisions of the act to the payment of wages to any class of persons employed in any industrial establishment or class of establishments specified by the Central Government or a State Government under Clause (h) of Section 2 (ii) [Section 1 (5)].

3. In case of industrial establishments owned by the Central Government, such notification can be issued with the concurrence of the Central Government [proviso to Section 1 (5)].

4. In various States the Act has been extended to shops and establishments also.

DEFINITIONS

1. Employed person [Section 2 (i)]. 'Employed person' is the legal representative of a deceased employed person.

2. Employer [Section 2 (ia)]. 'Employer' is the legal representative of a deceased employer.

When there is a manager who is entrusted with the affairs of a company, the directors cannot be said to be employers [Superintendent & Remembrancer of Legal Affairs *Vs*. B.C. Saha, (1974) 45 F.J.R. 489].

3. Factory. [Section 2 (ib)]. It is defined in Section 2 (m) of the Factories Act, 1948 and includes any place to which the provisions of the Factories Act, 1948 have been applied under Section 85 (1) of that Act.

4. Industrial or Other Establishment [Section 2 (ii)]. It means any :

(a) tramway service, or motor transport service engaged in carrying passengers or goods or both by road for hire or reward;

(aa) air transport service other than such service belonging to or exclusively employed in the military, naval or air force of the Union or the Civil Aviation Department of the Government of India;

(b) dock, wharf or jetty;

(c) inland vessel, mechanically propelled;

(d) mine, quarry or oil-field;

(e) plantation;

(f) workshop or other establishment in which articles are produced, adapted or manufactured, with a view to their use, transport or sale;

(g) establishment in which any work relating to the construction, development or maintenance of buildings, roads, bridges or canals, or relating to operations connected with navigation, irrigation or supply of water or relating to the transmission or distribution of electricity or any other form of power is being carried on;

(h) any other establishment or class of establishment which the Central Government or a State Government may, having regard to the nature thereof, the need for protection of persons employed therein and other relevant circumstances, specify, by notification in the Official Gazette.

5. Mine [Section 2 (iia)]. It has the meaning assigned to it in Section 2 (10 (f) of the Mines Act, 1952.

6. Plantation [Section 2 (iii)]. It has the meaning assigned to it in Section 2 (f) of the Plantation Labour Act, 1951.

7. Railway Administration [Section 2 (v)]. It has the meaning assigned to it in Section 2 (32) of the Railways Act, 1989.

8. Wages [Section 2 (vi)]. 'Wages' means all remuneration (whether by way of salary, allowances or otherwise) expressed in terms of money or capable of being so expressed which would, if the terms of employment, express or implied, were fulfilled, be payable to a person employed in respect of his employment or of work done in such employment. Simply stated, 'wages' means all remuneration due to any worker or employee if the terms of contract of employment are fulfilled.

Wide Definition of Wages. The definition of expression 'wages; is made sufficiently wide by including within the expression;

(a) any remuneration payable under any award or settlement between the parties or order of a Court;

(b) any remuneration to which the person employed is entitled in respect of overtime work or holidays or any leave period;

(c) any additional remuneration payable under the terms of employment (whether called a bonus or by any other name);

(d) any sum which by reason of the termination of employment of the person employed is payable under any law, whether with or without deductions, but does not provide for the time within which the payment is to be made;

(e) any sum to which the person employed is entitled under any scheme framed under any law for the time being in force.

What does the Expression 'Wages' not include?

(1) any bonus (whether under a scheme of profit-sharing or otherwise) which does not form part of the remuneration payable under the terms of employment or which is not payable under any award or settlement between the parties or order of a Court;

(2) the value of any house accommodation, or of the supply of light, water, medical attendance or other amenity or of any service excluded from the computation of wages by a general or special order of the State Government;

(3) any contribution paid by the employer to any pension or provident fund, and the interest which may have accrued thereon;

(4) any travelling allowances or the value of any travelling concession;

(5) any sum paid to the employed person to defary special expenses entailed on him by the nature of his employment;

(6) any gratuity payable on the termination of employment in cases other than those specified in Clause (d) above.

Parts of the Definition of the Expression 'Wages'

1. The first part declares that 'wages' means all remuneration which would, if the terms of the contract of employment, express or implied, were fulfilled, be payable to a person employed, in respect of his employment. This clause presents no difficulty whatsoever for it declares in an unambiguous language that an employee is entitled to receive wages in accordance with the terms of his contract.

2. The second part says that the expression 'wages' shall include any bonus or other remuneration of the nature aforesaid which would be so payable, *i.e.*, payable in accordance with the terms of the contract.

3. The third part declares that the expression 'wages' shall include 'any sum' payable to such person by reason of the termination of his employment. The language of this clause is wide enough to embrace not a sum payable to an employee under the terms of a contract but also a sum payable to him under the provisions of any law.

RULES FOR PAYMENT OF WAGES (Sections 3 to 6)

1. Responsibility for Payment of Wages (Sections 3)

Every employer shall be responsible for the payment to persons employed by him of all wages required to be paid under the Payment of Wages Act (Sections 3). But in the case of persons employed (otherwise than by a contractor) in factories, industrial establishments or upon railways the following persons shall also be responsible for the payment of wages :

(i) in factories, the person named as the manager;

(ii) in industrial or other establishments, the person, if any, who is responsible to the employer for the supervision and control of the industrial or other establishment;

(iii) upon railways (otherwise than in factories), the person nominated by the railway administration in this behalf for the local area concerned (Proviso to Section 3).

2. Fixation of Wage-Periods (Section 4)

Every person responsible for the payment of wages under Section 3 shall fix periods, known as wage-periods, in respect of which such wages shall be payable [Section 4 (1)]. A wage-period shall not exceed one month [Section 4 (2)].

3. Time of Payments of Wages (Section 5)

(i) *Wages to be paid before 7th or 10th day* : The wages of every person employed upon or in any railway, factory or industrial or other establishment upon or in which less than 1,000 persons are employed, shall be paid before the expiry of 7th day of the following wage-period. In case the number of workers exceeds 1,000, the wages shall be paid before the 10th day of following wage-period [Section 5 (1)].

In the case of persons employed on a dock, wharf or jetty or in a mine, the balance of wages due on completion of the final tonnage account of the ship or wagons loaded or unloaded, as the case may be, shall be paid before the expiry of the 7th day from the day of such completion [Proviso to Section 5 (1)].

(ii) *Wages in Case of Termination of Employment* : Where the employment of any person is terminated by or on behalf of the employer, the wages earned by him shall be paid before the expiry of the 2nd working day from the day on which his employment is terminated [Section 5 (2)]. Where the employment of any person in an establishment is terminated due to the closure of the establishment for any reason other than a weekly or other recognised holiday, the wages earned by him shall be paid before the expiry of the 2nd day from the day on which his employment is so terminated [Proviso to Section 5 (2)].

(iii) *Exemption* : The State Government may, by general or special order, exempt the person responsible for the payment of wages from the operation of the above provisions in certain cases [Section 5 (3)].

(iv) *Wages to be paid on a Working Day* : All payment of wages shall be made on a working day [Section 5 (4)].

4. Medium of Payment of Wages (Section 6)

All wages shall be paid in current coin or currency notes or both (Section 6). Payment of wages in kind is not permitted. In order to save the worker from carrying cash on the pay day and mis-spending it, a Proviso has been added to Section 6 by the Payment of Wages (Amendment) Act, 1976. According to it, the employer may after obtaining the written authorisation of the employed person, pay him the wages either by cheque or by crediting the wages in his bank account. The provision in the Amendment Act for paying wages by cheque or depositing wages in bank account will also inculcate the banking habit among the workers and also make the process of payment simpler for the employer.

DEDUCTIONS FROM WAGES (Sections 7 to 13)

Section 7 provides that the wages of an employed person shall be paid to him without deductions of any kind except those authorised by or under the Payment of Wages Act, 1936 [Section 7 (1)].

Kinds of Deductions

The deductions from wages of an employed person referred to in Section 7 (1) may be of the following kinds only, namely;

1. Deductions for Fines [Sections 7 (2) (a) and 8]

(i) No fine shall be imposed on any employed person save in respect of such acts or omissions on his part as the employer, with the previous approval of the State Government or of the prescribed authority, may have specified by a notice [Section 8 (1)].

(ii) The notice specifying the acts and omissions for which fines may be imposed shall be exhibited in the prescribed manner on the premises (and in case of persons employed upon a railway, at prescribed place or places) in which the employment is carried on [Section 8 (2)].

(iii) No fine shall be imposed on an employed person until he has been given an opportunity of showing cause against the fine and has completed the age of 15 years [Section 8 (3) and (5)].

(iv) The total amount of fine which may be imposed in any one wage period on any employed person shall not exceed 3 per cent of the wages payable to him in respect of that wage-period [Section 8 (4)]. Such a fine shall not be recovered from the employed person by instalments or after the expiry of 60 days from the day on which it was imposed [Section 8 (6)].

(v) Every fine shall be deemed to have been imposed on the day of the act or omission in respect of which it was imposed [Section 8 (7)].

(vi) All fines and all realisations thereof shall be recorded in a register to be kept by the person responsible for the payment of wages, in such form as may be prescribed. All realisations of fines shall be applied only to such purposes as are beneficial to the person employed in the factory [Section 8 (8)].

2. Deductions for Absence from Duty [Section 7 (2) (b) and 9]

Deductions may be made on account of the absence of an employed person from duty [Section 7 (2) (b)] from the place or places where, by the terms of his employment, he is required to work. The absence may be for the whole or any part of the period during which he is so required to work [Section 9 (1)]. But the ratio between the amount of such deductions and the wages payable shall not exceed the ratio between the period of absence and total period within such wage-period [Section 9 (2)]. It has however been held in K.S.R.T. Employees' Assn. *Vs*. General Manager, K.S.R.T., (1985) Lab. I.C. 552 (Ker.) that in a strike by workers in a public utility like transport service, if employees absent for a part of the day without notice, deduction of full day's wages would not be unjustified or illegal.

If, however, 10 or more employed persons, acting in concert, absent themselves without due notice and without reasonable cause, the deduction for absence from duty from any such person may include such amount not exceeding his wages for 8 days as may be due to the employer in lieu of notice [Proviso to Section 9 (2)]. In this regard any employed person shall be deemed to be absent from the place where he is required to work if he refuses, in pursuance of a stay-in-strike or for any other cause which is not reasonable in the circumstances, to carry out his work (Explanation to Section 9.)

3. Deductions for Damage or Loss [Sections 7 (2) (c, (m), (n) and (o) and 10]

A deduction for damage to or loss of *goods expressly* entrusted to the employed person for custody or for money for which he is required to account shall not exceed the amount of the damage or loss caused to the employer by the neglect or default of the employed person. Same is the case as regards losses sustained by a railway administration on account of any rebates or refunds incorrectly granted by the employed person [Section 7 (2) (c) and 10 (1)].

Section 10 (1-A) also provides that a deduction for damage or loss shall not be made until the employed person has been given an opportunity of showing cause against the deduction. A similar opportunity shall also be given to the employed person in case of deductions for recovery of losses sustained by a railway administration on account of :

(i) acceptance by the employed person of counterfeit or base coins or mutilated or forged currency notes [Section 7 (2) (m)];

(ii) the failure of the employed person to invoice, to bill, to collect or to account for the appropriate charges due to the railway administration. The loss may relate to fares, freight, demurrage, wharfage and cranage or in respect of sale of food in catering establishments or in respect of sale of commodities in grain shops or otherwise [Section 7 (2) (n)];

(iii) any rebates or refunds incorrectly granted by the employed person where such loss is directly attributable to his neglect or default [Section 7 (2) (o)].

Section 10 (2) requires that all deductions and realisations in respect of damage to or loss of goods shall be recorded in a register to be kept by the person responsible for the payment of wages under Section 3.

4. Deductions for Services [Sections 7 (2) (d), (e) and 11]

A deduction for house accommodation [Section 7 (e) (d)] and such amenities and services supplied by the employer as have been authorised by the State Government [Section 7 (2) (e)] shall not be made from the wages of an employed person, unless such services have been accepted by him as a term of employment or otherwise. Deductions in respect of these services shall not exceed the value thereof. In case of deductions as regards services and amenities, the State Government may impose conditions (Section 11).

5. Deductions for Recovery of Advances [Section 7 (2) (f) and 12]

A deduction for recovery of an advance given to an employed person is subject to the following conditions :

(i) recovery of an advance of money given before employment began shall be made from the first payment of wages in respect of complete wage-period, but no recovery can be made of such advance given for travelling expenses;

(ii) recovery of an advance of money given after employment began shall be subject to such conditions as the State Government may impose;

(iii) recovery of advances of wages not already earned shall be subject to any rules made by the State Government in this regard. The State Government may regulate the extent to which such advances may be given and the instalments by which they may be recovered (Section 12).

The advance may be of any nature (including advance for travelling allowance or conveyance allowance) and the interest due in respect thereof, or for adjustment of over-payment of wages [Section 7 (2) (f)].

Deductions for adjustment of over-payment of wages is also authorised under the Act [Section 7 (2) (f)]. But there is no provision in the Act limiting the period within which the employers should made the deduction for adjustment of over-payment of wages [M.G. Koshi *Vs.* A.D. Cotton Mills, A.I.R. (1959) Ker. 332].

6. Deductions for Recovery of Loans [Sections 7 (2) (fff) and 12-A]

Deductions for loans granted for house-building or other purposes and the interest due in respect thereof [Section 7 (2) (fff)] approved by the State Government shall be subject to any rules made by the State Government regulating the extent to which such loans may be granted and the rate of interest payable thereon (Section 12-A).

7. Deductions for Payments to Co-operative Societies and Insurance Schemes [Sections 7 (2) (f) and (k) and 13]

These deductions shall include :

(i) deductions for payments to Co-operative Societies approved by the State Government or to a scheme of insurance maintained by the Indian Post Office [Section 7 (2) (f)] and

(ii) deductions made with the written authorisation of the person employed for the payment of any premium on his life insurance policy to the Life Insurance Corporation of India or for the purchase of securities of the Government of India or of any State Government or for being deposited in any Post Office Saving Bank in furtherance of any saving scheme of any such Government [Section 7 (2) (k)].

These deductions shall be subject to such conditions as the State Government may impose (Section 13).

8. Other Deductions

(i) deductions of income-tax payable by the employed person [Section 7 (2) (g)];

(ii) deductions required to be made by order of a Court or other authority competent to make such order [Section 7 (2) (h)];

(iii) deductions for payments to Co-operative Societies of advances from any provident fund to which the Provident Fund Act, 1925 applies or any recognised provident fund (as defined in Section 58-A of the Indian Income-tax Act, 1922) or any provident fund approved in this behalf by the State Government [Section 7 (2) (i)];

(iv) deductions for payment of insurance premia on Fidelity Guarantee Bonds [Section 7 (2) (i)];

(v) deductions for recovery of losses sustained by a railway administration on account of any default by the employed person. The default may consist of acceptance of counterfeit or base coins or forged currency notes, or allowing of excess rebates or refunds [Section 7 (2) (m)];

(vi) deductions made, with the written authorisation of the employed person, for contribution to the Prime Minister's National Relief Fund or to such other Fund as may be specified by the Central Government [Section 7 (2) (p); This Clause was added by the Payment of Wages (Amendment) Act, 1976] and

(vii) deductions for contributions to any insurance scheme framed by the Central Government for the benefit of its employees [Section 7 (2) (q); This Clause was added by the Payment of Wages (Amendment) Act, 1977].

Limit on Deductions [Section 7 (3)]

The total amount of deductions which may be made under the above heads [Section 7 (2)] in a wage-period from the wages of any employed person shall not exceed 75 per cent of such wages in cases where such deductions are wholly or partly made for payments to Co-operative Societies under Section 7 (2) (f). In any other case, they shall not exceed 50 per cent of such wages [Section 7 (3)]. Where the total deductions authorised under Section 7 (2) exceed 75 per cent, or as the case may be, 50 per cent of the wages, the excess may be recovered in such manner as may be prescribed [Proviso to Section 7 (3)].

MAINTENANCE OF REGISTERS AND RECORDS (Section 13-A)

Every employer shall maintain registers and records giving the following particulars of the persons employed by him :

(a) the work performed by them;

(b) the wages paid to them;

(c) the deductions made from their wages;

(d) the receipts given by them [Section 13-A (1)].

The registers and records shall be in such form as may be prescribed. They shall be preserved for a period of 3 years after the date of the last entry made therein [Section 13-A (2)].

ENFORCEMENT OF THE ACT

1. Inspectors (Section 14)

(i) *Appointment* : An Inspector of Factories appointed under Section 8 (1) of the Factories Act, 1948 shall be an Inspector for the purposes of the Payment of Wages Act in respect of all factories within the local limits assigned to him [Section 14 (1)].

The State Government may also, by notification in the Official Gazette, appoint such other persons as it thinks fit to be Inspectors for the purposes of the Act. It may define the local limits within which and the class of factories and industrial or other establishments in respect of which they shall exercise their functions [Section 14 (3)]. It may also appoint Inspectors for the purposes of the Act in respect of persons employed upon a railway (otherwise than in a factory) to whom the Act applies [Section 14 (2)].

(ii) *Powers and Functions of Inspectors* : An Inspector may :

(a) make such examination and inquiry as he thinks fit in order to ascertain if the provisions of the Act or rules made thereunder are being observed;

(b) with such assistants, if any, as he thinks fit, enter inspect and search any premises of any railway, factory or industrial or other establishment at any reasonable time for the purpose of carrying out the object of the Act;

(c) supervise the payment of wages to persons employed upon any railway or in any factory or industrial or other establishment;

(d) require by a written order the production at such place, as may be prescribed, of any register of record maintained in pursuance of the Act. He may also take on the spot or otherwise statements of any persons which he considers necessary for carrying out the purposes of the Act;

(e) seize or take copies of registers or documents or portions thereof as he may consider relevant in respect of an offence under this Act which he has reason to believe has been committed by an employer;

(f) exercise such other powers as may be prescribed [Section 14 (4)].

But no person shall be compelled under Section 14 (4) to answer any question or make any statement tending to incriminate himself [Proviso to Section 14 (4)].

The provisions of the Code of Criminal Procedure, 1973 shall, so far as may be, apply to any search or seizure as they apply to any search or seizure made under the authority of a warrant issued under Section 94 of the said Code [Section 14 (4-A)].

(iii) *Inspector deemed to be a Public Servant* : Every Inspector shall be deemed to be a public servant within the meaning of the Indian Pennal Code, 1860 [Section 14 (5)].

(iv) *Facilities to be afforded to Inspectors* : Every employer shall afford an Inspector all reasonable facilities for making any entry, inspection, supervision, examination or inquiry under the Act (Section 14-A).

2. Claims Arising out of Deductions from Wages or Delay in Payment of Wages and Penalty for Malicious or Vexatious Claims (Section 15)

(i) *Authority for Decision* : The scheme of Payment of Wages Act is that all claims arising out of deductions from wages or delay in the payment of wages are to be decided by the Authority appointed by the State Government under Section 15 and not by a Civil Court [Marute M. Mullik *Vs.* Polson Ltd. (1970) Lab. I.C. 308]. It was further observed in Authority Sabastian Almenda *Vs.* Taylor R.M., A.I.R. (1956) Bom. 737 that the Authority under the Payment of Wages Act constitutes a Court or a Tribunal of summary jurisdiction and the clear object of the Legislature in setting up this Court or Tribunal is to give facilities to the employee to recover his wages as expeditiously as possible [Rameshwar Lal. *Vs.* Jogender Dass, A.I.R. (1970) Ori. 76].

(ii) *Who may be appointed Authorities*? : Section 15 empowers the State Government to appoint some person as the Authority to hear and decide for any specified area all claims arising out of (a) deductions from the wages, or (b) delay in payment of the wages of persons employed or paid in that area, including all matters incidental to such claims. The appointment shall be made by notification in the Official Gazatte. The following may be appointed as the Authority as aforesaid :

(a) a presiding officer of any Labour Court or Industrial Tribunal, constituted under the Industrial Disputes Act, 1947, or under any corresponding law relating to the investigation and settlement of industrial disputes in force in the State, or

(b) any Commission for Workmen's Compensation, or

(c) any other officer with experience as a Judge of a Civil Court or as a stipendiary Magistrate [Section 15 (1)].

(iii) *Number of Authority* : The State Government may, where it considers necessary so to do, appoint more than one Authority for any specified area,. It may, by general or special order, also provide for the distribution or allocation of work to be performed by them under this Act [Proviso to Section 15 (1)].

(iv) *Powers of Authorities appointed under Section 15* : Section 18 provides that every Authority appointed under Section 15 (1) shall have all the powers of a Civil Court under the Code of Civil Procedure, 1908, for the purpose of :

(a) taking evidence and enforcing the attendance of witnesses and

(b) compelling the production of documents.

Further, every such Authority shall be deemed to be a Civil Court for all the purposes of Section 195 and of Chapter XXVI of the Code of Criminal Procedure, 1973.

(v) *Who may file Application*? : An application for claims arising under the Act may be filed by :

(a) the person employed himself, or

(b) any legal practitioner, or

(c) any official of a registered trade union authorised in writing to act on his behalf, or

(d) any Inspector under the Act, or

(e) any other person acting with the permission of the Authority appointed under Section 15 (1) [Section 15 (2)].

(vi) *Application to be filed Within 12 Months* : Every application for claims under the act shall be presented within 12 months from the date on which the deduction from the wages was made or from the date on which the payment of the wages was due to be made [Proviso 1 to Section 15 (2)]. An application may also be admitted after 12 months if the applicant satisfies the Authority that there was a sufficient cause for not making the application within 12 months [Proviso 2 to Section 15 (2)].

(vii) *Procedure* : When any application for claims under the Act is entertained, the Authority shall hear the applicant and the employer or other persons responsible for the payment of wages under Section 3, or give them an opportunity of being heard. The Authority shall make such further inquiry as may be necessary. It may direct the refund to be made to the employed person of the amount deducted or the payment of the delayed wages, together with such compensation as it may think fit. The compensation shall not exceed 10 times the amount improperly deducted, and Rs. 25 in case of delayed wages. Even where the deducted or delayed wages are paid before the disposal of the application, the Authority may direct the payment of such compensation as it may think fit. This amount of compensation shall however not exceed Rs. 25 [Section 15 (3)].

(viii) *No Direction if the Authority is satisfied* : No direction for the payment of compensation shall be made in the case of delayed wages if the Authority is satisfied that the delay was due to :

(a) a *bona fide* error or dispute; or

(b) the occurrence of an emergency or the existence of exceptional circumstances; or

(c) the failure of the employed person to apply for or accept payment [Proviso to Section 15 (3)].

(ix) *Malicious or Vexatious Application* : If the Authority hearing an application is satisfied that the application was malicious or vexatious, it may direct a penalty not exceeding Rs. 50 to be paid to the employer or other person responsible for payment of wages, by the person presenting the application [Section 15 (4) (a)]. The authority may further direct that a penalty not exceeding Rs. 50 to be paid to the State Government by the employer or other person responsible for the payment of wages in cases where the applicant ought not to have been compelled to seek redress under Section 15 [Section 15 (4) (b)].

(x) *Dispute as to Legal Representatives* : Where there is any dispute as to the person or persons being the legal representative or representatives of the employer or of the employed person, the decision of the Authority on such dispute shall be final [Section (4-A)].

(xi) *Inquiry under Section 15 is a Judicial Proceeding.* Any inquiry under Section 15 shall be deemed to be a judicial proceeding within the meaning of Sections 193, 219 and 228 of the Indian Penal Code, 1860 [Section 15 (4-B)].

(xii) *Recovery of Amount* : Any amount directed to be paid under Section 15 may be recovered :

(a) if the Authority is a Magistrate, by the Authority as if it were a fine imposed by him as Magistrate and

(b) if the Authority is not a Magistrate, by any Magistrate to whom the Authority makes application in this behalf, as if it were a fine imposed by such Magistrate [Section 15 (5)].

3. Single Application in respect of Claims (Section 16)

A single application may be presented under Section 15 on behalf of or in respect of any number of employed persons belonging to the same unpaid group. When a single application is made, every person on whose behalf such application is presented may be awarded maximum compensation to the extent specified in Section 15 (3) [Section 16 (2)].

Employed persons are said to belong to the same unpaid group if they are borne on the same establishment and ·

(i) if deductions have been made from their wages in contravention of the Act for the same cause and during the same wage-period or periods, or

(ii) if their wages for the same wage-period or periods have remained unpaid after the day fixed by Section 5 [Section 16 (1)].

The Authority may deal with any number of separate pending applications, presented under Section 15 in respect of persons belonging to the same unpaid group, as a single application [Section 16 (3)].

4. Appeal (Section 17)

(i) *Preferring* : An appeal may be preferred in a Presidency-town before the Court of Small Causes and elsewhere before the District Court against :

(a) an order dismissing either wholly or in part an application made under Section 15 (2), or

(b) a direction made under Section 15 (3) by the Authority to refund to the employed person the amount deducted from wages or under Section 15 (4) by the Authority for payment of penalty to the employer.

The appeal may be preferred within 30 days of the date on which the order or direction was made [Section 17 (1)].

The Court may, if it thinks fit, submit any question of law for the decision of the High Court and, if it so does, shall decide the question in conformity with such decision [Section 17 (4)].

(ii) *Who may Prefer Appeal*? :

(a) the employer or other person responsible for the payment of wages under Section 3, if the total sum directed to be paid by way of wages and compensation exceeds Rs. 300 or such direction has the effect of imposing on the employer or the other person a financial liability exceeding Rs. 1,000 [Section 17 (1) (a)]; or

(b) an employed person, if the total amount of wages claimed to have been withheld from the employed person exceeds Rs. 20 or from the unpaid group to which the employed person belongs or belonged exceeds Rs. 50. The appeal may also be made by any legal practitioner or any official of a registered trade union authorised in writing to act on behalf of the employed person or any Inspector under the Act, or any other person permitted by the Authority to make an application under Section 15 (2) [Section 17 (1) (b)]; or

(c) any person directed to pay a penalty under Section 14 (4) [Section 17 (1) (c)].

Where an employed prefers an appeal under Section 17, the authority against whose decision the appeal has been preferred may, and if so directed by the Court shall, pending the decision of the appeal, withhold payment of any sum in deposit with it [Section 17 (3)].

5. Penalty for Offences under the Act (Section 20)

(i) *Penalty for Delaying Payment of Wages Within the Prescribed Period or Making Unauthorised Deductions* : Whoever being responsible for the payment of wages to an employed person delays payment of wages within the period laid down under the Act or makes unauthorised deductions shall be punishable with fine which shall not be less than Rs. 200 but which may extend to Rs. 1,000 [Section 20 (1)].

(ii) *Penalty for not Paying Wages on a Working Day or in Current Coin or not Recording Fines or not Displaying the Abstracts of the Act* : Not paying the wages on a working day, or not paying wages in current coin or currency or both, or not recording the fines or amounts realised for damage or loss in a register, or not displaying by notice abstracts of the Act the rules, are also offences punishable with a fine which may extend to Rs. 500 for each offence [Section 20 (2)].

(iii) *Penalty for Failure to maintain, furnish Records and Returns* : Whoever being required under the Act to maintain any records or registers or to furnish any information or return :

(a) fails to maintain such register or record; or

(b) wilfully refuses or without lawful excuse neglects to furnish such information or return; or

(c) wilfully furnishes or causes to be furnished any information or return which be knows to be false; or

(d) refuses to answer or wilfully gives a false answer to any question necessary for obtaining any information required to be furnished under the Act;

shall, for each such offence, be punishable with fine which shall not be less than Rs. 200 but which may extend to Rs. 1,000 [Section 20 (3)].

(iv) *Penalty for obstructing, etc. Inspector* : Whoever —

(a) wilfully obstructs an Inspector in the discharge of his duties under the Act; or

(b) refuses or wilfully neglects to afford an Inspector any reasonable facility for making any entry, inspection, examination, supervision, or inquiry authorised by or under the Act in relation to any railway, factory or industrial or other establishment; or

(c) wilfully refuses to produce on the demand of an Inspector any register of other document kept in pursuance of the Act; or

(d) pervents or attempts to prevent any person from appearing before an Inspector acting in pursuance of his duties under the Act;

shall be punishable with fine which shall not be less than Rs. 200 but which may extend to Rs. 1,000 [Section 20 (4)].

(v) *Subsequent Offence* : If any person who has been convicted of any offence punishable under the Act is again guilty of an offence involving contravention of the same provision, he shall be punishable on a subsequent conviction with imprisonment for a term which shall not be less than 1 month but which may extend to 3 months, or with fine which shall not be less than Rs. 500 but which may extend to Rs. 3,000 or with both [Section 20 (5)]. But no cognizance shall be taken of an earlier conviction made more than 2 years before the date of the commission of the present offence [Proviso to Section 20 (5)].

(vi) *Additional Fine for Failure to pay Wages by the Fixed Date* : If any person fails or wilfully neglects to pay the wages of any employed person by the fixed date, he shall, without prejudice to any other action that may be taken against him, be punishable with an additional fine which may extend to Rs. 100 for each day for which such failure or neglect continues [Section 20 (6)]. The words 'additional fine' do not contemplate a fine subsequent to one imposed earlier

[Kanta Press *Vs.* Prescribed Authority, (1988) 56 F.L.R. 301 (All.) (D.B.)].

MISCELLANEOUS

1. Bar of Suits (Section 22). No Court shall entertain any suit for the recovery of wages or of any deduction from wages in so far as the sum so claimed :

(i) forms the subject of an application under Section 15 which has been presented by the plaintiff and which is pending before the Authority appointed under that Section or of an appeal under Section 17; or

(ii) has formed the subject of a direction under Section 15 in favour of the plaintiff; or

(iii) has been adjudged, in any proceeding under Section 15, not to be owed to the plaintiff; or

(iv) could have been recovered by an application under Section 15.

2. Protection of Action taken in Good Faith (Section 22-A). No suit, prosecution or other legal proceedings shall lie against the Government or any officer of the Government for anything which is in good faith done or intended to be done under the Act.

3. Contracting out (Section 23). Any contract or agreement whereby an employed person relinquishes any right conferred by the Act shall be *null and void* in so far as it purports to deprive him of such right [Armugham *Vs.* Jawahar Mills, A.I.R., (1956) Mad. 76].

If a deduction is unauthorised, no agreement, even if true, could give an employer a right to make such deduction [*Bharat Airways Ltd.* v. *S.R. Chakrabarti*, (1956) 1 L.L.J. 89].

4. Display by Notice of Abstracts of the Act (Section 25). The person responsible for the payment of wages to persons employed in a factory or an industrial or other establishment shall cause to be displayed a notice containing such abstracts of the Act and of the rules made thereunder in English and in the language of the majority of the persons employed in the factory or an industrial or other establishment, as may be prescribed.

5. Payment of Undisbursed Wages in Case of Death of Employed Person (Section 25-A). In case of death of an employed person or in case of his whereabouts not being known, all amounts payable to him as wages, shall :

(i) be paid to the person nominated by him in this behalf in accordance with the rules made under the Act;

(ii) be deposited with the prescribed Authority; or

(iii) where no nomination has been made, or

(iv) where for any reasons such amounts cannot be paid to the person nominated.

The prescribed Authority shall deal with the amounts deposited in the prescribed manner. The above rule is subject to the other provisions of the Act [Section 25-A (1)].

Where the amounts payable by an employer as wages are disposed of in manner referred to in Section 25-A (1), the employer shall be discharged of his liability to pay those wages [Section 25-A (2)].

6. Rule-making Power (Section 26)

(i) *Rules to regulate Procedure of Authorities* : The State Government may make rules to regulate the procedure to be followed by the Authorities and Courts referred to in Sections 15 and 17 [Section 26 (1)].

(ii) *Contravention of Rule Punishable with Fine* : In making any rule under Section 26, the State Government may provide that a contravention of the rule shall be punishable with fine which may extend to Rs. 200 [Section 26 (4)].

(iii) *Previous Publication of Rules* : All rules made under Section 26 shall be subject to the condition of previous publication, and the date to be specified under Section 23 (3) of the General Clauses Act, 1897 shall not be less than 3 months from the date on which the draft of the proposed rules was published [Section 26 (5)].

(iv) *Rules made by the Central Government to be laid before Parliament* : Every rule made by the Central Government under Section 26 shall be laid, as soon as may be after it is made, before each House of Parliament while it is in session for a total period of 30 days. This period of 30 days may be comprised in one session or in 2 or more successive sessions. If both Houses agree in making any modification in the rule, the rule shall thereafter have effect only in such modified form. If both Houses agree that the rule should not be made, it shall have no effect. But any such modification or annulment of the rule shall be without prejudice to the validity of anything previously done under that rule [Section 26 (6)].

QUESTIONS FOR EXERCISE

1. Under the Payment of Wages Act. 1936, define 'wages' and 'industrial establishment'.
2. State the rules regarding fixation of wage-periods. On whom does the responsibility for payment of wages lie under the Payment of Wages Act, 1936?

3. Describe the time of payment of wages in railways, factories and industrial establishments under the Payment of Wages Act, 1936.
4. Describe an employer's liability for paying wages. Is he entitled to make any deductions at the time of payment of wages?
5. What is meant by wages according to the Payment of Wages Act, 1936? Who is responsible for the payment of wages under the Act?
6. The Payment of Wages Act, 1936 provides that the wages are to be paid in a particular form at regular intervals and without any unauthorised deductions. Explain.
7. X, an employee, enters into a contract with his employer Y to accept his wages in kind and not in money. Can X later on demand his wages in cash?
8. What are the provisions of the Payment of Wages Act, 1936 regarding deduction from wages for absence from duty?
9. What are the provisions of the Payment of Wages Act, 1936 with regard to deductions which may, and which may not, be made from wages?
10. How can the deduction from wages for damage or loss caused to the employer by the neglect or default of the employed person may be made and to what extent?

PRACTICAL PROBLEMS

1. A fine is imposed on a employed person on 1st January 2000. The employer seeks to recover the fine on 7th March 2000. Can he recover? State reasons for your answer.
   [**Hint** : The employer cannot recover [Section 8 (6)]].
2. An employer imposes a fine on an employee who is 15 years' old and deducts it from his wages. What provisions of the Payment of Wages Act, 1936 does he violate and what is the remedy available to the employee?
   [**Hint** : The employer violates Section 8 (5) and the employee can recover the amount of fine deducted from his wages under Section 15 (2) (Sections 8 (5), 15 (2)].
3. An employer made alteration in the wage structure as a result of which certain allowances previously paid to an employee were stopped. His total wages, however, were not less than before. Does stopping of these allowances amount to deduction from the wages? Will an application under Section 15 (2) lie for this?

[**Hint :** The stopping of allowance does not amount to 'deduction' bad as such no application will lie under Sec. 15 (2)].

4. An employee committed an act in respect of which a fine was imposed. No prior notice specifying this particular act in respect of which fine could be imposed had been exhibited. The employer deducted the fine in 4 instalments from the wages of the employee. What provisions of the Act does the employer violate?
   [**Hint :** The employer violates the provisions of Sections 8 (2) and 8 (6)].

5. 12 employed persons acting in concert absent themselves for 2 days without due notice and without reasonable cause. What is the maximum amount that may be deducted on account of the absence from duty of these persons?

   [**Hint :** Wages for 10 days, *i.e.*, two days' wages for absence plus 8 days' wages for not giving due notice (Proviso to Section 9 (2))].

6. While working on a machine, a worker accidentally breaks a valuable testing appliance. The employer deducts the value of the appliance from the wages of the worker. Is the deduction justified?
   [**Hint :** No, as the loss cannot be directly attributable to the worker's neglect or default (Sections 7 (2) (c) and 10)].

7

The Minimum Wages Act, 1948

The Minimum Wages Act was passed in 1948. It enabled the Central and State Governments to fix minimum rates of wages payable to employees in a selected number of 'sweated' industries. The Act applies to the whole of India.

Objective of the Act

The Object of the Act is to secure the welfare of the workers in a competitive market by fixing the minimum rates of wages in certain employments. The Legislature intended to apply the Act to those industries or localities in which, by reason of causes such as unorgainsed labour or absence of machinery for regulation of wages, wages paid to workers were inadequate in the light of the general level of wages and subsistence level, [Bhikusa Yamasa Kshatriya *Vs.* Sangammer Akola Taluka, Bidi Kamgar Union, A.I.R. (1963) S.C. 806].

DEFINITIONS

1. Adolescent [Section 2 (a)]. 'Adolescent' is a person who has completed his 14th year of age but not completed his 18th year.

2. Adult [Section 2 (aa)]. 'Adult' is a person who has completed his 18th year of age.

3. Appropriate Government [Section 2 (b)]. In relation to any scheduled employment carried on by or under the authority of the Central Government or a railway administration, or in relation to a mine, oilfield or major port, or any corporation established by a Central Act, Appropriate Government means the Central Government [Section 2 (b) (i)].

In relation to any other scheduled employment (which means an employment specified in the Schedule to the Act), the appropriate Government means the State Government [Section 2 (b) (ii)].

4. Child [Section 2 (bb)]. 'Child' is a person who has not completed his 14th year of age.

5. Competent Authority [Section 2 (c)]. 'Competent authority' is the authority appointed by the appropriate Government by notification in its Official Gazette to ascertain from time to time the cost of living index number applicable to the employees employed in the scheduled employments (*i.e.*, employments specified in the Schedule to the Act) specified in such notification.

6. Cost of Living Index Number [Section 2 (d)]. In relation to employees in any scheduled employment in respect of which minimum rates of wages have been fixed, 'Cost of living index number' means the index number ascertained and declared by the competent authority by notification in the Official Gazette to be the cost of living index number applicable to employees in such employment.

7. Employer [Section 2 (e)]. 'Employer' is any person who employs, whether directly or through another person, or whether on behalf of himself or any other person, one or more employees, in any scheduled employment in respect of which minimum rates of wages have been fixed under the Act.

Who are the Employers?

(i) in a factory where there is carried on any scheduled employment in respect of which minimum rates of wages have been fixed under the Act, any person named as manager of the factory under Section 7 (1) (f) of the Factories Act, 1948;

(ii) in any scheduled employment under the control of any Government in India in respect of which minimum rates of wages have been fixed under the Act, the person or authority appointed by such Government for the supervision and control of employees or where no person or authority is so appointed, the head of the department;

(iii) in any scheduled employment under any local authority in respect of which minimum rates of wages have been fixed under the Act, the person appointed by such authority for the supervision and control of employees or where no person is so appointed, the chief executive officer of the local authority;

(iv) in any other case where there is carried on any scheduled employment in respect of which minimum rates of wages have been fixed under the Act, any person responsible to the owner of the supervision and control of the employees or for the payment of wages.

8. Scheduled employment [Section 2 (g)]. It means an employment specified in the Schedule to the Act (reproduced below), or any process or branch of work forming part of such employment.

THE SCHEDULE
[Sections 2 (g) and 27]

PART I

1. Employment in any woollen carpet making or shawl weaving establishment.

2. Employment in any rice mill, flour mill or dal mill.

3. Employment in any tobacco (including *bidi* making) manufactory.

4. Employment in any plantation, that is to say, any estate which is maintained for the purpose of growing cinchona, rubber, tea or coffee.

5. Employment in any oil mill.

6. Employment under any local authority.

7. Employment on the construction or maintenance of roads or in building operations.

8. Employment in stone-breaking or stone-crushing.

9. Employment in any lac manufactory.

10. Employment in any public motor transport.

11. Employment in any mica works.

12. Employment in public motor transport.

13. Employment in tanneries and leather manufactory.

14. Employment in gypsum mines.

15. Employment in barytes mines.

16. Employment in bauxite mines.

17. Employment in managanese mines.

18. Employment in maintenance of buildings and employment in the construction and maintenance of runways.

19. Employment in china clay mines.

20. Employment in kyanite mines.

21. Employment in copper mines.

22. Employment in clay mines covered under the Mines Act, 1952.

23. Employment in magnesite mines covered under the Mines Act, 1952.

24. Employment in white clay mines.

25. Employment in stone mines.

26. Employment in steatite (including the mines producing seapstone and tale).

27. Employment in ochre mines.

28. Employment in asbestos mines.
29. Employment in fire clay mines.
30. Employment in chromite mines.
31. Employment in quartizite mines.
32. Employment in quartz mines.
33. Employment in silica mines.
34. Employment in graphite mines.
35. Employment in felspar mines.
36. Employment in laterite mines.
37. Employment in dolomite mines.
38. Employment in redoxide mines.
39. Employment in wolfram mines.
40. Employment in iron ore mines.
41. Employment in granite mines.
42. Employment in rock phosphate mines.
43. Employment in hematite mines.
44. Employment in loading and unloading in :
    (i) railways, goods sheds,
    (ii) docks and ports.
45. Employment in marble and calcite mines.

PART II

9. Employment in Agriculture. It is in any form of farming, including the cultivation and tillage of the soil, dairy farming, the production, cultivation, growing and harvesting of any agricultural or horticultural commodity, the raising of live-stock, bees or poultry, and any practice performed by a farmer or on a farm as incidental to or in conjunction with farm operations (including any forestry or timbering operations and the preparations for market and delivery to storage or to market or to carriage for transportation to market of farm produce.)

10. Wages [Section 2 (h)]. 'Wages' means all remuneration, capable of being expressed in terms of money, which, would, if the terms of the contract of employment, express or implied, were fulfilled, be payable to a person employed in respect of his employment or work done in such employment. It includes house rent allowance but does not include :

(i) the value of —

(a) any house accommodation, supply of light, water, medical attendance, or

(b) any other amenity or any service excluded by general or special order of the appropriate Government;

(ii) any contribution paid by the employer to any Pension Fund Provident Fund or under any scheme of social insurance;

(iii) any travelling allowance or the value of any travelling concession;

(iv) any sum paid to the person employed to defray special expenses entailed on him by the nature of his employment; or

(v) any gratuity payable on discharge.

11. Employee [Section 2 (i)]. 'Employee' is any person who is employed for hire or reward to do any work, skilled or unskilled, manual or clerical, in a scheduled employment in respect of which minimum rates of wages have been fixed. The term includes an out-worker to whom any articles or materials are given out by another person to be made up, cleaned, washed, altered, onamented, finished, repaired, adapted or otherwise processed for sale for the purpose of the trade or business of that other person where the process is to be carried out either in the home of the out-worker or in some other premises not being premises under the control and management of that other person. The term also includes an employee declared to be an employee by the appropriate Government. It does not however include any member of the Armed Forces of the Union.

FIXATION AND REVISION OF WAGES (Sections 3 to 5)

1. Fixing of Minimum Rates of Wages (Section 3)

(i) *The Responsibility for fixing the Minimum Rates of Wages* : It is that of the appropriate Government. Section 3 provides that the appropriate Government :

(a) shall fix the minimum rates of wages payable to employees employed in an employment specified in Part I or Part II of the Schedule (reproduced earlier) and in an employment added to either Part by notification in the Official Gazette [Section 3 (1) (a)];

(b) may, in respect of employees employed in an employment specified in Part II of the Schedule, instead of fixing minimum rates of wages for the whole State, fix such rates for a part of the State or for any specified class or classes of such employment in the whole State or part thereof [Proviso to Section 3 (1) (a)];

(c) shall review at such intervals not exceeding 5 years, the minimum rates of wages so fixed and revise the minimum rates if necessary [Section 3 (1) (b)].

(ii) *Minimum Number of Employees* : The appropriate Government may refrain from fixing minimum rates of wages in respect of any scheduled employment in which there are in the whole State less than 1,000 employees engaged in such employment. But if at any time, the appropriate Government comes to a finding after an inquiry that the number of employees in any scheduled employment has risen to 1,000 or more, it shall fix minimum rates of wages payable as soon as may be after such finding [Section 3 (1-A)].

2. Fixations of Minimum Rates. The appropriate Government may fix :

(i) a minimum rate of wages for time work (referred to as 'a minimum time rate');

(ii) a minimum rate of wages for piece work (referred to as 'a minimum piece rate');

(iii) a minimum rate of remuneration to apply in the case of such employees employed on piece work for purpose of securing to such employees a minimum rate of wages on a time work basis (referred to as 'a guaranteed time rate');

(iv) a minimum rate (whether a time rate or a piece rate) to apply in substitution for the minimum rate which would otherwise be applicable, in respect of overtime work done by employees (referred to as 'overtime rate') [Section 3 (2)].

3. Different Minimum Rates. In fixing or revising minimum rates of wages, different minimum rates of wages may be fixed for :

(i) different scheduled employments;

(ii) different classes of work in the same scheduled employment;

(iii) adults, adolescents, children and apprentices;

(iv) different localities [Section 3 (3) (a)].

Further in fixing or revising minimum rates of wages under Section 3, minimum rates of wages may be fixed by any one or more of the following wage-periods, namely :

(i) by the hour,

(ii) by the day,

(iii) by the month, or

(iv) by such other larger wage-period as may be prescribed.

Where such rates are fixed by the day or by the month, the manner of calculating wages for a month or for a day, as the case may be, may be indicated [Section 3 (3) (b)]. Also where any wage-periods have been fixed under Section 4 of the Payment of Wages

Act, 1936, minimum wages shall be fixed in accordance therewith [Proviso to Section 3 (3) (b)].

4. Content of Minimum Rate of Wages (Section 4)

Any minimum rate of wages fixed or revised by the appropriate Government in respect of scheduled employments under Section 3 may consist of :

(i) a basic rate of wages and a special allowance (hereinafter referred to as the 'cost of living allowance'). The rate of cost of living allowance shall be adjusted at such intervals and in such manner as the appropriate Government may direct. The rate-shall accord as nearly as practicable with the variation in the cost of living index number applicable to such workers; or

(ii) a basic rate of wages with or without the cost of living allowance, and the cash value of the concessions in respect of supplies of essential commodities at concessional rates, where so authorised; or

(iii) an all inclusive rate allowing for the basic rate, the cost of living allowance and the cash value of the concessions, if any [Section 4 (1)].

The cost of living allowance and the cash value of the concessions in respect of supplies of essential commodities at concessional rates shall be computed by the competent authority. The computation shall be done by the competent authority at such intervals and in accordance with such directions as may be specified or given by the appropriate Government [Section 4 (2)].

5. Procedure for fixing and revising Minimum Wages (Section 5)

Section 5 provides 2 separate modes of procedure for fixing and revising minimum wages and the primary object of both the procedures is to enable the Government to reach a balanced conclusion with regard to fixation of a minimum wage. In one case a committee [Section 5 (1) (a)] is appointed and in the other a notification [Section 5 (1) (b)] is made and objections are invited [Mohan Bros. *Vs*. State, A.I.R. (1967) Punj. 491; P. Gangadharan *Vs*. State, A.I.R. (1968) Ker. 218].

(i) The Provisions of Section 5 : In fixing minimum rages of wages in respect of any scheduled employment for the first time or in revising minimum rates of wages so fixed, the appropriate Government shall follow either of the following two methods :

(a) *Appointment of Committees* : The appropriate Government shall appoint as many committees and sub-committees as it considers necessary to hold inquiries and advise it in respect of fixation or revision of minimum rates of wages, as the case may be [Section 5 (1) (a)]; or

(b) *Publication of Proposals in the Official Gazette* : The appropriate Government shall, by notification in the Official Gazette, publish its proposals for the information of persons likely to be affected by the fixation or revision of minimum rates of wages. It shall also specify a date on which the proposals will be taken into consideration. The date so specified shall not be less than 2 months from the date of the notification [Section 5 (1) (b)].

After considering the advice of the committee or committee [under Section (1) (a)] or all representations received by it before the date specified in the notification [under Section 5 (1) (b)], the appropriate Government shall, by notification in the Official Gazette, fix or revise the minimum rates of wages in respect of each scheduled employment. The fixation or revision shall come into force on the expiry of 3 months from the date of the issue of notification, unless the notification otherwise provides [Section 5 (2)]. The power of the Government under Section 5 (2) to issue notification revising minimum wages includes power to give retrospective effect to notification [Mizar Govinda Annappa Pai & Sons *Vs.* State of Karnataka, (1986) Lab. I.C. 1555 (Kant.)].

(ii) *Consultation with Advisory Board* : Where the appropriate Government proposes to revise the minimum rates of wages by the mode specified in Section 5 (1) (b), it shall also consult the Advisory Board [constituted under Section 7] [Proviso to Section 5 (2)].

(iii) *Government not bound to accept the Recommendation of the Committee Appointed Under Section 5 (1) (a)* : A committee appointed under Section 5 (1) (a) is only an advisory body and the Government is not bound to accept its recommendation in every case [Management of All Tea Estates in Assam *Vs.* Indian National Trade Union Congress, A.I.R. (1957) S.C. 206]. Further any irregularity in the constitution of this committee or a procedure adopted by it cannot affect the validity of the notification issued by the appropriate Government under Section 5 (1) (b) [Edwards Mills Co. Ltd., Marwar *Vs.* State of Ajmer, A.I.R. (1955) S.C. 25]. If no advise is given by the Committee or if inadequate advice is given, Section 5 does not deprive the appropriate Government of its power and duty to fix or revise the minimum rates of wages [Tourist Hotel *Vs.* State of A.P., (1975) 1.L.L.J. 211].

The notification of the Government that employees who are in receipt of higher wages than those fixed under the notification should continue to enjoy the same is not warranted by the provisions of the

Act. The Government cannot convert a voluntary payment into a compulsory payment [Bengal Motion Picture Employees' Union *Vs.* Kohinoor Pictures Pvt. Ltd., A.I.R. (1964) Cal. 519].

6. Correction of Errors (Section 10). The appropriate Government may, at any time, by notification in the Official Gazette, correct clerical or arithmetical mistakes in any order fixing or revising minimum rates of wages under the Act, or errors arising therein from any accidental slip or omission [Section 10 (1)]. Every such notification shall, as soon as may be after it is issued, be placed before the Advisory Board (constituted under Section 7) for information [Section 10 (2)].

ADVISORY BOARD AND CENTRAL ADVISORY BOARD (Sections 7 to 9 and 29)

1. Advisory Board (Section 7)

(i) *Appointment* : For the purpose of co-ordinating the work of committees and sub-committees appointed under Section 5 and advising the appropriate Government generally in the matter of fixing and revising minimum rates of wages, the appropriate Government shall appoint an Advisory Board (Section 7).

(ii) *Procedure* : No procedure is prescribed in the Act for the Advisory Board to function. It can devise its own procedure [State of Rajasthan *Vs.* Hari Ram Nathwani, A.I.R. (1976) S.C. 277].

(iii) *Composition of Committees and Advisory Board (Section 9)* : Each of the committees, Sub-committees and the Advisory Board shall consist of persons to be nominated by the appropriate Government representing employers and employees in the scheduled employments, who shall be equal in number, and independent persons not exceeding 1/3rd of its total number of members. One of the independent persons shall be appointed the Chairman by the appropriate Government.

2. Central Advisory Board (Section 8)

(i) *Objectives of Appointment* : The Central Government shall appoint a Central Advisory Board :

(a) for the purpose of advising the Central and State Governments in the matters of the fixation and revision of minimum rates of wages and other matters under the Act and

(b) for co-ordinating the work of the Advisory Boards [Section 8 (1)].

(ii) *Composition of the Central Advisory Board* : It shall consist of persons nominated by the Central Government representing employers and employees in the scheduled employments, who shall be equal in number, and independent persons not exceeding 1/3rd of its total number of members. One of the independent persons shall be appointed the Chairman of this Board by the Central Government [Section 8 (2)].

(iii) *Rules of Working* : According to Section 29, the Central Government may, subject to the condition of previous publication, by notification in the Official Gazette, make rules prescribing the term of office of the members, the procedure to be followed in the conduct of business, the method of voting, the manner of filling up casual vacancies in membership and the quorum necessary for the transaction of business of the Central Advisory Board.

SAFEGUARDS IN PAYMENT OF MINIMUM WAGES (Sections 11 to 18)

1. Wages in Kind (Section 11)

Minimum wages payable under the Act shall be paid in cash [Section 11 (1)]. But where it has been the custom to pay wages wholly or partly in kind, the appropriate Government may, by notification in the Official Gazette, authorise the payment of minimum wages either wholly or partly in kind [Section 11 (2)].

The appropriate Government may also by notification in the Official Gazette authorise the provision of the supply of essential commodities at concessional rates [Section 11 (3)].

The cash value of wages in kind [under Section 11 (2)] and of concession in respect of supplies of essential commodities at concessional rates authorised under Section 11 (2) and (3) shall be estimated in the prescribed manner [Section 11 (4)].

2. Payment of Minimum Rate of Wages (Section 12)

Where in respect of any scheduled employment minimum wages have been fixed, the employer shall pay to every employee wages at a rate not less than the minimum rate of wages fixed for that class of employees in the employment. Such wages shall be paid without any deductions except as may be authorised. Where the contract rate of wages is higher, the staturory obligation does not come into play [Section 12 (1)].

Section 12 does not affect the provisions of the Payment of Wages Act, 1936 [Section 12 (2)].

3. Fixing Hours for a Normal Working Day, etc. (Section 13)

(i) *Functions of* Government : In regard to any scheduled employment where minimum rates of wages have been fixed, the appropriate Government may :

(a) fix the number of hours of work which constitute a normal working day, inclusive of one or more specified intervals;

(b) provide for a day of rest in every period of 7 days and for payment of remuneration in respect of such day of rest;

(c) provide for payment for work on a day of rest at a rate not less than the overtime rate [Section 13 (1)].

(ii) *Conditions of Application of Provisions of Section 13 (1)* : In relation to the following classes of employees, the provisions of Section 13 (1) shall apply only to such extent and subject to such conditions as may be prescribed;

(a) employees engaged on urgent work, or in any emergency which could not have been foreseen or prevented;

(b) employees engaged in work in the nature of preparatory or complementary work which must necessarily be carried on outside the limits laid down for the general working in the employment concerned;

(c) employees whose employment is essentially intermittent;

(d) employees engaged in any work which for technical reasons has to be completed before the duty is over;

(e) employees engaged in work which could not be carried on except at times dependent on the irregular action of natural forces [Section 13 (2)].

(iii) *Intermittent Employment* : The employment of an employee is essentially intermittent when it is declared to be so by the appropriate Government. The appropriate Government declares an employment as intermittent on the ground that the daily hours of duty of the employee normally include periods of inaction during which the employee may be on duty but is not called upon to display either activity or sustained attention [Section 13 (3)].

4. Rates of Overtime {Sections 14}

(i) Where an employee, whose minimum rate of wages is fixed under this Act, by the hour, by the day or by such longer wage-period as may be prescribed, works overtime, the employer shall pay him for every hour or for part of an hour so worked in excess, wages at the rates fixed for overtime work under the Act or under any law of the appropriate Government, whichever is higher [Section 14 (1)].

(ii) The provisions of the Minimum Wages Act, 1948 do not prejudice the operation of the provisions of Section 59 of the Factories Act, 1948 in any case where those provisions are applicable [Section 14 (2)].

5. Wages of Worker Who works for less than Normal Working Day (Section 15)

Sometimes an employee whose minimum rate of wages has been fixed by the day may work on any day on which he was employed for a period less than the requisite number of hours constituting a normal working day. In that case he is entitled to receive wages in respect of work done by him on that day as if he had worked for a full normal working day except :

(i) where his failure to work is caused by his unwillingness to work and not by omission of the employer to provide him with work and

(ii) in such other cases and circumstances as may be prescribed.

6. Wages for Two or More Classes of Work (Section 16)

Where an employee does two or more classes of work to each of which a different minimum rate of wages is applicable, the employer shall pay to such employee in respect of the time respectively occupied in each such class of work, wages at not less than the minimum rate in force in respect of each such class.

7. Minimum Time Rate Wages for Piece Work (Section 17)

Where an employee is employed on piece work for which minimum time rate and not a minimum piece rate has been fixed under the Act, the employer shall pay to such employee wages at not less than the minimum time rate.

8. Maintenance of Registers and Records (Section 18)

Every employer shall maintain registers and records giving particulars of employees employed by him, the work performed by them, the wages paid to them, the receipts given by them and such other particulars as may be prescribed [Section 18 (1)]. He shall also keep exhibited notices in the prescribed form containing prescribed particulars in the prescribed manner in the factory, workshop or place where the employees in the scheduled employment may be employed. In the case of out-workers, he shall keep these notices exhibited in such factory, workshop or place as may be used for giving out-work to them [Section 18 (2)].

The appropriate Government may, by rules made under the Act, provide for the issue of wage books or wage slips to employees employed in any scheduled employment in respect of which minimum rates of wages have been fixed. It may also prescribe the manner in which entries shall be made and authenticated in such wage books or wage slips by the employer or his agent [Section 18 (3)].

ENFORCEMENT OF THE ACT
(Sections 19 to 21)

1. Inspectors (Section 19)

(i) *Appointment* : The appropriate Government may, by notification in the Official Gazette, appoint Inspectors for the purposes of the Act, and define the local limits within which they shall exercise their functions [Section 19 (1)].

(ii) *Powers and Functions* : The powers and functions of the Inspectors so appointed are almost similar to those of the Inspectors appointed under the Payment of Wages Act, 1936. The Inspectors have to see that the Provisions of the Minimum Wages Act are complied with.

(iii) *Local Limits* : The words 'local' limits' in Section 19 (1) do not exclude appointment of Inspector for the whole of the State [P.N. Dubey *Vs.* State of U.P., (1978) F.L.R. 334, a case decided under Section 8 (1) of the Factories Act, 1948].

(iv) *Powers of Inspectors* : An Inspector may :

(a) enter at all reasonable hours, with such assistants as he thinks fit, any premises or place where employees are employed or work is given out to out-workers in any scheduled employment in respect of which minimum rates of wage have been fixed, for the purpose of examining any register, record of wages or notices required to be kept or exhibited by or under the Act or rules made thereunder, and require the production thereof for inspection;

(b) examine any person whom he finds in any such premises or place and who, he has reasonable cause to believe, is an employee employed therein or an employee to whom out-work is given;

(c) require any person giving out-work and any out-workers, to give any information, which is in his power to give, with respect to the names and addresses of the persons to, for and from whom the work is given out or received, and with respect to the payments to be made for the work;

(d) seize or take copies of such register, record of wages or notices as he may consider relevant in respect of an offence under the Act which he has reason to believe has been committed by an employer and

(e) exercise such other powers as may be prescribed [Section 19 (2)].

(v) *Authority of Inspectors* : Any person required to produce any document or thing or to give any information by an Inspector under Section 19 (2) shall be deemed to be legally bound to do so within the meaning of Sections 175 and 176 of the Indian Penal Code, 1860 [Section 19 (4)].

Every Inspector shall be deemed to be public servant within the meaning of the Indian Penal Code, 1860 [Section 19 (3)].

2. Claims (Section 20)

(i) *Area of Claim Authority* : The appropriate Government may, by notification in the Official Gazette, appoint an Authority to hear and decide for any specified area all claims :

(a) arising out of payment of less than the minimum rates of wages, or

(b) in respect of the payment of remuneration for the days of the rest [under Sec. 13 (1) (b)] or for work done on days of rest [under Section 13 (1) (c)]; or

(c) in respect of wages at the overtime rate (under Section 14), to employees employed or paid in that area [Section 20 (1)].

(ii) *Persons to be an Authority under the Act* : The Authority under the Act may be :

(a) any Commissioner for Workmen's Compensation, or

(b) any officer of the Central Government exercising functions as a Labour Commissioner for any region, or

(c) any officer of the State Government not below the rank of a Labour Commissioner, or

(d) any other officer with experience as a Judge of a Civil Court or as a stipendiary Magistrate [Section 20 (1)].

(iii) *Which Person may apply for Claim*? Where an employee has any claim, any of the following persons may apply to the Authority for hearing and deciding the case :

(a) the employee himself, or

(b) any legal practitioner, or

(c) any official of a registered Trade authorised in writing to act on his behalf, or

(d) any Inspector, or

(e) any person acting with the permission of the Authority [Section 20 (2)].

(iv) *Processing of Claim Application* : When an application under Section 20 (2) is filed by a person other than the employee, the Authority must inquire into the competence of such a person to file the same [A.P. State Handloom Weavers' Co-op. Society *Vs*. Authority under the Minimum Wages Act, (1986) 1 L.L.N. 934 (A.P.)]. The plea that an Inspector filling an application under Section 20 (2) is not validly appointed is not maintainable when it is not shown that any substantial injury or failure of justice has resulted thereby [Ajanta Talkies, Allahabad *Vs*. Dy. Labour Commr., (1979) Lab. I.C. 659].

Every application under Section 20 (2) shall be presented within 6 months from the date on which the minimum wages or other amount became payable [Proviso 1 to Section 20 (2)]. It may be admitted after 6 months when the applicant satisfies the Authority that he had sufficient cause for not making the application within such period [Proviso 2 to Section 20 (2)].

(v) *Amount of Compensation* : When any application is entertained, the Authority shall hear the applicant and the employer or give them an opportunity of being heard. After such further inquiry, if any, as it may consider necessary, the Authority may direct :

(a) in the case of a claim arising out of payment of less than the minimum rates of wages, the payment to the employee of the amount by which the minimum wages payable to him exceed the amount actually paid, together with the payment of such compensation as the Authority may think fit, not exceeding 10 times the amount of such excess;

(b) in any other case, the payment of the amount due to the employee, together with the payment of such compensation as the Authority may think fit, not exceeding Rs. 10.

(c) The Authority may direct payment of such compensation in cases where the excess or the amount due is paid by the employer to the employee before the disposal of the application. The discretion of the Authority under Section 20 (3) to award compensation is without prejudice to any other penalty to which the employer may be liable under the Act [Section 20 (3)].

(d) Any amount directed to be paid under Section 20 may be recovered by the Authority as if it were a fine imposed by the Authority as a magistrate [Section 20 (5)].

(e) Every direction of the Authority under Section 20 shall be final [Section 20 (6)].

(vi) *Malicious or Vexatious Application* : If the authority hearing any application is satisfied that it was either malicious or vexatious, it may direct that a penalty not exceeding Rs. 50 be paid to the employer by the person presenting the application [Section 20 (4)].

(vii) *Powers of the Authority* : The Authority shall have all the powers of a Civil Court under the Code of Civil Procedure, 1908, for the purpose of :

(i) taking evidence,

(ii) enforcing the attendance of witnesses and

(iii) compelling the production of documents.

Every such Authority shall be deemed to be a Civil Court for all the purposes of Section 195 and Chapter XXXV of the Code of Criminal Procedure, 1898 (now 1973) [Section 20 (7)].

3. Single Application in respect of a Number of Employees (Section 21). Subject to such rules as may be prescribed, a single application may be presented under Section 20 on behalf or in respect of any number of employees employed in the scheduled employment in respect of which minimum rates of wages have been fixed. In such cases the maximum compensation which may be awarded under Section 20 (3) shall not exceed 10 times the aggregate amount of such excess or Rs. 10 per head, as the case may be [Section 21 (1)].

The Authority may deal with any number of separate pending applications presented under Section 20 in respect of employees in the scheduled employment (in respect of which minimum rates of wages have been fixed), as a single application presented under Section 21 (1) and the provisions of Section 21 (1) shall apply accordingly [Section 21 (2)].

OFFENCES AND PENALTIES

1. Penalties for certain offences (Section 22)

Any employer who :

(i) pays to any employee less than the minimum rates of wages fixed for that employee's class of work, or less than the amount due to him under the provisions of the Act, or

(ii) contravenes any rule or order made under Section 13,

shall be punishable with imprisonment for a term which may extend to 6 months, or with fine which may extend to Rs. 500, or with both [Section 22].

In imposing any fine for an offence under Section 22, the Court shall take into consideration the amount of any compensation already awarded against the accused in any proceedings taken under Section 20 (Proviso to Section 22).

2. General Provision for Punishment of Other Offences (Section 22-A)

Any employer who contravenes any provision of the Act or of any rule or order made thereunder shall, if no other penalty is provided for such contravention by the Act, be punishable with fine which may extend to Rs. 500.

3. Cognizance of Offences (Section 22-B)

No Court shall take cognizance of a complaint against any person for an offence :

(i) involving payment of less than the minimum wages unless an application in respect of the facts constituting such offence has been duly presented under Section 20 and granted and the appropriate Government or an officer authorised by it in this behalf has sanctioned the making of the complaint;

(ii) involving contravention of any rule or order made under Section 13 or Section 22-A except on a complaint made by, or with the sanction of, an Inspector [Section 22-B (1)].

(iii) Further, no Court shall take cognizance of an offence :

(a) under Section 22, unless complaint thereof is made within 1 month of the grant of sanction under Section 22-B;

(b) under Section 22-A, unless complaint thereof is made within 6 months of the date on which the offence is alleged to have been committed [Section 22-B (2)].

4. Offences by Companies (Section 22-C)

(i) If the person committing any offence under the Act is a company, every person who, at the time the offence was committed, was in charge of, and was responsible to, the company for the conduct of the business of the company as well as the company shall be deemed to be guilty of the offence and shall be liable to be proceeded against and punished accordingly [Section 22-C (1)]. Such person shall not be liable to any punishment provided in the Act if he proves that the offence was committed without his knowledge or that he exercised all due diligence to prevent the commission of such offence [Proviso to Section 22-C (1)].

(ii) Further where an offence under the Act has been committed by a company and it is proved that the offence has been committed with the consent or connivance of, or is attributable to any neglect on the part of, any director, manager, secretary or other officer of the company, such director, manager, secretary or other officer of the company shall also be deemed to be guilty of that offence and shall be liable to be proceeded against and punished accordingly [Section 22-C (2)].

(iii) For the purposes of Section 22-C :

(a) 'company' means any body corporate and includes a firm or other association of individuals and

(b) 'director' in relation to a firm means a partner in the firm (Explanation to Section 22-C).

MISCELLANEOUS
(Sections 22-D to 30)

1. Payment of Undisbursed Amounts Due to Employees (Section 22-D). All amounts payable by an employer to an employee as the amount of minimum wages or otherwise due to the employee under the Act shall be deposited with the prescribed authority if such amount could not or cannot be paid to the employee :

(i) on account of his death before payment, or

(ii) on account of his whereabouts not being known.

The prescribed authority shall deal with the money so deposited in such manner as may be prescribed.

2. Protection against Attachment of Assets of Employer with Government (Section 22-E). Any amount deposited with the appropriate Government by an employer to secure the due performance of a contract with that Government and other amount due to such employer from that Government in respect of such contract shall not be liable to attachment under any decree or order of any Court in respect of any debt or liability incurred by the employer other than any debt or liability incurred by the employer towards any employee employed in connection with the contract aforesaid.

3. Application of Payment of Wages Act, 1936 to Scheduled Employments (Section 22-F). Notwithstanding anything contained in the Payment of Wages Act, 1936, the appropriate Government may, by notification in the Official Gazette, direct that all or any of the provisions of the said Act shall apply to wages payable to employees in such scheduled employments as may be specified in the notification [Section 22-F (1)].

Where all or any of the provisions of the Payment of Wages Act, 1936 are applied to wages payable to employees in any scheduled employment under Section 22-F (1), the Inspector appointed under the Minimum Wages act shall be deemed to be the Inspector for the purpose of enforcement of the provisions so applied within the local limits of his jurisdiction [Section 22-F (2)].

4. Exemption of Employer from Liability in Certain Cases (Section 23). Where an employer is charged with an offence against this Act, he shall be excused from liability if he can show that some other person was responsible for the offence and that :

(i) he has used diligence to enforce the execution of the Act and

(ii) the said other person committed the offence in question without his knowledge consent or connivance.

In such a case, the other person shall be convicted of the offence and shall be liable to the like punishment as if he were the employer and the employer shall be discharged (Section 23).

In seeking to prove as aforesaid, the employer may be examined on oath, and the evidence of the employer or his witness, if any, shall be subject to cross-examination by or on behalf of the person whom the employer charges as the actual offender and by the prosecution (Proviso to Section 23).

5. Bar of Suits (Section 24). No Court shall entertain any suit for the recovery of wages in so far as the sum so claimed :

(i) forms the subject of an application under Section 20 which has been presented by or on behalf of the plaintiff, or

(ii) has formed the subject of a direction under Section 20 in favour of the plaintiff, or

(iii) has been adjudged in any proceeding under Section 20 not to be due to the plaintiff, or

(iv) could have been recovered by an application under Section 20.

6. Contracting Out (Section 25). Any contract or agreement, whether made before or after the commencement of the Act, whereby an employee either relinquishes or reduces his right to a minimum rate of wages or any privilege or concession accruing to him under the Act shall be *null and void* in so far as it purports to reduce the minimum rate of wages fixed under the Act.

7. Exemptions and Exceptions (Section 26). The appropriate Government may : (i) direct that the provisions of this Act shall not apply in relation to the wages payable to disabled employees [Section 26 (1)];

(ii) exempt by notification in the Official Gazette some specified scheduled employments from the application of some or all of the provisions of the Act [Section 26 (2)];

(iii) direct that the provisions of the Act shall not apply to the wages payable by an employer to a member of his family who is living with him and is dependent on him [Section 26 (3)].

A member of the employer's family in this regard is deemed to include his or her spouse or child or parent or brother or sister [Explanation to Section 26 (3)].

(iv) The appropriate Government may, having regard to the terms and conditions of service applicable to any class of employees in a scheduled employment generally or in a scheduled employment in a local area, direct, by notification in the Official Gazette, that the provisions of this Act or any of them shall not apply in relation to such employees, if they are in receipt of wages exceeding the prescribed limit [Section 26 (2-A].

8. Power of Appropriate Government to add to Schedule (Section 27). If the appropriate Government intends to add to the Schedule any employment in respect of which it is of opinion that minimum rates of wages should be fixed, it must give by notification in the Official Gazette not less than 3 months' notice of its intention so to do. After that the appropriate Government may, by like notification in the Official Gazette, add to the Schedule the employments in respect of which it is of opinion that minimum rates of wages should be fixed.

9. Power of Central Government to give Directions (Section 28). The Central Government may give directions to a State Government as to the carrying into execution of this Act in the State.

10. Power of Central Government to make Rules (Sections 29 and 30-A). (i) *Making Rules* : The Central Government may, subject to the condition of previous publication, by notification in the Official Gazette, make rules prescribing the term of office of the members, the procedure to be followed in the conduct of business, the method of voting, the manner of filling up casual vacancies in membership and the quorum necessary for the transaction of business of the Central Advisory Board (Section 29).

(ii) *Rules to be laid before Parliament (Section 30-A)* : Every rule made by the Central Government under this Act shall be laid as soon as may be after it is made before each House of Parliament while it is in session for a total period of 30 days. This period of 30 days may be comprised in one session or in 2 or more successive sessions. If both Houses agree in making any modification in the rule, the rule shall thereafter have effect only in the modified form. If both Houses agree that the rule should not be made, the rule thereafter have no effect. But any such modification or annulment shall be without prejudice to the validity of anything previously done under that rule.

11. Power of the Appropriate Government to make Rules (Section 30). The appropriate Government may, subject to the condition of previous publication, by notification in the Official Gazette, make rules for carrying out the purposes of the Act.

QUESTIONS FOR EXERCISE

1. State the object of the Minimum Wages Act, 1948.
2. Describe the importance of the Minimum Wages Act, 1948.
3. Define the following terms as used in the Minimum Act, 1948 :
   (a) employer, (b) employee, (c) cost of living index number, (d) scheduled employments and (e) wages.

4. Explain the procedure for fixing Minimum wages. What is the composition of such minimum rate of wages?
5. What is the procedure for fixing and revising minimum wages?
6. What is meant by 'Scheduled Employments' under the Minimum Wages Act, 1948? Define and enumerate some of them with your own comments.
7. Describe the constituents of any minimum rate of wages fixed or revised by the appropriate Government in respect of Scheduled Employments.
8. Describe the functions of Advisory Board and Central Advisory Board constituted under the Minimum Wages Act, 1948. Explain their composition.
9. What remedy is available to a worker who has been paid less than the minimum rate of wages?
10. Discuss and explain the rule regarding the following :
    (a) Worker who works less than the normal working day and
    (b) Wages to an employee who does two or more classes of work.
11. How can an employee take action if he is getting less than the minimum wages? What is the procedure for the final determination of the dispute?
12. What are the provisions of the Minimum Wages Act, 1948 relating to claims arising out of payment of less than the minimum rates of wages of employees?
13. What are the provisions of the Minimum Wages Act, 1948 in connection with protection against attachment of assets of employer with Government?
14. What is the procedure of hearing claims relating to disputes in respect of payment of minimum rates of wages?
15. How are the Inspectors appointed for the purposes of the Minimum Wages Act, 1948? What are their powers?
16. What are the powers of the appropriate Government in the matter of fixing minimum rates of wages.
17. What constitutes the minimum rate of wages under the Minimum Wages Act, 1948.

PART THREE
WORKING CONDITION

8

Industrial Health

WHO "Health is a state of complete physical, mental and social well being and not merely the absence of disease." The industrial health is a state complete physical, mental and social well being of an industrial organisation including all its employees."

OBJECTIVES OF INDUSTRIAL HEALTH

(1) To Prevent Disease and Injury to Industrial Workers. It has two aspects Health Hazards and Health risks.

(i) *Health Hazards* : These are common to all situations.

(ii) *Health Risks* : These differ from industry to industry and time to time.

Health risks can be considerably reduced by providing proper working conditions and by adopting proper safety measures against these risks.

(2) To Conserve Health and Prevent Occupational Disease. According to Veil, "The aim of industrial hygiene is the promotion and maintenance of the highest degree of the physical, social and mental well being of the workers, the prevention of the factors which are responsible for the ill health in the organisation".

IMPORTANCE OF INDUSTRIAL HEALTH

Where a large number of worker spend a great deal of their time in an organisation, their environment is not usually conductive to a healthy life. Malnutrition, insanity, advance psychological conditions and the stress and strain under which they work are injurious to their health. Efficiency is related to employee health. A high rate of absenteeism and turnover, industrial discontent and indiscipline, poor performance and low productivity are the symptoms of bad industrial health. A well devised industrial health, programmme may lead to mere labour turnover, less absenteeism and reduced industrial discontent and indiscipline, high performance and efficiency.

FACTORS PROMOTING INDUSTRIAL HEALTH

1. Legislative measures
2. Special advisory committee
3. Improvement in diet and housing conditions
4. Regular medical check up
5. Education and training in industrial health
6. Study of environmental factors
7. Control upon noise
8. Control upon temperature
9. Proper lightening arrangement
10. Proper cafetaria facility

1. Legislative Measures. The Government of India have enacted following labour legislations protecting the health of the industrial workers. The Factories Act. 1948, The Mines Act 1952, The Plantation Labour Act 1901, The Indian Dock Labourers Act 1934, The Motor Transport Workers Act 1961, the coal Mines (conservation and safety) Act 1952, The Employees State Insurances Act 1948. Under these acts several provisions have been made to protect the health of industrial workers from the occupational diseases. These pertain to both the curative and the preventive aspects of the industrial health. The employes are responsible for carrying out the provisions of the concerned acts.

2. Special Advisory Committee. A special Advisory Committee on Industrial Health has been set up under the Indian Research Fund. Association to conduct research on health problems peculiar to Indian industries. Following problems have been investigated :

(i) Incident of intoxication in printing process.

(ii) Sickness and absenteeism due to accident.

(iii) Assessment of toxicity of industrial dust and fumes.

(iv) Effects of Excess noise on workers.

3. Improvement in Diet and Housing Conditions. Malnutrition and insanitary conditions of living are the main causes of bad health. Hence, efforts should be made towards improving the diet and housing conditions before concentrating on the improvement of medical facilities.

4. Regular Medical Check Up. As suggested by National Commission on Labour, there should be a thorough medical check up of new employees and regular periodic check up of all employees from time to time. This will help to meet the following objectives :

(i) Detect and provide for remediable diseases,

(ii) Eliminate those whose health is not fit for job and those who suffer from communicable diseases and

(iii) Maintain the health of those who are healthy.

5. Study of Environment Factors. Every employer should study the effects of environmental factors on the health of the workers of his industry and devise preventive measures.

6. Education & Training in Industrial Health. An Industrial Health and Safety Bulletin is being published regularly by the Govt. of India to educate the workers. A special course in industrial hygiene has been introduced at the All India Institute of Hygiene and Public Health.

7. Control Upon Noise. Efforts have been made to reduce the noise to the minimum because too much noise causes mental fatigue and disturbance to the workers in their work.

8. Control Upon Temperature. Temperature of the factory premises should be suitable for health. It should neither be too hot nor too cold.

9. Lighting Arrangement. Lighting Arrangement should be made properly in factories. These are of two types natural and artificial. Artificial lighting is more important than natural lighting in an industrial enterprise. Care should be taken that the lighting arrangements should be optimum and suitable. Direction of light should not have adverse effect upon the eyes and health of workers. While arranging for the light the structure of building and the colour of paints should also be considered.

10. Proper Cafetaria Facility. Cafeteria facilities should be provided to the employees at reasonable price so that they can get the refreshment as and when they require.

GOVERNMENTAL MACHINING TO IMPROVE INDUSTRIAL HEALTH

The Government of India have taken following steps to protect the health of the workers :

1. Special Advisory Committee. Indian Government have set up a special Advisory Committee on Industrial Health under the Indian Research Fund Association. It is responsible for conducting research on the problems of health in Indian Industries. Important problems to be investigated by this committee are :

(i) Effect of noise on the health of worker

(ii) Effect of intoxication in printing press etc.

(iii) Sickness and absenteeism due to industrial accidents.

2. Control and Supervision. Inspectors of factories have been appointed in almost all the state to keep an eye upon the implementation of safety measures in industries. These inspectors visit the factories of their area and monitor the implementation of safety measures in them. Medical inspectors have also been appointed in many states.

3. Legislative Measures. Indian Government have passed several Acts to provide health protection to the workers. These are : Factories Act 1948; Indian Mines Act 1952; Indian Dock Labourers act 1934; Motor Transport Act 1961; Coal Mines Conservation and Safety Act 1952 and Employees State Insurance Act 1948. Provisions of these acts provide protection to the industrial workers with regard to health.

QUESTIONS FOR EXERCISE

1. Describe the objectives and importance of industrial health.
2. What factors are important in creating good industrial health? What is Indian Government doing in this direction?

9

The Industrial Employment (Standing Orders) Act, 1946

DEFINITIONS OF RECRUITMENT

1. *William F. Glueek* : "Recruiting refers to those sets of activities an organisation uses to attract job candidates possessing the appropriate characteristics to help the organisation reach its objectives."

2. *Lloyd. L. Byars and Leslie W. Rue* : "Recruitment involves seeking and attracting a pool of people from which qualified candidates for job vacancies can be chosen."

SUB-SYSTEMS OF RECRUITMENT

There are four sub-systems in recruitments which can be divided into further sub-systems as shown below :

1. Sources. Finding out and developing the sources where the required number and kind of employees are/will be available.

2. Techniques. Developing suitable techniques to attract the desirable candidates.

3. Attraction. Employing the techniques to attract candidates.

4. Stimulation. Stimulating as many candidates as possible and making them to apply for jobs irrespective of number of candidates required. In order to increase selection ratio *i.e.*, number of applications per one job vacancy the management has to attract more candidates to select the most suitable candidates out of the total candidates available and due to lower yield ratio. Recruitment aims at increasing the number of applicants. Selection selects the suitable candidates automatically eliminating the unsuitable candidates.

NATURE OF RECRUITMENT

A number of factors make performance of recruitment a complex one. Increasing the selection ratio is not as easy because of the hurdles created by the internal/external which influence an orgainsation.

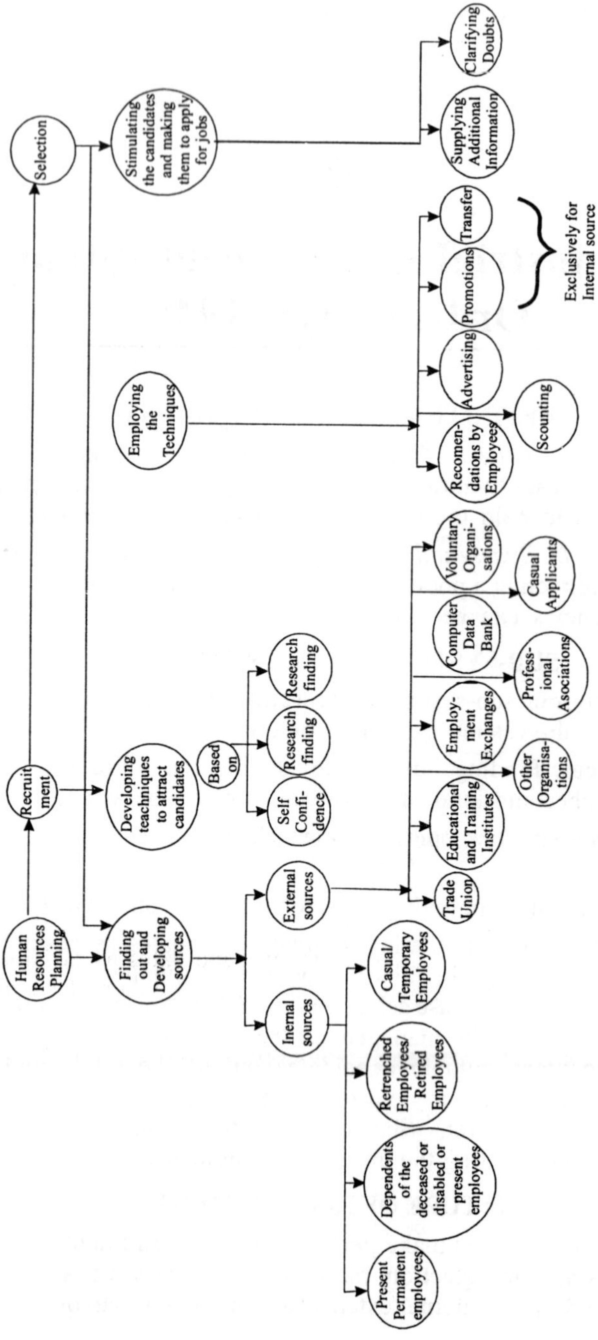

Fig. 1. Sub-systems of Recruitment

HURDLES IN SEARCHING FOR PROSPECTIVE EMPLOYEES

(i) Organisational Policy regarding filling up of certain percentage of vacancies by internal candidates.

(ii) Local candidates (sons of soil).

(iii) Influence of trade unions.

(iv) Government regulations regarding reservations of certain number of vacancies to candidates based on community/region/caste/sex.

(v) Influence or recommendations, nepotism etc.

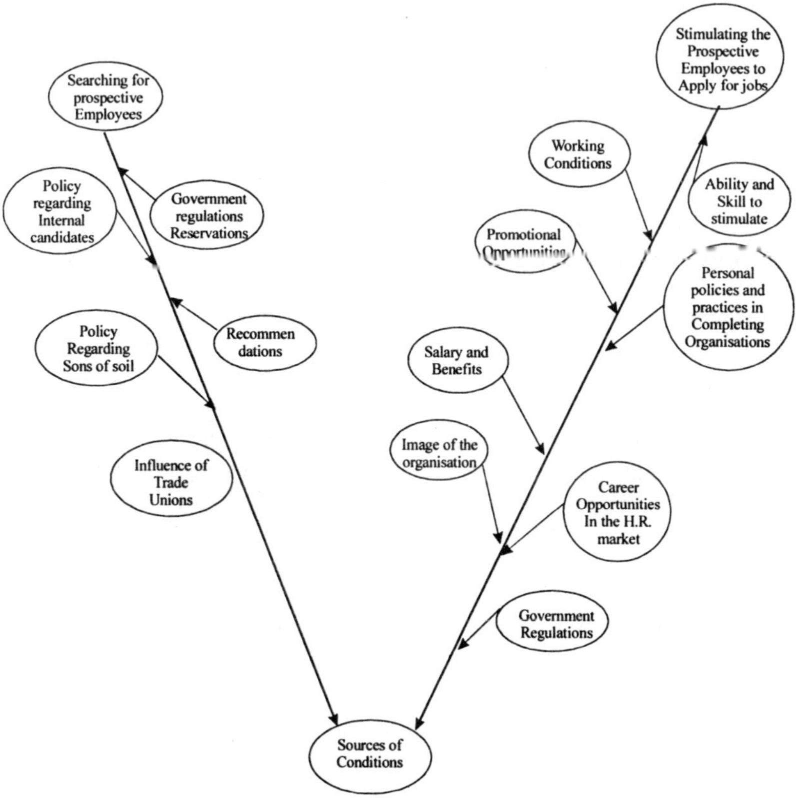

Fig. 2. Hurdles in the Recruitment functions

2. Hurdles by the internal factors such as :

(i) working conditions;

(ii) promotional opportunities;

(iii) salary levels, type and extent of benefits;

(iv) other personal policies and practices;

(v) image of the organisations and

(vi) ability and skill of the management to stimulate the candidates.

3. Hurdles by external factors.

(i) personnel policies and practices of various organisations regarding working conditions, salary, benefits, promotional opportunities, employee relations etc.;

(ii) Career opportunities in other organisations and

(iii) Government regulations. However, the degree of compile-rity of recruitment function can be minimised by formulating sound policies.

RECRUITMENT POLICY

Recruitment policy takes into consideration the Government's reservation policy, policy regarding sons of soil etc., personnel policies of other organisations regarding merit, internal sources, social responsibility in absorbing minority sections, women etc. In any organisation, the recruitment policy is derived from its personal policy. The former is a part of the latter. Recruitment policy depends on the organisation's personnel policy like enriching the organisation's human resources or serving the community by absorbing the worker sections and disadvantaged people of the society, motivating the employees through internal promotions improving the employee loyalty tot he organisation by absorbing the retrenched or laid off employees or casual/temporary employees or dependents of present/former employees etc.

According to Dale Yadar and Paul D. Standohar, general personnel policies provide following variety of guidelines to be spelt out in recruitment policy :

1. Abiding by the public policy and relevant law on selection;

2. Providing the employees the security and continuous employment;

3. Integrating the organisational needs and individual needs;

4. Providing the freedom and opportunity to employees to utilise their talent, skill and knowledge to the maximum extent;

5. Treating all the employees fairly and equally in all employment relationships including salary, benefits, promotions and transfers;

6. Protecting women and minority candidates;

7. Providing suitable jobs which can be handled easily by physically-handicapped and to those employees who are partially disabled due to accidents during the course of duty and to those who cannot do their present jobs due to health reasons.

FACTORS AFFECTING RECRUITMENT POLICY

1. Government policies;
2. Personnel policies of other competing organisations;
3. Organisation's personnel policies;
4. Recruitment sources;
5. Recruitment needs;
6. Recruitment cost;
7. Selection criteria and preference etc.

Before 1946, conditions of employment obtaining in several industrial establishments were governed by contract between the employers and their employees. In many cases they were not reduced to writing and were governed by oral agreements. The conditions of service were not well-defined. There was ambiguity or doubt in regard to their nature and scope. Therefore, the Legislature took the view that the conditions of employment of industrial labour should be well-defined and precisely known to both the parties. With this object, Industrial Employment (Standing Orders) Act, 1946, made relevant provisions for making Standing Orders which, constitute the statutory terms of employment between the industrial establishments in question and their employees.

Object of the Act

1. To define Conditions of Employment and Standing Orders. The object of the Act is "to require employers in industrial establishments to define with sufficient precision the conditions of employment under them and to make the said conditions known to workmen employed by them" (Preamble to the Act). Conditions of employment include, *inter alia*, the conditions of recruitment, discharge, disciplinary action, holidays of the workmen employed in industrial establishments, etc. The object of defining the conditions of employment is to avoid disputes arising from uncertainty and vagueness in the terms of employment. Standing orders are the rules made in this regard.

2. Formal Declaration of Terms and Conditions of Employment. Passed in 1946 the main object of the Act is to require the employers in industrial establishments to define formally the terms and conditions of employment in their establishments. In imposing this obligation on the employers, the Act intends that the terms and conditions of industrial employment should be well-defined and should be known to the employees before they accept the employment.

3. Uniformity of Terms and Conditions. Another object of thc Act is to introduce uniformity of terms and conditions of employment in respect of workmen belonging to the same category and doing the same or similar work under an industrial establishment.

Scope and Application of the Act

1. It applies to every industrial establishment wherein 100 or more workmen are employed, or were employed on any day of the preceding 12 months.

2. After giving not less than 2 months notice of its intention so to do the appropriate Government may also by notification in the Official Gazette, apply the provisions of the Act to any industrial establishment employing such number of persons less than 100 as may be specified in the notification [Section 1 (3)].

3. Once the Act becomes applicable to an industrial establishment, it does not cease to apply on account of fall in the number of workmen in that establishment below 100 [Balakrishna Pillai & Others *Vs*. Anant Engg. Works (Pvt.) Ltd. (1975) 2 L.L.J. 391].

Where the Act does not apply [Section 13-B] :

1. any industry to which the provisions of Chapter VII of the Bombay Industrial Relations Act, 1946 apply.

2. any industrial establishment to which the provisions of the Madhya Pradesh Industrial Employment (Standing Orders) Act, 1961 apply. But notwithstanding anything contained in the Madhya Pradesh Industrial Employment (Standing Orders) Act, 1961, the provisions of the Act shall apply to all industrial establishments under the control of the Central Government [Section 1 (4)].

3. The Act does not apply to an industrial establishment in so far as the workmen employed therein are persons to whom the following rules apply, *viz*,

(i) The Fundamental And Supplementary Rules,

(ii) The Civil Services (Classification, Control and Appeal) Rules,

(iii) The Civil Services (Temporary Service) Rules,

(iv) The Revised Leave Rules,

(v) The Civil Service Regulations,

(vi) The Civilians in Defence service (Classification, Control and Appeal) Rules, or

(vii) The Indian Railway Establishment Code, or

(viii) Any other rules or regulations that may be notified in this behalf by the appropriate Government in the Official Gazette.

The latest amendment to the Act was made in 1982.

DEFINITIONS

1. Appellate Authority [Section 2 (a)]. It is an authority appointed by the appropriate Government by notification in the Official Gazette to exercise the functions of an appellate authority under the Act. The area of the appellate authority may be specified in the notification. But in relation to an appeal pending before an Industrial Court or other authority immediately before the commencement of the Industrial Employment (Standing Orders) (Amendment) Act, 1963, that Court or authority shall be deemed to be the appellate authority.

2. Appropriate Government [Section 2 (b)]. In respect of Industrial establishments under the control of the Central Government or a railway administration or in a major port, mine or oilfield, it means the Central Government. In all other cases, appropriate Government means the State Government.

3. Certifying Officer [Section 2 (c)]. 'Certifying Officer' is a Labour Commissioner, or a Regional Labour Commissioner, and includes any other officer appointed by the appropriate Government, by notification in the Official Gazette, to perform all or any of the functions of a Certifying Officer under the Act.

4. Employer [Section 2 (d)]. 'Employer' is the owner of an industrial establishment to which this Act for the time being applies, and includes :

(i) in a factory, any person named under Section 7 (1) (f) of the Factories Act, 1948, as manager of the factory,

(ii) in any industrial establishment under the control of any department of any Government in India, the authority appointed by such Government in this behalf, or where no authority is so appointed, the head of the department;

(iii) in any other industrial establishment, any person responsible to the owner for the supervision and control of the industrial establishment.

5. Industrial Establishment [Section 2 (e)]. It is (i) an industrial establishment as defined in Section 2, (ii) of the Payment of Wages Act, 1936, or (iii) a factory as defined in Section 2 (m) of the Factories Act, 1948, or (iv) a railway as defined in Section 2 (39) of the Railways Act, 1989, or (v) the establishment of a person who, for the purpose of fulfilling a contract with the owner of any industrial establishment, employs workmen.

6. Standing Orders [Section 2 (g)]. The term 'Standing Orders' means rules relating to matters set out in the Schedule to the Act.

THE SCHEDULE
[See Sections 2 (g) and 3 (2)]
Matters to be provided in Standing Orders

(i) Classification of workmen, *e.g.*, whether permanent, temporary, apprentices, probationers, or *badlis*.

(ii) Manner of intimating to workmen periods and hours of work, holidays pay days and wage rates.

(iii) Shift working.

(iv) Attendance and late coming.

(v) Conditions of, procedure in applying for, and the authority which may grant leave and holidays.

(vi) Requirement to enter premises by certain gates, and liability to search.

(vii) Closing and reopening of sections of the industrial establishment, temporary stoppages of work and the rights and liabilities of the employer and workmen arising therefrom.

(viii) Termination of employment, and the notice thereof to be given by employer and workmen.

(ix) Suspension or dismissal for misconduct and acts or omissions which constitute misconduct.

(x) Means of redress for workmen against unfair treatment or wrongful exactions by the employer or his agents or servants.

(xi) Any other matter which may be prescribed.

7. Trade Union [Section 2 (h)]. It means a trade union for the time being registered the trade Unions Act, 1926.

8. Wages and workman [Section 2 (i)]. 'Wages' and 'workman' have the meanings respectively assigned to them in Section 2 (rr) and Section 2 (s) of the Industrial Disputes Act, 1947.

PROCEDURE FOR SUBMISSION OF DRAFT STANDING ORDERS (Section 3)

1. Submission of Draft. Within 6 months of the application of the Act to an industrial establishment, the employer shall submit to the Certifying Officer 5 copies of the draft standing orders proposed by him for adoption in his industrial establishment [Section 3 (1)].

2. Scope of Draft. Such draft standing orders shall cover every matter set out in the Schedule to the Act which may be applicable to the industrial establishment. Where model standing orders have been prescribed, the standing orders shall be, so far as is practicable, in conformity with such model [Section 3 (2)].

3. Standing Orders to be accompanied by Particulars of Workmen. The draft standing orders submitted under Section 3 shall be accompanied by a statement giving prescribed particulars of the workmen employed in the industrial establishment. They shall also give the name of the trade union, if any, to which the workmen belong [Section 3 (3)].

4. Employers in Similar Establishments may submit a Joint Draft. For the convenience of a group of employers in similar industrial establishments, they may submit a joint draft of standing orders under Section 3. But this is subject to the conditions as may be prescribed [Section 3 (4)].

PROCEDURE FOR CERTIFICATION OF STANDING ORDERS

1. Certification of Standing Orders (Section 5)

(i) *Copy of Draft Standing Orders to be sent to Trade Union or Workmen* : On receipt of the draft standing orders under Section 3, the Certifying Officer shall forward a copy thereof to the trade union, if any, of the workmen. Where there is no trade union, the copy of the draft standing orders shall be sent to the workmen in such manner as may be prescribed. The Certifying Officer will also send along with a copy of the draft a notice in the prescribed form requiring objections, if any, which the workmen may desire to make to draft standing orders. The objections shall be submitted to him within 15 days from the receipt of the notice [Section 5 (1)].

(ii) *Opportunity of hearing to Trade Union/Workmen to be provided* : The Certifying Officer shall give an opportunity to the employer and the trade union or such other representatives of the workmen as may be prescribed of being heard if any modification or addition to standing orders is to be made. After this formality is over he shall decide whether or not any modification or addition to the draft submitted by the employer is necessary to render the draft standing orders certifiable under this Act, and shall make an order in writing accordingly [Section 5 (2)].

(iii) *Certification* : The Certifying Officer shall thereupon certify the draft standing orders with the modifications, if any. He shall then within 7 days send copies of the certified standing orders authenticated in the prescribed representatives of the workmen [Section 5 (3)].

2. Conditions for Certification of Standing Orders (Section 4)

In certifying the standing orders, the Certifying Officer shall see that the conditions as laid down in Section 4 are complied with. According to Section 4, standing orders shall be certifiable under the Act if :

(a) provision is made therein for every matter set out in the Schedule which is applicable to the industrial establishment and

(b) The standing orders are otherwise in conformity with the provisions on the Act.

It is the function of the Certifying Officer or appellate authority to adjudicate upon the fairness or reasonableness of the provision of any standing order.

3. Appeals (Section 6)

(i) *Who can Appeal* : Any employer, workman, trade union or other prescribed representatives of the workmen aggrieved by the order of the Certifying Officer may, within 30 days from the date on which copies are sent under Section 5 (3), appeal to the appellate authority.

(ii) *Action of Appellate Authority* : The appellate authority shall by order in writing confirm the standing orders either in the form certified by the Certifying Officer or after amending the said standing orders. It may amend the standing orders by making such modifications thereof additions thereto as it thinks necessary to render the standing orders certifiable under the Act. The decision of the appellate authority shall be final [Section 6 (1)].

(iii) *Copies of Order* : Section 6 (2) lays down that the appellate authority shall, within 7 days of its order, send copies thereof to the Certifying Officer, to the employer and to the trade union or other prescribed representative of the workmen. The order shall be accompanied by the copies of the standing orders as certified by it and authenticated in the prescribed manner.

OTHER PROVISIONS RELATING TO STANDING ORDERS

1. Date of operation of Standing Orders (Section 7). Standing orders shall, unless an appeal is preferred, come into operation on the expiry of 30 days from the date on which authenticated copies thereof are sent under Section 5 (3). Where an appeal is preferred, standing orders shall come into operation on the expiry of 7 days from the date on which copies of the order of the appellate authority are sent under Section 6 (2).

2. Register of Standing Orders (Section 8.). A copy of all standing orders as finally certified under the act shall be filed by the Certifying Officer in a register in the prescribed form maintained for the purpose. The Certifying Officer shall furnish a copy thereof to any person applying therefor on payment of the prescribed fee.

3. Posting of Standing Orders (Section 9). The text of the standing orders as finally certified under the Act shall be prominently displayed by the employer in English and in the language understood by the majority of his workmen. The display shall be on special boards to be maintained for the purpose :

(a) at or near the entrance through which the majority of the workmen enter the industrial establishment and

(b) in all departments thereof where the workmen are employed.

4. Duration and Modification of Standing Orders (Section 10). Standing orders finally certified under the Act shall not, except on agreement between the employer and the workmen or a trade union or other representative body of the workmen, be liable to modification until the expiry of 6 months from the date on which the standing orders or the last modifications thereof came into operation [Section 10 (1)].

(i) Subject to the provisions of Section 10 (1), any employer or workman or a trade union or other representative body of the workmen, may apply to the Certifying Officer to have the standing orders modified. Such an application shall be accompanied by 5 copies of the modifications proposed to be made. Where modifications are proposed to be made by agreement between the employer and the workmen or a trade union or other representative body of the workmen, a certified copy of that agreement shall be filed along with the application [Section 10 (2)].

(ii) The provisions as contained in Sections 3 to 9 of the Act shall apply in respect of an application under Section 10 (2) as they apply to the certification of the first standing orders [Section 10 (3)].

(iii) The provisions as contained in Section 10 (2) shall not apply to an industrial establishment in respect of which the appropriate Government is the Government of the State of Gujarat or the Government of the State of Maharashtra [Section 10 (4)].

5. Payment of Subsistence Allowance (Section 10-A)

(i) *Subsistence Allowance at 50/75 Per Cent* : Section 10-A makes provision for payment of subsistence allowance by an employer to a workman who has been suspended by the employer pending investigation or inquiry into complaints or charges of misconduct against the workman. The subsistence allowance shall be payable :

(a) at the rate of 50 per cent of wages which the workman was entitled to immediately preceding the date of such suspension, for the first 90 days of suspension and

(b) at the rate of 75 per cent, of such wages for the remaining period of suspension if the delay in the completion of disciplinary proceedings against such workman is not directly attributable to the conduct of such workman [Section 10-A (1)].

(ii) *Dispute regarding Subsistence Allowance to be referred to Labour Court* : If any dispute arises regarding the subsistence allowance payable to a workman, the workman or the employer concerned may refer the dispute to the Labour Court, constituted under the Industrial Disputes Act, 1947, within the local limits of whose jurisdiction the industrial establishment wherein such workman is employed is situated. The Labour Court to which the dispute is so referred shall, after giving the parties an opportunity of being heard, decide the dispute and such decision shall be final and binding on the parties [Section 10-A (2)].

(iii) *If Subsistence Allowance more Beneficial under any Other Law, Provisions of That Law to apply* : Where provisions relating to payment of subsistence allowance under any other law for the time being in force in any State are more beneficial than the provisions of Section 10-A, the provisions of such other law shall be applicable to the payment of subsistence allowance in that State [Section 10-A (3)].

ENFORCEMENT OF THE ACT

1. Powers of Certifying Officers and Appellate Authorities (Section 11). Every Certifying Officer and appellate authority shall have all the powers of a Civil Court for the purposes of :

(i) receiving evidence,

(ii) administering oaths,

(iii) enforcing the attendance of witnesses and

(iv) compelling the discovery and production of documents.

2. Civil Court. Every Certifying Officer and appellate authority shall be deemed to be a Civil Court within the meaning of Sections 345 and 346 of the Code of Criminal Procedure, 1973 [Section 11 (1)].

3. Correction. Clerical or arithmetical mistakes in any order passed by a Certifying Officer or appellate authority, or errors arising therein from any accidental slip, or omission may, at any time, be corrected by the Officer or authority or the successor in office of such Officer or authority, as the case may be [Section 11 (2)].

4. Oral Evidence not admitted. No oral evidence having the effect of addition to or otherwise varying or contradicting standing orders finally certified under the act shall be admitted in any Court (Section 12).

MISCELLANEOUS

1. Temporary Application of Model Standing Orders (Section 12-A). When the Act becomes applicable to an industrial establishment for the first time, till the standing orders as finally certified under the Act come into operation under Section 7 in that establishment, the prescribed model standing orders shall be deemed to be adopted in that establishment [Section 12-A (1)].

The provisions of Section 12-A (1) shall not apply to an industrial establishment in respect of which the appropriate Government is the Government of the State of Gujarat or the Government of the State of Maharashtra [Section 12-A (2)].

2. Interpretation, etc., of Standing Orders (Section 13-A). Sometimes a question may arise as to the application or interpretation of a standing order certified under the Act. In such a case any employer or workman or a trade union or other representative body of the workmen may refer the question to any one of the Labour Courts constituted under the Industrial Disputes Act, 1947 and specified for the disposal of such proceedings by the appropriate Government by notification in the Official Gazette. The Labour Court to which the Question is so referred shall, after giving the parties an opportunity of being heard, decide the question. The decision of the Labour Court shall be final and binding on the parties.

3. Power to exempt (Section 14). The appropriate Government may, by notification in the Official Gazette, exempt, conditionally or unconditionally, any industrial establishment or class of industrial establishments, from all or any of the provisions of the Act.

4. Delegation of Powers (Section 14-A). The appropriate Government may, be notification in the Official Gazette, direct that any power exercisable by it shall be exercisable also :

(i) where the appropriate Government is the Central Government, by such officer or authority subordinate to the Central Government or by the State Government or by such officer or authority subordinate to the State Government, as may be specified in the notification;

(ii) where the appropriate Government is a State Government, by such officer or authority subordinate to the State Government as may be specified in the notification.

The matters in relation to which the powers are delegated and the conditions under which such delegation is made shall be specified in the direction.

5. Power to make rules (Section 15). The appropriate Government may, after previous publication, and by notification in the Official Gazette, make rules to carry out the purposes of the Act [Section 15 (1)].

6. Rules to be laid before Parliament. Every rule made by the Central Government under Section 15 shall be laid as soon as may be after it is made, before each house of Parliament while it is in session of a total period of 30 days. This period of 30 days may be comprised in one session or in 2 or more successive sessions. If both the Houses agree in making any modification in the rule, the rule shall thereafter have effect only in such modified form. If both the Houses agree that the rule should not be made, the rule shall thereafter be of no effect. However, any such modification or annulment shall be without prejudice to the validity of anything previously done under that rule [Section 15 (3)].

PENALTIES

1. An employer who fails to submit draft standing orders as required by Section 3 or who modifies the standing orders otherwise than in accordance with Section 10, shall be punishable with fine which may extend to Rs. 5,000. In the case of a continuing offence, he shall be punishable with a further fine which may extend to Rs. 200 for every day after the first during which the offence continues [Section 13 (1)].

2. An employer who does any act in contravention of the standing orders finally certified under the Act for his industrial establishment shall be punishable with fine which may extend to Rs. 100. In the case of a continuing offence, he shall be punishable with a further fine which may extend to Rs. 25 for every day after the first during which the offence continues [Section 13 (2)].

3. Prosecution for an offence punishable under Section 13 shall not be instituted except with previous sanction of appropriate Government [Section 13 (3)].

4. No Court inferior to that of a Presidency Magistrate or Magistrate of the second class shall try any offence under Section 13 [Section 13 (4)].

QUESTIONS FOR EXERCISE

1. Define the following terms as used in the Industrial Employment (Standing Orders) Act, 1946; (i) Appellate Authority, (ii) Appropriate Government, (iii) Employer, (iv) Industrial establishment, (v) Standing Orders, (vi) Workman.
2. What is need for having standing orders in industrial establishments?
3. Explain the procedure for certification of standing orders? What are the conditions for their certification? What is the effect of certification of standing orders? What is their duration?
4. What are the provisions relating to submission of draft standing orders?
5. Explain the matters to be provided for in the standing orders under the Industrial Employment (Standing Orders) Act, 1946.
6. Can standing orders be modified? What is the procedure for their modification? Is oral evidence in contradiction of standing orders admissible?
7. How are standing orders made known to workmen employed in an industrial establishment?
8. "Certified standing orders constitute statutory conditions of employment." Comment.

10

The Factories Act, 1948

In the olden days, the workers in factories were regarded as objects no better than the machines and tools used in it. Behaviour towards them did not qualify as human. And in many cases, the workers were no better off than slaves. In the days of British India, in the margarine blue factories of the country, many national leaders had to raise their voices in protest against the cruelty meted out to workers under the owners of the factories. In the South, too, owners of factories and mines did not treat their employees at all well. The worker was daunted into submission, and in many occupations the workers was often turned out without prior notice or any compensation. In cases of accident, fatal or incapacitating, the worker and his family were reduced to abject misery and impecunious poverty. When machines were invented, women and children were also added to the labour force, no concessions being made to their delicate condition and ideally exalted position in life. Even when leave was absolutely necessary for women it was not permitted and pregnant women were often turned out to work. The systems in the factory and working conditions were almost completely deplorable. The owner was concerned solely with his own profit, and the conditions in which works was carried on was not his concern. It was outside the sphere of his thinking to worry about air, light, sanitation, water, etc., that were or were not supplied in adequate quantities. There being no legal bar to the extent of work to be forced out of the labourer, the owners forced the poor workers to work for long hours on very small remuneration. Promotion was a term unheard of at that time. Incentives to workers were not required, and equally not tendered. In this way, exploitation was the rule of the day.

Historical Review

Designed primarily to protect children and to provide for some health and safety measures the first Factories Act in India was passed in 1881. It was followed by new Acts in 1891, 1911, 1922 and 1934. The Act of 1934 was passed to implement the recommendations of the Royal Commission on Labour in India and the conventions of the International Labour Organisation. Its working revealed a number of defects and weaknesses hampering effective administration the Act. The provisions of this Act regarding safety, health and welfare of workers were also found to be inadequate and unsatisfactory. In view of the large and growing industrial activities in the country a redical overhauling of the law relating to factories was necessary. Therefore, the Factories Act of 1948 was enacted.

The Factories Act. 1948

1. Start. The Factories Act, 1948 came into force on the 1st day of April, 1949. Its object is to regulate the conditions of work in manufacturing establishments which come within the definition of the term 'factory' as used in the Act.

2. Area. The Act extends to the whole of India including the State of Jammu and Kashmir. Unless otherwise provided, It also applies to factories belonging to the Central or any State Government (Section 116).

3. Amendment. The Act was substantially amended in 1987. Some provisions of the Amending Act came into force with effect from 1st December 1987 and others from 1st June 1988.

DEFINITION OF FACTORY

1. Meaning of Factory. According to Section 2 (m), 'factory' means any premises including the precincts thereof :

(i) whereon 10 or more workers are working or were working on any day of the preceding 12 months, and in any part of which a manufacturing process is being carried on with the aid of power, or is ordinarily so carried on, or

(ii) whereon 20 or more workers are working or were working on any day of the preceding 12 months, and in any part of which a manufacturing process is being carried on without the aid of power, or is ordinarily so carried on.

The term 'factory' does not include a mine subject to the operation of the Indian Mines Act, 1952 or a mobile unit belonging to the armed forces of the Union, a railway running shed or a hotel, restaurant or eating place.

In simple words, a factory is a premises whereon 10 or more persons are engaged if power is used, in a manufacturing process.

For computing the number of workers, all the workers in different groups and relays in a day shall be taken into account [Expl. 1 to Section 2 (m)].

For the purposes of Section 2 (m), the mere fact that an Electronic Data Processing Unit or a Computer Unit is installed in any premises or part thereof, shall not be construed to make it a factory if no manufacturing process is being carried on in such premises or part thereof [Expl. 2 to Section 2 (m) as introduced by the Amendment Act of 1987].

2. Meaning of Precincts. The definition of the term 'factory' in Section 2 (m) envisages premises which have precincts, as the expression used in the definition is 'premises including the precincts thereof. 'Precincts' are usually understood as a space enclosed by walls or fences. Where premises are buildings, they would include precincts. What are the precincts of particular premises is a question of fact to be determined according to the circumstances of each particular case. The word 'premises' is not to be confined in its meaning to buildings alone.

Example. A concrete apron of an airfield adjoining a hanger used for testing planes was enclosed by a security fence. Held, the airfield fell within the meaning of the precincts of factory [Wells *Vs.* Weather Ground Mech. Co. Ltd., (1951) All E.R. 588].

3. Whether any Establishment is a Factory. In order to determine whether any establishment is a factory, two things must be proved :

(1) that a manufacturing process is being carried on in any pat of the premises of that establishment and

(2) that there are prescribed number of workers working in any part of the premises where the manufacturing process is being carried on.

Mere fact that power is used in a premises is not the deciding factor; the power used must be in the aid of the manufacturing process [New Taj Mahal Hotel *Vs.* Inspector of Factories, (1956) 1 L.L.J. 273].

4. Examples. (a) Salt works which consist merely of open stretches of large areas of land with some temporary shelters [Ardeshir A. Bhiwandiwala *Vs.* State of Bombay. A.I.R. (1962) S.C. 29].

(b) Railway workshops [Indar Singh *Vs.* Secretary of State, A.I.R. (1929) Lah. 573].

(c) A premises where the manufacturing process is carried on with 7 persons employed permanently and 3 persons employed temporarily in repairs of part of machinery [Hari Krishan & Another *Vs.* State, A.I.R. (1959) All. 1974].

Important Terms.

For proper understanding of the meaning of the term 'factory', the following three terms should be clearly understood.

1. Manufacturing Process [Section 2 (k)]. It means any process for :

(i) making, altering, repairing, ornamenting, finishing, packing, billing, washing, cleaning, breaking up, demolishing, or otherwise treating or adapting any article or substance with a view to its use, sale, transport, delivery or disposal, or

(ii) pumping oil, water sewage, or any other substance, or

(iii) generating, transforming or transmitting power, or

(vi) composing types for printing, printing by letter press, lithography, photogravure or other similar process or book binding, or

(v) constructing, reconstructing, repairing, refitting, finishing, breaking up ships or vessels, or

(vi) preserving or storing any article in cold storage.

Some of the processes which have been held to be manufacturing processes are as follows :

(a) *Bidi* making [Chintaman Rao *Vs*. State of M.P., (1962) S.C.J. 388].

(b) Moulding and transformation of raw cinematography films into a finished product [Gemini Studio *Vs*. State, (1952-53) 4 F.J.R. 329].

(c) Work done in a salt work which consists of converting sea-water into salt [Ardeshir H. Bhiwandiwala *Vs*. State of Bombay, A.I.R. (1962) S.C. 29].

(d) Use of a refrigerator for treating or adapting any article with a view to its sale [New Taj Mahal Cafe Ltd. *Vs*. Inspector of Factories, (1956) 1 L.L.J. 273].

(e) Work of composition in printing business [V.K. Press *Vs*. Authority, A.I.R, (1955) All. 702].

(f) Use of electric motor for the purpose of lifting or pumping water [Syed Mooda Kazimi *Vs*. K.M. Sheriff, A.I.R. (1959) Mad. 542].

(g) Process of moistening, stripping and packing of tobacco leaves [V.P. Gopala Rao *Vs*. Public Prosecutor, A.I.R. (1970) S.C. 66].

(h) Activities of a petrol pump [Gateway Auto Services *Vs*. Regional Director, E.S.I. Corpn., (1981) Lab. I.C. 49].

In deciding whether a particular business is a manufacturing process or not, regard must be had to the circumstances of each particular case. To constitute manufacturing process, there must be some transformation, *i.e.*, the article must become commercially known as something different from which it acquires its existence.

2. Worker [Section 2 (1)]. (i) *Employed* : A worker is a person *employed*, directly or by or through any agency (including a contractor) with or without the knowledge of the principal employer. He may be employed for or without remuneration. But he must be employed in a manufacturing process, or in cleaning some part of the machinery or premises used for the manufacturing process, or in some other kind of work incidental to, or connected with, the manufacturing process, or the subject of the manufacturing process. A worker does not include any member of the armed forces of the Union.

(ii) *Relationship of Master and Servant* : The expression 'employed' in the above definition means that the relationship of master and servant must exist. It makes no difference whether the worker employed in the manufacturing process is paid wages or not or is paid wages on time-rate basis or piece-rate basis.

Whether a particular person is a worker depends upon the terms of contract between him and the employer. A worker does not include an independent contractor or his coolies or servants who are not under the control and supervision of the employer.

(iii) *Obligations of Workers (Section 111)* : A worker in a factory shall not :

(a) wilfully interfere with or misuse any appliance, convenience or other thing provided in the factory for the purposes of securing the health, safety or welfare of the workers therein;

(b) wilfully and without reasonable cause do anything likely to endanger himself or others and

(c) wilfully neglect to make use of any appliance or other thing provided in the factory for the purposes of securing the health or safety of the workers therein [Section 111 (1)].

If any worker employed in a factory contravenes any of the provisions of Section 111 or any rule or order made thereunder, he shall be punishable with imprisonment for a term which may extend to 3 months, or with fine which may extend to Rs. 100 or with both [Section 111 (2)].

(iv) *Rights of workers, etc. (Section 111)* : A as introduced by the Amendment Act of 1987). Every worker shall have the right to :

(i) obtain from the occupier, information relating to workers' health and safety at work;

(ii) get trained within the factory wherever possible, or to get himself sponsored by the occupier for getting trained in a training centre or institute, duly approved by the Chief inspector, where training is imparted for workers' health and safety at work;

(iii) represent to the Inspector directly or through his representative in the matter of inadequate provision for protection of his health or safety in the factory.

3. Power [Section 2 (g)]. It means electrical energy, or any other form of energy which is mechanically transmitted and is not generated by human or animal agency.

(i) *Different Departments to be Separate Factories or 2 or More Factories to be a Single Factory (Section 4)* : The occupier of a factory may apply to the State Government that the different departments or branches of the factory of the occupier be treated as separate factories. He may also apply to the State Government that 2 or more factories of the occupier specified in the application be treated as a single factory. The State Government may, by an order in writing, accede to the request of the occupier.

(ii) *Exemption during Public Emergency (Section 5)* : In any case of public emergency the State Government may, by notification in the Official Gazette, exempt any factory or class or description of factories from all or any of the provisions of this Act except Section 67 (which deals with prohibition of employment of young persons). This exemption may be for a specified period not exceeding 3 months at a time and subject to such conditions as the State Government may think fit to impose.

Public emergency means a grave emergency whereby the security of India or of any part of the territory thereof is threatened, whether by war or external aggression or internal disturbance [Expl. to Section 5].

Section 86 empower the State Government to exempt certain workshops or workplaces attached to public institutions maintained for the purposes of education, training, research or reformation, from all or any of the provisions of the Act.

(iii) *Certain Premises deemed to be a Factory (Section 85)* : The State Government may, by notification in the Official Gazette, declare any establishment carrying on a manufacturing process to be a factory for the purpose, of the Act even though the number of persons employed therein is less than the prescribed minimum number of workers. If the manufacturing process is being carried on by the owner only with the aid of his family, Section 85 will not apply.

DEFINITIONS

1. Adult [Section 2 (a)]. An 'adult' means a person who has completed his 18th year of age.

2. Adolescent [Section 2 (b)]. An 'adolescent' means a person who has completed his 15th year of age but has not completed his 18th year.

3. Child [Section 2 (c)]. A 'child' means a person who has not completed his 15th year of age.

4. Competent Person [Section 2 (c a) as introduced by the Amendment Act of 1987]. 'Competent person', in relation to any provision of the Act, means a person or an institution recognised as such by the Chief Inspector. The recognition must be for the purposes of carrying out tests, examinations and inspections required to be done in a factory under the provisions of the Act. This recognition must be given having regard to :

(a) the qualifications and experience of the person and the facilities available at his disposal; or

(b) the qualifications and experience of the person employed in such institution and facilities available therein with regard to the conduct of such tests, examinations and inspections.

It may be noted that more than one person or institution may be recognised as competent persons in relation to a factory.

5. Hazardous Process [Section 2 (c b) as introduced by the Amendment Act of 1987]. It means any process or activity in relation to an industry specified in the First Schedule where, unless special care is taken, raw material used therein or the intermediate or finished products, bye-products, wastes or effluents thereof would :

(a) cause material impairment to the health of the persons engaged in or connected therewith, or

(b) result in the pollution of general environment.

The State Government may, by notification in the Official Gazette, amend the First Schedule by way of addition, omission or variation of any industry specified in the First Schedule.

The definition of 'hazardous process' has been introduced by the Amendment Act of 1987.

6. Calendar Year [Section 2 (bb)]. It means the period of 12 months beginning with the 1st day of January in any year.

7. Young Person [Section 2 (d)]. A 'young person' means a person who is either a child or an adolescent.

8. Day [Section 2 (e)]. It means a period of 24 hours beginning at midnight.

9. Week [Section 2 (f)]. It means a period of 7 days beginning at midnight on Saturday night or such other night as may be approved in writing for a particular area by the Chief Inspector of Factories.

10. Prime Mover [Section 2 (h)]. It means any engine, motor or other appliance which generates or otherwise provides power.

11. Transmission Machinery [Section 2 (i)]. It means any shaft, wheel, drum, pulley system of pulleys, coupling, clutch, driving belt or other appliance or device by which the motion of a prime mover is transmitted to or received by any machinery or appliance.

12. Occupier [Section 2 (n)]. 'Occupier' of a factory means the person who has ultimate control over the affairs of the factory. In the case of a firm or other association of individuals, any one of the partners or members thereof shall be deemed to be the occupier. In the case of a company, the directors shall be deemed to be the occupier. In the case of a factory owned or controlled by the Central Government or any State Government or any local authority, the person or person appointed to manage the affairs of the factory by the Central Government, the State Government or the local authority, as the case may be, shall be deemed to be the occupier. The definition of 'occupier' has been considerably enlarged by the Amendment Act of 1987.

A partner in a firm who has ultimate control over the affairs of a factory is an occupier [*Sohanlal* v. *State of Rajasthan*, (1962) 1 L.L.J. 605]. An 'occupier' may be an owner, a lessee or a mere licensee, but he must have the right to occupy the property and dictate terms of management [*Emperor* v. *Jamshedji Nuservanji Modi*, A.I.R. (1931) Bom. 308]. He must be in possession of the factory and control its working. A mere servant charged with specific duties in regard to the control of the machinery, workmen or office is not an 'occupier'.

13. Shift and Relay [Section 2 (r)]. Where work of the same kind is carried out by 2 or more sets of workers working during different periods of the day, each of such sets is called a 'relay' and each of such periods is called a 'shift'.

14. References to Time of Day (Section 3). In the Factories Act references to time of day are references to Indian Standard Time, being 5-1/2 hours ahead of Greenwich Mean Time. But for any area in which Indian Standard Time is not ordinarily observed, the State Government may make rules (a) specifying the area, (b) defining the local mean time ordinarily observed therein, and (c) permitting such time to be observed in all or any of the factories situated in the area.

APPROVAL, LICENSING AND REGISTRATION OF FACTORIES

1. Procedure

(i) *Powers of State Government* : The State Government is empowered under Section 6 to make rules requiring the submission of plans, and approval, licensing and registration of factories. The effect of Section 6 is that before a site is used for a factory, previous permission in writing of the State Government or of the Chief Inspector has to be obtained. This permission is granted only when an applicant has duly complied with direction enjoined by Section 6.

(ii) *Application for Permission* : Under Section 6, the State Government may make rules requiring the submission of plans of factories to the Chief Inspector or the State Government, Section 6 further requires the previous permission in writing to be obtained for the site on which the factory is to be situated and for the construction or extension of the factory. An application for such permission may be made to the State Government or the Chief Inspector, along with the duly certified plans and specifications. The State Government may also make rules requiring the registration and licensing of factories and prescribing the fees payable for such registration and licensing and the renewal of licences. But no such licence shall be granted or renewed unless the notice specified in Section 7 (as discussed below) has been given [Section 6 (1)].

(iii) *Presumption of Permission if nothing is heard Within 3 Months* : If on an application to the State Government or the Chief Inspector for permission accompanied by plans and specification of a factory, nothing is heard within 3 months, the permission is deemed to be granted [Section 6 is heard within 3 months, the permission is deemed to be granted [Section 6 (2)].

(iv) *Appeal* : Where a State Government refuses to grant permission to the site, construction or extension of a factory or to the registration and licensing of a factory, the applicant may within 30 days of the date of such refusal appeal to the Central Government. Where a Chief Inspector refuses to grant such permission, the applicant may, within 30 days of refusal, appeal to the State Government [Section 6 (3)].

1. Notice by Occupier (Section 7)

(i) *Written Notice* : The occupier shall, at least 15 days before he begins to occupy or use any premises as a factory, send to the Chief inspector a written notice containing :

(a) the name and situation of the factory;

(b) the name and address of the occupier;

(c) the name and address of the owner of the premises or building (including the precincts thereof);

(d) the address to which communications relating to the factory may be sent;

(e) the nature of the manufacturing process to be carried on in the factory during the next 12 months;

(f) the total rated horse power installed or to be installed in the factory (not including the rated horse power of any separate standby plant);

(g) the name of the manager of the factory for the purposes of this Act;

(h) the number of worker likely to be employed in the factory; and such other particulars as may be prescribed [Section 7 (1)].

Before a factory engaged in a manufacturing process which is ordinarily carried on for less than 180 working days in an year resumes working, the occupier shall send a written notice to the Chief Inspector containing the particulars specified in Section 7 (1) at least 30 days before the date of the commencement of work [Section 7 (3)].

(ii) *Rules* : The rules regarding the plans and specifications of a factory are essential to ensure proper sanitation, ventilation, proper working conditions and other health measures.

2. General Duties of the Occupier (Section 7-A)

A new Section 7-A has been introduced by the Amendment Act of 1987, prescribing the general duties of the occupier in regard to the health, safety and welfare of the workers in his factory. According to it, every occupier shall ensure, so far as is reasonably practicable, the health, safety and welfare of all workers while they are at work in the factory [Section 7-A (1)]. Section 7-A (2) enumerates the matters in regard to health, safety and welfare of the workers. These matters include :

(i) the provision and maintenance of plant and systems of work in the factory that are safe and without risks to health;

(ii) the arrangements in the factory for ensuring safety and absence of risks to health in connection with the use, handling, storage and transport of articles and substances.

(iii) the provision of such information, instruction, training and supervision as are necessary to ensure the health and safety of all workers at work;

(iv) (a) the maintenance of all places of work in the factory in a condition that is safe and without risks to health and (b) the provision and maintenance of such means of access to and egress from such places as are safe and without such risks;

(v) the provision, maintenance or monitoring of such working environment in the factory for the workers that is (i) safe, (ii) without risks to health, and (iii) adequate as regards facilities and arrangements for their welfare at work [Section 7-A (2)].

In addition to the above duties, every occupier shall also :

(i) prepare, and, a often as may be appropriate, revise, a written statement of his general policy with respect to (a) the health and safety of the workers at work, and (b) the organisation and arrangements for the time being in force for carrying out that policy and

(ii) bring the statement and any revision thereof to the notice of all the workers. In some cases as may be prescribed an occupier may be exempted from this duty [Section 7-A (3)].

3. General Duties of Manufactures, etc. as regards Articles and Substances for Use in Factories (Section 7-B)

A new Section, Section 7-B, has been introduced by the Amendment Act of 1987 prescribing the general duties of manufacturers, etc. as regards articles and substances for use in factories. The purpose of Section 7-B is also to ensure health and safety of the workers working in factories wherein these articles and substances are used. The provisions of Section 7-B are as follows :

1. Proper Design and Construction, Testing and Information. Every person who designs, manufactures, imports or supplies any article for use in any factory shall :

(i) ensure that the article is so designed and constructed as to be safe and without risks to the health of the workers when properly used;

(ii) carry out or arrange for the carrying out of such tests and examination as my be considered necessary for the effective implementation of the provisions of Clause (a);

(iii) take such steps as may be necessary to ensure that adequate information will be available :

(a) in connection with the use of the article in any factory;

(b) about the use for which it is designed and tested and

(c) about any conditions necessary to ensure that the article when put to such use, will be safe, and without risks to the health of the workers [Section 7-B (1)].

4. Articles designed or manufactured Outside India

Where an article is designed or manufactured outside India, it shall be obligatory on the part of the importer to see :

(i) that the article conforms to the same standards if such article is manufactured in India, or

(ii) if the standards adopted in the country outside for the manufacture of such article are above the standards adopted in India, that the article conforms to such standards [Proviso to Section 7-B (1)].

2. Research. Every person, who undertakes to design or manufacture any article for use in any factory, may carry out or arrange for the carrying out of necessary research. This may be necessary with a view to the discovery and the elimination or minimisation of any risks to the health or safety of the workers in which the design or article may give rise [Section 7-B (2)]. He need not repeat the testing, examination or research which has been carried out by some one else or at his instance if he can reasonably rely on the results of testing etc. for the purposes of Section 7-B (1) and (2) [Section 7-B (3)].

3. Duty to extend to Things done in Course of Business. Any duty imposed on any person by Section 7-B (1) and (2) shall extend only to things done in the course of business carried on by him and to matters within his control [Section 7-B (4)].

4. Undertaking by the User. Sometimes a person may design, manufacture, import or supply an article on the basis of a written undertaking by the user of such article to take the steps specified in the undertaking to ensure that the article will be safe and without risks to the health of the workers when properly used. Such an undertaking shall have the effect of relieving the person designing, manufacturing, importing or supplying the article from the duty imposed by Section 7-B (1) (a) to such extent as is reasonable having regard to the terms of the undertaking [Section 7-B (5)].

5. When Article not Properly Used. For the purposes of Section 7-B an article is not to be regarded as properly used if it is used without regard to any information or advice relating to its use which has been made available by the person who has designed, manufactured, imported or supplied the article [Section 7-B (6)].

For the purpose of Section 7-B 'article' shall include plant and machinery (Expl. to Section 7-B).

THE INSPECTING STAFF

1. Inspectors (Section 8). (i) *Appointment* : Section 8 provides for the appointment of Chief Inspector, Additional Chief Inspectors, Joint Chief Inspectors, Deputy Chief Inspectors, and Inspectors. According to it, the State Government may, by notification in the Official Gazette, appoint any person to be a Chief Inspector to exercise the powers conferred on him by the Factories Act. He shall also exercise the powers of an Inspector throughout the State [Section 8 (2)]. The State Government may also appoint, by notification in the Official Gazette, such persons as possess the prescribed qualifications to be Inspectors. It may assign to the Inspectors such local limits as it may thing fit [Section 8 (1)].

The State Government may, by notification in the Official Gazette, also appoint as many Additional Chief Inspectors, Joint Chief Inspectors, Deputy Chief Inspectors and as many other officers as it thinks fit to assist the Chief Inspector and to exercise such of the powers of the Chief Inspector as may be specified in the notification [Section 8 (2-A)].

Every Chief Inspector, Additional Chief Inspector, Joint Chief Inspector, Deputy Chief Inspector, Inspector, and every other officer appointed under Section 8 is deemed to be a public servant within the meaning of the Indian Penal Code, 1860 [Section 8 (7)].

No person who is or becomes directly or indirectly interested in a factory or in any process or business carried on therein or in any patent or machinery connected therewith shall act as a Chief Inspector, Additional, Inspector or any other officer appointed under Section 8 (2-A) [Section 8 (3)].

The State Government may also, by notification in the Official Gazette, appoint additional Inspectors within such local limits as it may assign to them respectively [Section 8 (5)].

In any area where there are more Inspectors than one, the State Government may declare the powers which such Inspectors shall respectively exercise and the Inspector to whom the prescribed notices are to be sent [Section 8 (6)].

(ii) *Powers of Inspectors (Section 9)* : An Inspector may, within the local limits for which he is appointed, —

(a) enter, with assistants who are in the service of the Government or any local or other public authority or with an expert, the premises of a factory,

(b) make examination of the premises, plant, machinery, article or substance;

(c) inquire into any accident or dangerous occurrence, whether resulting in bodily injury, disability or not, and take on the spot or otherwise statements of any person which he may consider necessary for such inquiry;

(d) require the production of any prescribed register or any other document relating to the factory;

(e) seize, or take copies of, any register, record or order document or any portion thereof, as he may consider necessary in respect of any offence under this Act, which he has reason to believe, has been committed;

(f) direct the occupier that any premises or any part thereof, or anything lying therein, shall be left undisturbed (whether generally or in particular respects) for so long as is necessary for the purpose of any examination under Clause (b);

(g) take measurements and photographs and make such recordings as he considers necessary for the purpose of any examination under Clause (b) taking with him any necessary instrument or equipment;

(h) In case of any article or substance found in any premises, being an article or substance which appears to him as having caused or is likely to cause danger to the health or safety of the workers, direct it to be dismantled or subject it to any process of test (but not so as to damage or destroy it unless the same is necessary for carrying out the purposes of this Act). Further, he may take possession of any such article or substance or a part thereof, and detain it for so long as is necessary for such examination;

(i) exercise such other powers as may be prescribed.

The above powers of an Inspector are subject to any rules which may be made by the State Government in this behalf.

(iii) *Additional Powers* : An Inspector has also the power :

(a) to require medical examination of a 'young person' working in a factory (Section 75) and also

(b) to take sample of any substance used, or intended to be used, in a factory for the purpose of finding out if the substance is injurious to the health of the workers (Section 91).

(iv) *Penalty for obstructing Inspector* (*Section* 95) : Whoever wilfully obstructs an Inspector in the exercise of any power conferred on him by or under the Act, or fails to produce on demand by an Inspector any registers or documents, shall be punished with imprisonment up to 6 months or with fine up to Rs. 10,000 or with both.

2. Certifying Surgeons (Section 10). (i) *Appointment* : The State Government may appoint qualified medical practitioners to be certifying surgeons for specified local limits or factories [Section 10 (1)]. A certifying surgeon may, with the approval of the State Government, authorise any qualified medical practitioner to exercise any of his powers [Section 10 (2)]. But no person shall be appointed a certifying surgeon who is or becomes the occupier of a factory or is or becomes directly or indirectly interested therein [Section 10 (3)]. The Sate Government may exempt any person or class of persons from the provisions of Section 10 (3) in respect of any factory or class or description of factories [Proviso to Section 10 (3)]. The exemption shall however be made by order in writing and subject to such conditions as may be specified in the order.

(ii) *Duties of Certifying Surgeons* : The certifying surgeon shall carry out such duties as may be prescribed in connection with :

(a) the examination and certification of young persons;

(b) the examination and persons engaged in factories in dangerous occupations or processes;

(c) the exercising of such medical supervision as may be prescribed for any factory where (i) cases of illness have occurred which it is reasonable to believe are due to the nature of the manufacturing process carried on, or other conditions of work prevailing, therein; (ii) by reason of any change in the manufacturing precess carried on or in the substances used therein, there is a likelihood of injury to the health of workers employed in that manufacturing process; (iii) young persons are, or are about to be, employed in any work which is likely to cause injury to their health [Section 10 (4)].

HEALTH, SAFETY AND WELFARE

The Act makes detailed provisions in regard to various matters relating to health, safety and welfare of the workers. These provisions impose upon the occupiers or managers certain obligations (a) to protect workers, unwary as well as negligent, from accidents and (b) to secure for them in employment, conditions conductive to their health, safety, and welfare. These provisions also require the occupiers or managers to maintain inspection staff and to make provisions for maintenance of health, cleanliness, prevention of overcrowding, and amenities like lighting, ventilation, drinking water, etc.

HEALTH

Chapter III (Sections 11 to 20) of the Act deals with the provisions ensuring the health of the workers in the conditions under which work is carried on in factories. These provisions are as follow :

1. Cleanliness (Section 11). Factory to be kept clean and free from effluvia and dirt. (i) Every factory shall be kept clean and free from effluvia arising from any drain, privy, or other nuisance. Accumulation of dirt and refuse shall be removed daily by some effective method. The floor of ever, work-room shall be cleaned at least once in every week by washing, using disinfectants, where necessary, or by some effectivc method.

(ii) *Effective Means of Drainage* : Where a floor is liable to become wet in the course of any manufacturing process to such an extent as is capable of being drained, effective means of drainage shall be provided.

(iii) *Use of Disinfectants, etc. : painting and varnishing.* Use of disinfectants, detergents, painting, repainting and varnishing, revarnishing, whitewashing or colourwashing shall be resorted to.

2. Disposal of Wastes and Effluents (Section 12). (i) *Treatment of Wastes and Effluents and their Disposal* : Effective arrangements shall be made in every factory for the treatment of wastes and effluents due to the manufacturing process carried on therein, so as to render them innocuous, and for their disposal [Section 12 (1)].

(ii) *Rules by the State Government prescribing Arrangements* : The State Government may make rules prescribing the arrangements to be made in this regard. It may also require that such arrangements shall be approved by such authority as may be prescribed [Section 12 (2)].

3. Ventilation and Temperature (Section 13). (i) *Maintenance of Adequate Ventilation and Temperature* : Effective and suitable provision shall be made in every factory for securing and maintaining in every workroom :

(a) adequate ventilation by the circulation of fresh air and

(b) such a temperature as will secure to workers therein reasonable conditions of comfort and prevent injury to health.

(ii) *Process Producing High Temperature to be separated* : The walls and roofs shall be of such materials and so designed that the temperature shall not be exceeded but kept as low as practicable. The process which produces high temperatures shall be separated from the workroom, by insulating the hot parts or by other effective means [Section 13 (1)].

(iii) *Standard of Adequate Ventilation and Temperature to be prescribed and Provision of Measuring Instruments* : The State Government may prescribe a standard of adequate ventilation and reasonable temperature for any factory direct that proper measuring instruments shall be provided and such records as may be prescribed shall be maintained [Section 13 (2)].

(iv) *Prescription of Measures by the State Government to reduce Temperatures* : Where excessively high temperatures can be reduced by such methods as whitewashing, spraying, or insulating and screening outside walls or roofs or windows, or by raising the level of the roof or by insulating the roof, the State Government may prescribe such of these or other methods as shall be adopted in the factory [Section 13 (3)].

(v) *Service of Notice by the Chief Inspector on the Occupier to adopt Measures for Reduction of Temperatures* : If it appears to the Chief Inspector that excessively high temperatures in any factory can be reduced by the adoption of suitable measures, he may serve on the occupier an order in writing specifying the measures which in his opinion should be adopted and requiring them to be carried out before a specified date [Section 13 (4)].

4. Dust and Fume (Section 14). (i) *Measures for Prevention of Inhalation or Accumulation of Dust and Fumes* : Where dust or fume or impurity of such a nature as is likely to be injurious or offensive to the workers is given off as a result of the manufacturing process being carried on in a factory, effective measures shall be taken in the factory for prevention of inhalation or accumulation of dust and fumes in workrooms. If for such a purpose any exhaust appliance is necessary, it shall be applied as near as possible to the point of origin of the dust, fume or other impurity and such point shall be enclosed so far as possible [Section 14 (1)].

(ii) *Exhaust for Internal Combustion Engine.* A stationary internal combustion engine shall not be operated unless the exhaust is conducted into the open air. Other internal combustion engines shall not be operated in any room unless effective measures have been taken to prevent accumulation of fumes therefrom which are injurious [Section 14 (2)].

5. Artificial Humidification (Section 15). (i) *Prescription of Standards of Humidification* : Ventilation and cooling of air. In respect of all factories in which the humidity of the air is artificially increased, the State Government may make rules prescribing standards of humidification. It may also make rules regulating the methods used for artificially increasing the humidity of the air. It may further make rules prescribing methods to be adopted for securing adequate ventilation and cooling of the air in the workrooms [Section 15 (1)].

(ii) *Water used for Artificial Humidification to be Clean* : In any factory in which the humidity of the air is artificially increased, the water used for the purpose shall be taken from a public supply or other source of drinking water, or shall be effectively purified before it is so used [Section 15 (2)].

6. Overcrowding (Section 16). (i) *Overcrowding Injurious to Health of Workers to be avoided* : There shall not be overcrowding in any room of the factory so as to be injurious to the health of the workers employed therein [Section 16 (1)].

(ii) *9.9/14.2 Cubic Metres of Space Per Worker* : There shall be at least 9.9. cubic metres (for the factories in existence at the time of the commencement of the Act) and 14.2 cubic metres (for the factories built after the commencement of the Act) of space for every worker. In calculating the space of 9.9 or 14.2 cubic metres, no account shall be taken of any space which is more than 4.2 metres above the level of the floor of the room [Section 16 (2)].

(iii) *Notice of Maximum of Workers to be employed in a Workroom* : If the Chief Inspector by order in writing so requires, there shall be posted in each workroom of the factory a notice specifying the maximum number of workers who may be employed in the workroom [Section 16 (3)].

7. Lighting (Section 17). (i) *Sufficient and Suitable Lighting in Every Part of Factory* : In every part of a factory where workers are working or passing there shall be provided and maintained sufficient and suitable lighting, natural or artificial, or both [Section 17 (1)].

(ii) *Glazed Windows and Skylights to be kept Clean* : All glazed windows and skylights used for the lighting of the workrooms shall be kept clean on both the inner and outer surfaces and free from obstruction [Section 17 (2)].

(iii) *Measures for Prevention of Glare and Formation of Shadows* : Effective provision shall also be made for the prevention of (a) glare, either directly from a source of light or by reflection from a smooth or polished surface; and (b) the formation of shadows to such an extent as to cause eye strain or the risk of accident to any worker [Section 17 (3)].

(iv) *Prescription of Standards of Sufficient and Suitable Lighting* : The State Government may prescribe standards of sufficient and suitable lighting for factories or for any class or description of factories or for any manufacturing process [Section 17 (4)].

8. Drinking Water (Section 18). (i) *Suitable Points for Wholesome Drinking Water* : In every factory, effective arrangements shall be made to provide and maintain at suitable points conveniently situated for all workers employed therein a sufficient supply of wholesome drinking water [Section 18 (1)].

(ii) *Drinking Points to be Legibly marked and to be Away from Urinal, latrine etc.* : All points for supply of drinking water shall be legibly marked 'drinking water' in a language understood by a majority of the workers employed in the factory. Such points shall be situated beyond 6 metres of any washing place, urinal, latrine, spittoon, open drain carrying sullage or effluent or any other source of contamination unless shorter distance is approved in writing by the Chief Inspector [Section 18 (2)].

(iii) *Cooling of Drinking Water Where More than 250 Workers employed* : In every factory wherein than 250 workers are ordinarily employed, provision shall be made for cooling drinking water during hot weather by effective means and for distribution thereof [Section 18 (3)].

9. Latrines and urinals (Section 19). (i) *Separate Latrines and Urinals for Male and Female Workers Conveniently Situated and Adequately lighted and ventilated* : In every factory, enclosed accommodation of latrines and urinals of prescribed types for male and female workers shall be provided for. Such accommodation shall be conveniently situated and accessible for workers at all times. It shall be adequately lighted and ventilated and maintained in a clean and sanitary condition. Sweepers shall also be employed for keeping clean latrines, urinals and washing places [Section 19 (1)].

(ii) *Latrine and Urinal Accommodation to be of Prescribed Sanitary Types and Floors and Walls to be glazed and cleaned* : In factories wherein more than 250 workers are ordinarily employed (a) all latrine and urinal accommodation shall be of prescribed sanitary types; (b) the floors and internal walls, up to a height of 90 centimeters, of the latrines and urinals and the sanitary blocks shall be laid in glazed tiles or otherwise finished to provide a smooth polished impervious surface; (c) the sanitary pan of latrines and urinals shall be thoroughly washed and cleaned at least once in every 7 days with suitable detergents or disinfectants, or with both [Section 19 (2)].

10. Spittoons (Section 20). (i) *Sufficient Number of Spittoons* : In every factory, there shall be provided a sufficient number of spittoons in convenient places and they shall be maintained in a clean and hygienic condition [Section 20 (1)].

(ii) *Display of Notice of Provision of Spittoons* : No person shall spit within the premises of a factory except in the spittoons provided for the purpose. A notice containing the provision of spittoons in the factory shall be prominently displayed at suitable places in the premises. The penalty for spitting anywhere except in the spittoons shall also be prominently displayed [Section 20 (3)]. penalty for spitting anywhere except in the spittoons shall also be prominently displayed [Section 20 (3)].

(iii) *Penalty* : Whoever spits in contravention of Section 20 (3) shall be punishable with fine not exceeding Rs. 5 [Section 20 (4)].

SAFETY

The safety provisions are absolute and obligatory in their character and the occupier of every factory is bound to follow them. They are contained in Chapter IV (Sections 21 to 41).

1. Fencing of Machinery (Section 21). (i) *Dangerous Part of Every Machinery to be securely fenced* : In every factory, every dangerous part of every machinery shall be securely fenced by safeguards of substantial construction which shall be constantly maintained and kept in position while the parts of machinery they are fencing are in motion or in use.

(ii) *Machineries covered by Section 21* : The following machineries are covered by Section 21. *viz.*,

(a) Every moving part of a prime mover, and every fly-wheel connected to a prime mover, whether the prime mover or fly-wheel is in the engine house or not;

(b) The headrace and tailrce of every water-wheel and water turbine;

(c) Any part of a stock-bar which projects beyond the headstock of a lathe;

(d) Every part of an electric generator, a motor or rotary convertor;

(e) Every part of transmission machinery and

(f) Every dangerous part of any other machinery [Section 21 (1)].

(iii) *Prescription of Further Precautions by State Government* : The State Government may by rules prescribe such further precautions as it may consider necessary in respect of any particular machinery or part thereof [Section 21 (2)].

2. Work on Near Machinery in Motion (Section 22). (i) *Examination of Machinery in Motion by a Trained Adult Male Worker* : Where in any factory it becomes necessary to examine any part of machinery while the machinery is in motion, such examination shall be made only by a specially trained adult male worker wearing tight fitting clothing. The clothing shall be supplied by the occupier. The name of the person so engaged shall be entered in the prescribed register. Further he shall be furnished with a certificate of his appointment [Section 22 (1)].

(ii) *Restriction on Women and Young Persons* : No woman or young person shall be allowed to clean, lubricate or adjust any part of a machinery in motion if it would expose the woman or young person to risk of any injury from any moving part [Section 22 (2)].

3. Employment of Young Persons on Dangerous Machines (Section 23). (i) *Restriction on Young Persons to work on Dangerous Machines* : No young person shall be required or allowed to work on any machine to which this Section applies unless — (a) he has been fully instructed as to the dangers arising in connection with the machine and the precautions to be observed; and (b) he has received sufficient training to work on the machine, or is under adequate supervision by a person who has thorough knowledge and experience of the machine [Section 23 (1)].

(ii) *Machines Dangerous for Young Persons to be specified by the State Government* : The State Government shall specify machines which in its opinion are of such a dangerous character that young persons ought not to work at them unless the foregoing requirements are complied with [Section 23 (2)].

4. Striking Gear and Devices for cutting off Power (Section 24). (i) *Suitable Striking Gear to be provided, maintained and used* : In every factory, provided striking gear or other efficient mechanical appliance shall be provided and maintained and used to move driving belt to and from fast and loose pulleys which form part of transmission machinery. Driving belts when not in use shall not be allowed to rest or ride upon the shafting in motion [Section 24 (1)].

(ii) *Locking Device to prevent Accidental Starting of Transmission Machinery* : When a device, which can inadvertently shift from 'off' to 'on' position, is provided in a factory to cut off power, arrangements shall be provided for locking the device in safe position. This is to prevent accidental starting of the transmission machinery or other machines to which the device is fitted [Section 24 (3)].

5. Self-acting Machines (Section 25). *Traversing Part not allowed to run Within Distance of 45 Centimetres from any fixed Structure* : No traversing part of a self-acting machine in any factory and no material carried thereon shall be allowed to run on its outward or inward traverse within a distance of 45 centimetres from any fixed structure which is not part of the machine. This provision shall apply only if the space over which the traversing part of the self-acting machine runs is a space over which any person is liable to pass, whether in the course of his employment or otherwise.

6. Casing of New Machinery (Section 26). (i) *Casing to prevent Danger.* All machinery driven by power and installed in any factory after 1st April 1949, every set screw, bolt or key on any revolving shaft, spindle, wheel or pinion shall be so sunk, encased or otherwise effectively guarded as to prevent danger. Further, all spur, worm and other toothed or friction gearing not requiring frequent adjustments while in motion shall be completely encased unless it is safely situated [Section 26 (1)].

(ii) *Penalty* : If any one sells or lets on hire either directly or as an agent, any machine which does not comply with the provisions of Section 26, he shall be punishable with imprisonment up to 3 months or with fine up to Rs. 500 or with both [Section 26 (2)].

7. Prohibition of Employment of Women and Children Near Cotton-Openers (Section 27). No woman or child shall be employed in any part of a factory for pressing cotton in which a cotton-opener is at work. If the feed-end of a cotton-opener is in a room separated from the delivery end by a partition extending to the roof or to a specified height, women and children may be employed on the side of the partition where the feed-end is situated.

8. Hoists and Lifts (Section 28). (i) *Hoists and Lifts to be of Good Mechanical Construction, and to be Properly maintained and examined Once in every 6 Months* . In every factory every hoist and lift shall be of good mechanical construction, sound material, and adequate strength. Further it shall be sufficiently protected by enclosures fitted with gates. It shall also be properly maintained and shall be thoroughly examined by a competent person at least once in every 6 months. A register containing the prescribed particulars of every such examination shall be kept. The maximum safe working load shall also be plainly marked on every hoist or lite, and no load greater than such load shall be carried thereon. The cage of every hoist or life used for carrying persons shall be fitted with a gate on each side from which access is afforded to a landing. The gate shall be fitted with interlocking or other efficient device to secure that the cage cannot be moved unless the gate is closed.

(ii) For the purposes of Section 28, no lifting machine or appliance shall be deemed to be a hoist or lift unless it has a platform or cage, the direction or movement of which is restricted by a guide or guides (Expl. to Section 28 added by the Amendment Act of 1987).

9. Lifting Machines, Chains, Ropes and Lifting Tackles (Section 29). (i) *Cranes and Lifting Machines etc. to be of good construction and to be examined once in every 12 months* : In every factory, cranes and other lifting machines (and every chain, rope and lifting tackle for the purpose of raising or lowering persons, goods or materials) shall be of good construction, sound material, adequate strength, free from defects and properly maintained. They shall be thoroughly examined by a competent person at least once in every 12 months. A register containing the prescribed particulars of every such examination shall be kept [Section 29 (1) (a)].

(ii) *Cranes and Lifting Machines not to be loaded Beyond Safe Working Load* : The aforesaid machines shall not, except for the purpose of test, be loaded beyond the safe working load which shall be plainly marked thereon together with an identification mark and duly entered in the prescribed register. Where this is not practicable, a table showing the safe working loads of the aforesaid machinery in use shall be displayed in prominent positions on the premises [Section 29 (1)(b)].

(iii) *Crane not to approach within 6 Metres of a Place Where any Person is employed or working* : If any person is employed or working on or near the wheel track of a travelling crane in any place where he would be liable to be struck by the crane, effective measures shall be taken to ensure that the crane does not approach within 6 metres of that place [Section 29 (1)(c)].

10. Revolving Machinery (Section 30). (i) *Notice of Maximum Safe Working Speed of Grindstone or Abrasive Wheel, etc. to be kept Near Machine* : In every factory in which the process of grinding is carried on, there shall be permanently kept near each machine a notice indicating (a) the maximum safe working peripheral speed of every grindstone or abrasive wheel, (b) the speed of the shaft or spindle upon which the wheel is mounted, and (c) the diameter of the pulley upon such shaft or spindle necessary to secure such safe working peripheral speed [Section 30 (1)].

(ii) *Speeds not to be exceeded* : (a) The speeds indicated in notices under Section 30 (1) shall not be exceeded [Section 30 (2)].

(b) Effective measures shall be taken in every factory to ensure that the safe working peripheral speed of every revolving vessel, cage, basket, fly-wheel, pulley, disc or similar appliance driven by power is not exceeded [Section 30 (3)].

11. Pressure Plant (Section 31). (i) *Safe Working Pressure not to be exceeded* : If in any factory any plant or any machinery or part thereof is operated at a pressure above atmospheric pressure, effective measures shall be taken to ensure that the safe working pressure is not exceeded [Section 31 (1)].

(ii) *Rule-making Power of the State Government providing for Examination and Exemption* : The State Government may make rules providing for the examination and testing of any plant or machinery and providing for additional safety measures [Section 31 (2)].

12. Floors, Stairs and Means of Access (Section 32). In every factory :

(i) all floors, steps,. stairs, passages and gangways shall be of sound construction and properly maintained. Further they shall be kept free from obstructions and substances likely to cause persons to slip and handrails shall be provided where necessary;

(ii) there shall, so far as is reasonably practicable, be provided and maintained safe means of access to every place at which any person is at any time required to work;

(iii) When any person has to work at a height from where he is likely to fall, provision shall be made, so far as is reasonably practicable, by fencing or otherwise, to ensure the safety of the person so working. This restriction is not applicable if the place provides secure foothold and, where necessary, secure handhold.

13. Pits, Sumps, Openings in Floors, etc. [Section 33]. (i) *Pits, Sumps, etc. to be securely covered or fenced* : In every factory, pits, sumps, fixed vessels, tanks, openings in the ground or in the floor shall be securely covered or securely [Section 33 (1)].

(ii) *Exemption* : The State Government may, by order in writing, exempt any factory in respect of any vessel, sump, tank, pit or opening from compliance with the above provision [Section 33 (2)].

(iii) *Securely fencing a Pit* : It means covering or fencing it in such a way that it ceases to be a source of danger to those who have occasion to go near there [State of Mysore *Vs.* Narayana Raghvendra, (1967) 2 L.L.J. 616].

14. Excessive Weights (Section 34). (i) *Prohibition on lifting or carrying of Excessive Weights* : No person shall be employed in any factory to lift, carry or move any load so heavy as to be likely to cause him injury [Section 34 (1)].

(ii) *Maximum Weights to be lifted or carried to be prescribed* : The State Government may make rules precribing the maximum weights which may be lifted,. carried or moved by adult men, adult women, adolescents and children employed in factories or in any class or description of factories or in carring on any spedified process [Section 34 (2)].

15. Protection of Eyes (Section 35). In very factory, screen or suitable goggles shall be provided for the protection of persons employed on, or in immediate vicinity of, mechanical or other processes which invlove any danger or injury to workers' eyesight. The risk of injury to the eyes may be from particles or frangments thrown off in the course of the process or by reason of exposure to excessive light.

16. Precautions against Dangerous Fumes (Section 36). (i) *Prohibition on Entry into any Chamber, Tank, Vat, Pit, Pipe etc. : where any gas, fume etc. is present.* No person shall be required or allowed to enter any chamber, tank, vat, pit, pipe, flue or other confined space in any factory in which any gas, fume, vapour or dust is likely to be present to such an extent as to involve risk to persons being overcome thereby, unless it is provided with a manhole of adequate size or other effective means of agress [Section 36 (1)].

(ii) *Practicable Measures to be taken for removal of Gas, Fume etc.* : No person shall be required or allowed to enter any confined space as is referred to in Section 36 (1), until all prcticable measures have been taken to remove any gas, fume, vapour or dust, which may be present so as to bring its level within the permissible limits and to prevent any ingress of such gas, fume, vapour or dust and unless :

(a) a certificate in writing has been given by a competent person, based on a test, carried out by himself that the space is reasonably free from dangerous gas, fume, vapour or dust; or

(b) such person is wearing suitable breathing apparatus and a belt securely attached to a rope, the free end of which is held by a person outside the confined space [Section 36 (2)].

17. Precautions regarding the Use of Portable Electric Light (Section 36-A). No portable electic light or any other electric appliance of voltage exceeding 24 volts shall be permitted for use inside any chamber, tank, vat, pit, fule or other confined space in a factory, unless adequate safety devices are provided. If any inflammable gas, fume or dust is likely to be present in such chamber, tank, vat, pit, flue or other confined space, no lamp or light other than that of flame-proof construction shall be permitted to be used in the factory.

18. Precautions against Explosive or Inflammable Dust, Gas, etc. (Section 37). (i) *Practicable Measures to prevent Explosion on Ignition of Gas, Fume etc.* : when in any factory any manufacturing process produces dust, gas, fume or vapour which is likely to explolde on ignition, all practicable measures shall be taken to prevent any such explosion by :

(a) effective enclosure of the plant or machinery used in the process,

(b) removal or prevention of the accumulation of such dust, gas, fume or vapour and

(c) exclusion or effective enclosure of all possible sources of ignition [Section 37 (1)].

(ii) *Provision of Chokes, Vents etc.* : When the plant or machinery cannot withstand the probable pressure which an explosion would produce, all practicable measures shall be taken to restrict the spread any effects of the explosion. This shall be done by the provision in the plant or machinery of chokes, baffles, vents or other effective appliances [Section 37 (2)].

(iii) *Special Measures Where Explosive or Inflammable Gas or Vapour is under Pressure Greater than Atmospheric Pressure* : Where any part of the plant or machinery in a factory contains an explosive or inflammable gas or vapour under pressure greater than atmospheric pressure, that part shall not be opened unless special measures prescribed for that are taken [Section 37 (3)]. These measures are as follows :

(a) The flow of gas or vapour shall be effectively stopped by a stop-valve or other means;

(b) All Practicable measures shall be taken to reduce the pressure to the atomspheric pressure and

(c) Where the fastening of such part has been loosened or removed, the fastening shall be secured or securely replaced [Section 37 (3)].

Further, a plant, tank or vessel containing explosive or inflammable substance shall not be welded, brazed, soldered or cut by applying heat untill such substance and fumes are rendered non-explosive and non-inflammable [Section 37 (4)].

(iv) *Exemption* : The State Government may by rules exempt any factory from compliance with all or any of the provisions of Section 37 [Section 37 (5)].

19. Precautions in Case of Fire (Section 38 as substituted by the Amendment Act of 1987). (i) *Practicable Measures to prevent Outbreak of Fire an Its Spread* : In every factory, all practicable measures shall be taken to prevent outbreak of fire and its spread, both internally and externally, and to provide and maintain :

(a) safe means of escape for all persons in the event of a fire and

(b) the necessary equipment and facilities for extinguishing fire [Section 38 (1)].

(ii) *Familiarity of Workers with Means of Escape* : Effective measures shall be taken to ensure that in every factory all the workers are familiar with the means of escape in case of fire and have been adequately trained in the routine to be followed in such cases [Section 38 (2)].

(iii) *Rule-making Power of the State Government* : The State Government may make rules, in respect of any factory or class or description of factories, requiring the measures to be adopted to give effect to the above provisions [Section 38 (3)].

(iv) *Additional Measures* : If the Chief inspector, having regard to the nature of the work carried on in any factory, the construction of such factory, special risk to life or safety, or any other circumstances, is of the opinion that the measures provided in the factory are inadequate, he may, by order in writing, require that such additional measures as he may consider reasonable and necessary be provided in the factory before such date as is specified in the order [Section 38 (4)].

20. Power to require Specifications of Defective Parts or Tests of Stability (Section 39). If it appears to the Inspector that any building or part of a building, machinery or plant in a factory may be dangerous to human life or safety, he may ask the occupier or the manager or both of the factory :

(i) to furnish drawings, specifications and other particulars as may be necessary to determine whether such building, ways, machinery or plant can be used with safety; or

(ii) to carry out the tests in the specified manner and inform the Inspector of the results thereof.

21. Safety of Building and Machinery (Section 40). (i) *Service of Order by Inspector on Occupier to take Specified Measures in Case of Dangerous Building or Machinery or Plant* : If any building or part of a building or machinery or plant in a factory is in such a condition that it is dangerous to human life or safety, the Inspector may serve on the occupier or the manager or both of the factory an order in writing specifying the measures which in his opinion shall be adopted and requiring them to be carried out before a specified date [Section 40 (1)].

(ii) *Prohibition of Use Where Danger is imminent* : Where it appears to the Inspector that the use of any such building, machinery, etc. involves imminent danger to human life or safety, he may prohibit its use until it has been properly repaired or altered [Section 40 (2)].

22. Maintenance of Building (Section 40-A). Where it appears to the Inspector that any building or any part of a building in a factory is in such a state of disrepair as is likely to lead to conditions detrimental to the health and welfare of the workers, he may serve on the occupier or manager or both of the factory an order in writing specifying the measures which should be taken. He may further require such measures to be carried out before such date as is specified in the order.

23. Safety Officers (Section 40-B). In every factory (i) wherein 1,000 or more workers are ordinarily employed, or (ii) wherein, in the opinion of the State Government, any manufacturing process or operation is carried on, which process or operation involves any risk of bodily injury, poisoning or disease, or any other hazard to health, to the persons employed in the factory, the occupier shall, if so required by the State Government by notification in the Official Gazette, employ such number of Safety Officers as may be specified in that notification [Section 40-B) (1)]. The duties, qualifications and conditions of service of Safety Offices shall be such as may be prescribed by the State Government [Section 40-B (2)].

Power to make Rules to supplement the Above Provisions (Section 41)

The State Government may make rules requiring the provision in any factory of such further devices and measures for securing the safety of persons employed therein as it ay deem necessary.

PROVISIONS RELATING TO HAZARDOUS PROCESSES (New Chapter IVA, Section 41-A to 41-H as introduced by the Amendment Act of 1987)

1. Site Appraisal Committees (Section 41-A)

(i) *Constitution of the Committee* : The State Government may, for purposes of advising it to consider applications for grant of permission for the initial location of a factory involving a hazardous process or for the expansion of any such factory, appoint a Site Appraisal Committee.

The Committee shall consist of :

(a) the Chief inspector of the State who shall be its Chairman;

(b) a representative of the Central Board for the Prevention and Control of Air Pollution referred to in Section 3 of the Water (Prevention and Control of Pollution) Act, 1974;

(c) a representative of the Central Board for the Prevention and Control of Air Pollution referred to in Section 3 of the Air (Prevention and Control of Pollution Act), 1981;

(d) a representative of the State Board appointed under Section 4 of the Water (Prevention and Control of Pollution) Act, 1974;

(e) a representative of the State Board for the Prevention and Control of Air Pollution referred to in Section 5 of the Air (Prevention and Control of Pollution) Act, 1981;

(f) a representative of the Department of Environment in the State;

(g) a representative of the Meteorological Department of the Government of India;

(h) an expert in the field of occupational health;

(i) a representative of the Town Planning Department of the State Government and

(j) not more than 5 other members who may be co-opted by the State Government. The co-opted members shall be (i) a scientist having specialised knowledge of the hazardous process which will be involved in the factory, (ii) a representative of the local authority within whose jurisdiction the factory is to be established and (iii) not more than 3 other persons as deemed fit by the State Government [Section 41-A (1)].

Where any process relates to a factory owned or controlled by the Central Government or to a corporation or a company owned or controlled by the Central Government, the State Government shall co-opt in the Site Appraisal Committee a representative nominated by the Central Government as a member of that Committee [Section 41-A (3)].

(ii) *Functions of the Committee* : The Site Appraisal Committee shall examine an application for the establishment of a factory involving a hazardous process. It shall make its recommendation to the State Government within a period of 90 days of the receipt of such application in the prescribed form [Section 41-A (2)].

The Site Appraisal Committee shall have power to call for any information from the person making an application for the establishment or expansion of a factory involving a hazardous process [Section 41-A (4)].

(iii) *No further Approval required* : Where the State Government has granted approval to an application for the establishment or expansion of a factory involving a hazardous process, it shall not be necessary for an applicant to obtain a further approval from the Central Board or the State Board established under the Water (Prevention and Control of Pollution) Act, 1974 and the Air (Prevention and Control of Pollution) Act, 1981 [Section 41-A (5)].

2. Compulsory Disclosure of Information by the Occupier (Section 41-B)

(i) *Disclosure to Whom* : The occupier of every factory involving a hazardous process shall disclose all information regarding dangers, including health hazard. He shall also disclose the measures to overcome such hazards arising from the exposure to or handling of the materials or substances in the manufacture, transportation, storage and other processes. This information is required to be disclosed to (a) the workers employed in the factory, (b) the Chief Inspector, (c) the local authority within whose jurisdiction the factory is situate, and the general public in the vicinity [Section 41-B (1)].

The information so furnished stall include accurate information as to the quantity, specifications and other characteristics of wastes and the manner of their disposal [Section 41-B (3)].

(ii) *Policy with regard to Health and Safety of Workers* : The occupier shall, at the time of registering the factory involving a hazardous process, lay down a detailed policy with respect to the health and safety of the workers employed therein. He shall intimate such policy to the Chief Inspector and the local authority. Thereafter, he shall, at such intervals as may be prescribed, inform the Chief Inspector and the local authority of any change made in the said policy [Section 41-B (2)].

(iii) *On-site Emergency Plan and Disaster Control Measures* : Every occupier shall, with the approval of the Chief Inspector, draw up an on-site emergency plan and detailed disaster control measures for his factory. He shall also make known to the workers employed therein and to the general public living in the vicinity of the factory the safety measures required to be taken in the event of an accident taking place [Section 41-B (4)].

(iv) *Information to the Chief Inspector before Commencement* : If a factory proposes to engage in a hazardous process, the occupier of the factory shall, within a period of 30 days before the commencement of such process, inform the Chief Inspector of the nature and details of the process in such form and in such manner as may be prescribed [Section 41-B (5)]. If the occupier contravenes this provision the licence issued under Section 6 to such factory shall, notwithstanding any penalty to which the occupier or factory shall be subjected to under the provisions of this Act, be liable for concellation [Section 41-B (6)].

(v) *Handling, Usage, Transportation of Hazardous Substances* : The occupier of a factory involving a hazardous process shall, with the previous approval of the Chief Inspector, lay down measures for the handling, usage, transportation and storage of hazardous substances inside the factory premises. He shall also lay down the measures for the disposal of such substances outside the factory premises. He shall also publicise these measures in the manner prescribed among the workers and the general public living in the vicinity [Section 41-B (7)].

3. Specific Responsibility of the Occupier in relation to Hazardous Processes (Section 41-C). Every occupier of a factory involving any hazardous process shall :

(i) maintain accurate and up-to-date health records or, as the case may be, medical records, of the workers in the factory who are exposed to any chemical, toxic or any other harmful substances which are manufactured, stored, handled or transported. Such records shall be accessible to the workers subject to such conditions as may be prescribed;

(ii) appoint persons who possess qualifications and experience in handling hazardous substances and are competent to supervise such handling within the factory and to provide at the working place all the necessary facilities for protecting the workers in the manner prescribed;

Where any question arises as to the qualifications and experience of a person so appointed, the decision of the Chief Inspector shall be final.

(iii) provide for medical examination of every worker :

(a) before such worker is assigned to a job involving the handling of or working with a hazardous substance and

(b) while continuing in such job, and after he has ceased to work in such job, at intervals not exceeding 12 months in such manner as may be prescribed.

4. Power of Central Government to appoint Inquiry Committee (Section 41-D)

(i) *Appointment of an Inquiry Committee in the Event of Occurrence of an Extraordinary Situation* : The Central Government may, in the event of the occurrence of an extraordinary situation involving a factory engaged in a hazardous process, appoint an Inquiry Committee to inquire into the standards of health and safety observed in the factory. The object of appointing the Committee is to find out the causes of any failure or neglect in the adoption of any measures or standards prescribed for the health and safety of the workers employed in the factory or the general public affected or likely to be affected due to such failure or neglect and for the prevention and recurrence of such extraordinary situation in future in such factory or elsewhere [Section 41-D (1)].

(ii) *Membership of the Committee and Its Tenure of Office* : The Committee shall consist of a Chairman and 2 other members. The terms of reference of the Committee and the tenure of office of its members shall be such as may be determined by the Central Government according to the requirements of the situation [Section 41-D (2)].

(iii) *Recommendations of the Advisory Committee* : The recommendations of the Committee shall be advisory in nature [Section 41-D (3)].

5. Emergency Standards (Section 41-E)

(i) Sometimes standards of safety may not have been prescribed in respect of a hazardous process or class of hazardous processes, or the standards so prescribed may be inadequate. In such a case if the Central Government is satisfied, it may direct the Director General of Factory Advise Service and Labour Institutes or any institution specialised in matters relating to standards of safety in hazardous processes, to lay down emergency standards for enforcement of suitable standards in respect of such hazardous processes [Section 41-E (1)].

(ii) The emergency standards so laid down shall, until these are incorporated in the rules made under this Act, be enforceable and have the same effect as if they had been incorporated in the rules made under this Act [Section 41-E (2)].

6. Permissible Limits of Exposure of Chemical and Toxic Substances (Section 41-F)

(i) The maximum permissible threshold limits of exposure of chemicals and toxic substances in manufacturing process (whether hazardous or otherwise) in any factory shall be of value indicated in the Second Schedule [Section 41-F (1)]. The Second Schedule, added by the Amendment Act of 1987, lays down permissible levels of certain chemical substances in work environment.

(ii) The Central Government may at any time for the purpose of giving effect to any scientific proof obtained from specialised institutions of experts in the field, by notification in the Official Gazette, make suitable changes in the said Schedule [Section 41-F (2)].

7. Workers' Participation in Safety Management (Section 41-G)

(i) *Appointment of a Safety Committee* : The occupier shall, in every factory where a hazardous process takes place, or where hazardous substances are used or handled, set up a safety Committee. The Committee shall consist of equal number of representatives of workers and management to promote co-operation between the workers and the management in maintaining proper safety and health at work. It shall review periodically the measures taken in that behalf [Section 41-G (1)].

(ii) *Composition of the Safety Committee* : The tenure of office of the members of the Safety Committee and their rights and duties shall be such as may be prescribed [Section 41-G (2)].

(iii) *Exemption* : The State Government may, by order in writing and for reasons to be recorded, exempt the occupier of any factory or class of factories from setting up the Safety Committee [Proviso to Section 41-G (1)].

8. Right of Workers to warn about Imminent Danger (Section 41-H)

(i) *Apprehension of Danger to be brought to Notice* : Sometimes the workers employed in a factory engaged in a hazardous process may have reasonable apprehension that there is a likelihood of imminent danger to their lives or health due to any accident. In such a case they may bring such danger to the notice of the occupier, agent manager or, any other person who is incharge of the factory or the process concerned directly or through their representatives in the Safety Committee. They may also simultaneously bring the danger to the notice of the Inspector [Section 41-H (1)].

(i) *Duty of Occupier, etc.* : It shall be the duty of the occupier, agent, manager or the person incharge of the factory or process to take immediate remedial action if he is satisfied about the existence of such imminent danger and send report forthwith of the action taken to the nearest Inspector [Section 41-H (2)].

(ii) *Reference of Matter to Inspector* : If the occupier, agent, manager or the person incharge is not satisfied about the existence of any imminent danger as apprehended by the workers, he shall, nevertheless, refer the matter forthwith to the nearest Inspector. The decision of the Inspector on the question of the existence of such imminent danger shall be final [Section 41-H (3)].

9. Penalty for Contravention of the Provisions of Sections 41-B, 41-C and 41-H [New Section 96-A as introduced by the Amendment Act of 1987]

Whoever fails to comply with or contravenes any of the provisions of Sections 41-B, 41-C or 41-H or the rules made thereunder shall, in respect of such failure or contravention be publishable with imprisonment for a term which may extend to 7 years and with fine which may extend to Rs. 2,00,000. In case the failure or contravention continues, the defaulter shall be punishable with additional fine which may extend to Rs. 5,000 for every day during which such failure or contravention continues after the conviction for the first such failure or contravention [Section 96-A (1)]. If this failure or contravention continues beyond a period of 1 year after the date of conviction, the offender shall be punishable with imprisonment for a term which may extend to 10 years [Section 96-A (2)].

WELFARE

Chapter V (Section 42 to 50) of the Act deals with facilities for the welfare of workers. The various provisions in this regard are as follows :

1. Washing Facilities (Section 42). In every factory (a) adequate and suitable facilities (separately and adequately screened for the use of male and female workers) shall be provided and maintained for the use of the workers therein; and (b) such facilities shall be conveniently accessible and shall be kept clean.

2. Facilities for storing and drying Clothing (Section 43). The State Government may make rules requiring the provision of suitable places for keeping clothing of workers not worn during working hours and for the drying of wet clothing in respect of any factory or class of factories.

3. Facilities for sitting (Section 44). (i) *Provision of sitting Arrangement for Workers obliged to work in a Standing Position* : In every factory, suitable arrangements for sitting shall be provided and maintained for all workers who are obliged to work in a standing position. This has been done in order that the workers may take advantage of any opportunities for rest which may occur in the course of their work [Section 44 (1)].

(ii) *Provision of seating Arrangement for Workers Doing Work Which can be done in a Sitting Position* : If the workers in any factory engaged in a particular manufacturing process or working in a particular room are able to do their work efficiently in a sitting position, the Chief Inspector may require the occupier of the factory to provide such seating arrangements as may be practicable [Section 44 (2)].

(iii) *Exemption* : The State Government may, by notification in the Official Gazette, exempt any factory or class of factories or manufacturing process from the application of the provisions of Section 44 [Section 44 (2)].

4. First-aid Appliances (Section 45). (i) *At least one First-aid Box with prescribed Contents for Every 150 Workers* : There shall in every factory be provided and maintained so as to be readily accessible during all working hours, first-aid boxes or cupboards with the prescribed contents. There shall be at least one such box for every 150 workers ordinarily employed at any one time in the factory [Section 45 (1)].

(ii) *First-aid box to have prescribed Contents* : Only the prescribed contents shall be kept in a first-aid box or cupboard [Section 45 (2)].

(iii) *First-aid box to be in the Charge of Responsible Person* : Each first aid box or cupboard shall be kept in the charge of a separate responsible person who holds a certificate in the first-aid treatment recognised by the State Government. Further, such person shall always be readily available during the working hours of the factory [Section 45 (3)].

(iv) *Ambulance Room in a Factory employing more than 500 Workers* : In every factory wherein more than 500 workers are ordinarily employed there shall be provided and maintained an ambulance room containing the prescribed equipment.

The room shall be in the charge of such medical and nursing staff as may be prescribed and those facilities shall always be made readily available during the working hours of the factory [Section 45 (4)].

5. Canteens (Section 46). (i) *Canteen in Factory employing more than 250 Workers : the State Government may make Rules* : The State Government may make rules requiring that in any specified factory wherein more than 250 workers are ordinarily employed, a canteen or canteens shall be provided and maintained by the occupier for the use of the workers [Section 46 (1)].

(ii) *Provisions in Rules* : The rules made by the State Government as to canteens may provide for (a) the date by which canteen shall be provided, (b) the standards in respect of construction, accommodation, furniture and other equipment of the canteen, (c) the foodstuffs to be served therein and the charges which may be made thereof, (d) the constitution of a managing committee for the canteen and representation of the workers in the management of the canteen; (e) the items of expenditure in the running of the canteen which are not to be taken into account in fixing the cost of foodstuffs and which shall be borne by the employer, and (f) the delegation to the Chief Inspector, subject to such conditions as may be prescribed, of the power to make rules under Clause (c) [Section 46 (2)].

6. Shelters, Rest Rooms and Lunch Rooms (Section 47). (i) *Provision for Shelters, Rest Rooms, Lunch Rooms in Factories employing more than 150 Workers* : In every factory wherein more than 150 workers are ordinarily employed, there shall be a provision for shelters, rest rooms and a suitable lunch room where workers can eat meals brought by them with provision for drinking water. However, any canteen maintained in accordance with the provisions of Section 46 shall be regarded as part of this requirement. Where a lunch room exists, no workers shall eat any food in the workroom [Section 47 (1)].

(ii) *Shelters etc. : to be sufficiently lighted, ventilated and cooled.* The shelters or rest rooms or lunch rooms shall be sufficiently lighted and ventilated and shall be maintained in a cool and clean condition [Section 47 (2)].

7. Creches (Section 48). (i) *Provision of Creches in Factories employing more than 30 Women Workers* : In every factory wherein more than 30 women workers are ordinarily employed, there shall be provided and maintained a suitable room or rooms for use of children under the age of 6 years of such women [Section 48 (1)].

(ii) *Creches to be adequately lighted and ventilated and to be under the Charge of Trained Women* : Rooms for use of children shall provide adequate accommodation, shall be adequately lighted and ventilated. Further they shall be maintained in a clean and sanitary condition and shall be under the charge of women trained in the care of children and infants [Section 48 (2)].

(iii) *Prescription of Rules by the State Government* : The State Government may make rules prescribing the location and the standards in respect of construction, accommodation, furniture and other equipment of rooms for use of children. It may also make rules for the provision of additional facilities for the care of children belonging to women workers, including suitable provision of facilities (a) for washing and changing their clothing, (b) of free milk or refreshment or both for the children, and (c) for the mothers of children to feed them at the necessary intervals [Section 48 (3)].

8. Welfare Officers (Section 49). (i) *Employment of Welfare Officers in Factories employing 500 or more Workers* : In every factory wherein 500 or more workers are ordinarily employed the occupier shall employ in the factory such number of welfare officers as may be prescribed [Section 49 (1)].

(ii) *Duties, Qualifications and Conditions of Service to be prescribed by the State Government* : The State Government may prescribe the duties, qualifications and conditions of service of welfare officers [Section 49 (2)].

Even if a factory (say, a sugar factory) employs over 500 workers only for a few months in the year and not continuously, the occupier shall employ the prescribed number of welfare officers [Employers' Assn. of Northern India *Vs.* Secretary of Labour, A.I.R. (1952) All. 109].

(iii) *Power to make Rules (Section 50)* : The State Government may make rules :

(a) exempting, subject to compliance with such alternative arrangements for the welfare of workers as may be prescribed, any factory or class or description of factories from compliance with any of the provisions of Sections 42 to 49;

(b) requiring in any factory or class or description of factories that representatives of the workers employed in the factory shall be associated with the management of the welfare arrangements of the workers.

WORKING HOURS OF ADULTS

The rules as to the regulation of hours of work of adult workers in a factory and holidays are as follows :

1. Working Hours

(i) *Weekly Hours* (Section 51) : No adult worker shall be required or allowed to work in a factory for more than 49 hours in any week.

(ii) *Daily Hours* (Section 54) : Subject to the above rule (as contained in Section 51) no adult worker shall be required or allowed to work in a factory for more than 9 hours in any day. But in order to facilitate the change of shift, this limit may be exceeded. This can, however, be done with the previous approval of the Chief Inspector of Factories.

(iii) *Intervals for Rest* (Section 55) : The periods of work of adult workers in a factory each day shall be so fixed that no period shall exceed 5 hours. Further no worker shall work for more than 5 hours before he has an interval for rest of at least half an hour (Section 55 (1)]. The State Government or Chief Inspector may, by written order and for the reasons specified therein, exempt any factory from the provisions of Section 55 (1). But in that case also, the total number of hours worked without an interval shall not exceed 6 [Section 55 (2)].

2. Spreadover, Night Shifts and Overlapping Shifts

(i) *Spreadover* (Section 56) : The periods of work of an adult worker in a factory shall be so arranged that inclusive of his intervals for rest, they shall not spread over more than 10-1/2 hours in any day. But the Chief Inspector may for reasons to be specified in writing increase the spreadover up to 12 hours.

(ii) *Night Shifts* (Section 57) : Where a worker in a factory works on a shift which extends beyond midnight :

(a) his weekly or compensatory holiday for a whole day means a period of 24 consecutive hours beginning when his shift ends, and

(b) the following day for him shall be deemed to be the period of 24 hours beginning when such shift ends, and the hours he has worked after midnight shall be counted in the previous day.

(iii) *Prohibition of Overlapping Shifts* (Section 58) : Work shall not be carried on in any factory by means of a system of shifts so arranged that more than one relay of workers is engaged in work of the same kind at the same time [Section 58 (1)].

(iv) The State Government or the Chief Inspector may, by written order and for the reasons specified therein, grant exemption to any factory or class or description of factories or any department or section of a factory from the provisions of Section 58 (1) [Section 58 (2)].

3. Extra Wages for Overtime (Section 59)

(i) *Wages at Twice the Ordinary Rate* : Where a worker works in a factory for more than 9 hours in any day or more than 48 hours in any week, he shall in respect of overtime work be entitled to wages at the rate of twice his 'ordinary rate of wages' [Section 59 (1)].

(ii) *Ordinary Rate of Wages* : It means the basic wages plus such allowances, including the cash equivalent of the advantage accruing through the concessional sale to workers of foodgrains and other articles, as the worker is for the time being entitled to. It does not include a bonus and wages for overtime work [Section 59 (2)].

(iii) *Workers paid on Piece Rate Basis* : The time rate in case of workers paid on piece rate shall be deemed to be equivalent to the daily average of their full time earnings for the days on which they actually worked on the same or identical job during the month immediately preceding the calendar month during which the overtime work was done, and such time rates shall be deemed to be the ordinary rates of wages of those workers [Section 59 (3)]. But in the case of a worker who has not worked in the immediately preceding calender month on the same or identical job, the time rate shall be deemed to be equivalent to the daily average of the earnings of the worker for the days on which he actually worked in the week in which the overtime work was done [Proviso to Section 59 (3)].

(iv) *Cash Equivalent of the Concessional Sale of Foodgrains and Other Articles* : It shall be computed as often as prescribed on the basis of the maximum quantity of foodgrains and other articles admissible to a 'standard family'. Standard family means a family consisting of the worker, his or her spouse and 2 children below the age of 14 years requiring in all 3 'adult consumption units'. Adult consumption unit means the consumption unit of a male above the age of 14 years. The consumption unit of a female above the age of 14 years and that of a child below the age of 14 years shall be calculated at the rate of 0.8 and 0.6 respectively of one adult consumption unit [Section 59 (4)].

(v) *Rule-making Power of the State Government* : The State Government may make rules prescribing (a) the manner in which the cash equivalent of the advantage accruing through the concessional sale to a worker of foodgrains and other articles shall be computed, and (b) the registers that shall be maintained in a factory for the purpose of securing compliance with the provisions of [Section 59 Section (5)]

4. Restriction on Double Employment (Section 60)

No adult worker shall be required or allowed to work in any factory on any day on which he has already been working in any other factory save in such circumstances as may be prescribed.

5. Notice of Periods of Work for Adult Workers (Section 61)

(i) *Notice to be displayed at Some Conspicuous Place* : A notice of periods of work for adult workers shall be displayed and correctly maintained in every factory. It shall show clearly for every day the periods during which adult workers may be required to work [Section 61 (1)]. The notice shall be in English and in a language understood by the majority of the workers in the factory. It shall be displayed at some conspicuous and convenient place at or near the main entrance to the factory and shall be maintained in a clean and legible condition [Section 108 (2)].

(ii) *Periods to be fixed Beforehand* : (a) The periods shown in the notice shall be fixed beforehand and shall not contravene the provisions of weekly and daily hours, weekly holidays, intervals for rest, spreadover and prohibition of overlapping shifts [Section 61 (2)].

(b) Where all the adult workers in a factory are required to work during the same period, the manager shall fix generally the periods [Section 61 (3)].

(iii) *Classification of Workers* : (a) Where all the adult workers in a factory are not required to work during the same periods, the manager of the factory shall classify them into groups according to the nature of their work indicating the number of workers in each group [Section 61 (4)].

(b) For each group which is not required to work on a system of shifts, the manager of the factory shall fix the periods during which the group may be required to work [Section 61 (5)].

(iv) Groups working on a system of shifts. (a) Where any group is required to work on a system of shifts and the relays are not to be subject to predetermined periodical changes of shift, the manager shall fix the periods during which each relay of the group may be required to work [Section 61 (6)].

(b) Where any group is to work on a system of shifts an the relays are subject to predetermined periodical changes of shifts, the manager shall draw up a scheme of shifts. This provision has been made so that the periods during which any relay of the group may be required to work and the relay which will be working at any time of the day may be ascertained for any day [Section 61 (7)].

(v) *Form of Notice of Periods of Work* : The State Government may prescribe forms of the notice of periods of work for adults and the manner in which it shall be maintained [Section 61 (8)].

(vi) *Copy of Notice in Duplicate and any Change to be sent to Inspector* : (a) A copy of the notice shall be sent in duplicate to the Inspector before the day on which work is begun in the factory [Section 61 (9)].

(b) Any proposed changes in the system of work in any factory which will necessitate a change in the notice shall be notified to the Inspector in duplicate before the change is made. Further, except with the previous sanction of the Inspector, no such change shall be made until 1 week has elapsed since the last change [Section 61 (10)].

6. Register of Adult Workers (Sections 62 and 63)

(i) The manager of every factory shall maintain a register of adult workers showing (a) the name of each adult worker in the factory, (b) the nature of his work, (c) the group, if any, in which he is included, (d) where his group works on shifts, the relay to which he is allotted, and (e) such other particulars as may be prescribed.

(ii) The register shall be available to the Inspector at all times during working hours, or when any work is being carried on in the factory.

(iii) If the Inspector is of opinion that any muster-roll or register maintained as part of the routine of a factory gives the above particulars in respect of workers, he may direct that such muster-roll or register shall be treated as the register of adult workers in that factory [Section 62 (1)].

(iv) No adult worker shall be required or allowed to work in any factory unless his name and other particulars have been entered in the register of adult workers [Section 62 (1-A)].

(v) The State Government may prescribe the form of the register of adult workers, the manner in which it shall be maintained and the period for which it shall be preserved [Section 62 (2)]. Further no adult worker shall be required or allowed to work in any factory otherwise than in accordance with the notice of periods of work for adults displayed in the factory and the entries made beforehand against his name in the register of adult workers of the factory (Section 63).

HOLIDAYS

1. Weekly Holidays (Section 52). Every adult worker in a factory shall be allowed a holiday during a week. As such no adult worker shall be required or allowed to work in a factory on the first day of the week which is a Sunday. But the manager can substitute for Sunday any of the 3 days preceding or following it. He shall, however, deliver a notice at the office of the Inspector of his intention to require the worker to work on that day. Such notice shall also be displayed in the factory. No substitution can, however, be made which results in any worker working for more than 10 days consecutively without a holiday for a whole day [Section 52 (1)].

Where any worker works on a Sunday and has had a holiday on one of the 3 days immediately before it, Sunday shall, for the purpose of calculating his weekly hours of work, be included in the preceding week [Section 52 (3)].

2. Compensatory Holidays (Section 53). Where a worker is deprived of any of the weekly holidays under Section 52 or by any of the rules made by the State Government exempting a factory from the provisions of Section 52, he shall be allowed compensatory holidays of equal number to the holidays so lost. Such compensatory holidays shall be allowed within the month in which the holidays were due to the workman or within 2 months immediately following that month [Section 53 (1)].

The State Government may prescribe the manner in which the compensatory holidays shall be allowed [Section 53 (2)].

3. Further Restrictions on Employment of Women (Section 66). These are discussed later in this Chapter under the heading "Employment of Women".

EMPLOYMENT OF YOUNG PERSONS

1. Prohibition of Employment of Young Children (Section 67). No child who has not completed his 14th year shall be required or allowed to work in a factory.

2. Non-adult Workers to carry Tokens (Section 68). A child who has completed his 14th year or an adolescent may be allowed to work in a factory if :

(i) a certificate of fitness for such work is in the custody of the manager of the factory and

(ii) such child or adolescent carries, while he is at work, a token giving a reference to such certificate.

A provision is made for a certificate of fitness under Section 69. Such a certificate entitles a young person who has completed his 14th year to work in a factory as a child. But if the young person has completed his 15th year, the certificate of fitness entitles him to work in a factory as an adult.

3. Certificate of Fitness (Section 69). (i) *Meaning and Procedure* : It is a certificate granted to a young person by a certifying surgeon after examining him and ascertaining his fitness for work in a factory. An application for such examination may be made by the young person himself or by his guardian. It shall, however, be accompanied by a document signed by the manager of the factory that such person will be employed therein if certified to be fit for work in a factory. The manager of the factory may also apply for such examination of the young person. The certifying surgeon shall examine the place of work and the manufacturing process before granting a certificate unless he has the personal knowledge of it [Section 69 (1)].

(ii) *Certificate of Fitness to entitle a Young Person to work as a Child or Adult* : The certifying surgeon, after examination, may grant to a young person or may renew a certificate of fitness to work in a factory as :

(a) a child, if he is satisfied (i) that the young person has completed his 14th year, (ii) that he has attained the prescribed physical standards, and (iii) that he is fit for such work;

(b) an adult, if he is satisfied (i) that the young person has completed his 15th year and (ii) that he is fit for a full day's work in a factory [Section 69 (2)].

(iii) *Certificate Valid for 12 Months* : A certificate of fitness granted or renewed is valid for 12 months from the date of issue, but is can be renewed. It may be issued subject to conditions in regard to nature the work in which the young person may be employed, or requiring re-examinations of the young person before the expiry of the period of 12 months [Section 69 (3)].

(iv) *Revocation of Certificate of Fitness* : A certificate of fitness can be revoked any time by the certifying surgeon if the holder of it is no longer fit to work in the capacity stated therein a factory [Section 69 (4)]. Where a certifying surgeon refuses to grant or renew a certificate of fitness, or revokes a certificate, he shall, if so requested, state his reasons in writing for so doing [Section 69 (5)].

(v) *Fees Payable by the Employer* : Fees for a certificate of fitness or its renewal shall be payable by the occupier and shall not be recoverable form the young person, his parents or guardian [Section 69 (7)].

(vi) *Effect of Certificate of Fitness* (Section 70) : An adolescent who has been granted a certificate of fitness to work in a factory as an adult and who carries a token giving reference to the certificate shall be deemed to be an adult for the purposes of hours of work of an adult and the annual leave [Section 70 (1)].

No female adolescent or a male adolescent who has not attained the age of 17 years but who has been granted a certificate of fitness to work in a factory as an adult shall be required or allowed to work in any factory except between 6 A.M. and 7 P.M. [Section 70 (1-A) as introduced by the Amendment Act of 1987].

The State Government may, by notification in the Official Gazette, in respect of any factory or group or class or description of factories :

(i) vary the limits laid down in Section 70 (1-A), but no female adolescent can be employed between 10 P.M. and 5 A.M.;

(ii) grant exemption from the provisions of Section 70 (1-A) in case of serious emergency where national interest is involved [Proviso to Section 70 (1-A)].

An adolescent who has not been granted a certificate of fitness to work in a factory as an adult is deemed to be a child for all the purposes of the Factories Act (Section 70 (2); Jhunjhunwala *Vs.* B.K. Patnaik, (1964) 2 L.L.J. 551).

4. Working Hours and Notice of Periods of Work for Children (Section 71 and 72). (i) *Working Hours Limited to 4-1/2* : No child shall be employed or permitted to work in any factor —

(a) for more than 4-1/2 hours in any day;

(b) during the night [Section 71 (1)].

'Night' means a period of at least 12 consecutive hours which shall include the interval between 10 P.M. and 6 A.M. [Expl. to Section 71 (1)].

(ii) *Period of Work of Children Limited to 2 Shifts* : The period of work of all children employed in a factory shall be limited to 2 shifts. These shifts shall not overlap spread over more than 5 hours each. Each child shall be employed in only one of the relays which shall not, except with the previous permission in writing of Chief Inspector, be changed more frequently than once in a period of 30 days [Section 71 (2)].

(iii) *Child Workers entitled to Weekly Holidays.* The provisions of weekly holidays (Section 52) shall apply also to child workers and not exemption from these provisions may be granted in respect of any child [Section 71 (3)].

(iv) *Prohibition if the Child Worker has already been working in Another Factory* : No child shall be required or allowed to work in any factory on any day on which he has already been working in another factory [Section 71 (4)].

(v) *Female Child to work only between 8 A.M. to 7 P.M.* : No female child shall be required or allowed to work in any factory except between 8 A.M. and 7 P.M. [Section 71 (5) as introduced by the Amendment Act of 1987].

(vi) *Display of Notice of Work of Child Workers* : There shall be displayed and correctly maintained in every factory in which children are employed a notice of periods of work for children showing clearly for every day the periods during which children may be required or allowed to work [Section 72 (1)]. The provisions of Section 61 (8), (9) and (10) (discussed earlier) also apply to the notice required under Section 72 (1) [Section 72 (3)].

(vii) *Fixation of Periods of Work Beforehand* : The periods shown in the notice shall be fixed beforehand in accordance with the method laid down for adult workers [Section 72 (2)].

5. Register of Child Workers (Section 73). (i) The manager of every factory in which children are employed shall maintain a register of child workers showing (a) the name of each child worker in the factory, (b) the nature of his work, (c) the group, if any, in which he is included, (d) where his group works on shifts, the relay to which he is allotted, and (e) the number of his certificate of fitness. The register shall be available to the Inspector at all times during working hours or when any work is being carried on in a factory [Setion 73 (1)].

(ii) No child worker shall be required or allowed to work in any factory unless his name and other particulars have been entered in the register of child workers [Section 73 (1-A)].

(iii) The State Government may prescribe the form of the register of child workers, the manner in which it shall be maintained and the period for which it shall be preserved [Section 73 (2)].

(iv) The hours of work of a child shall correspond with the notice of periods of work for children displayed in the factory and the entries made beforehand against his name in the register of child workers (Section 74).

6. Power to require Medical Examination (Section 75). An Inspector may direct the manager of a factory to have a person or young person medically examined by a certifying surgeon when he is of opinion :

(i) that the person working in the factory without a certificate of fitness is a young person, or

(ii) that the young person working in the factory with a certificate of fitness is no longer fit to work in the capacity stated in the certificate, and that such a person shall not be employed or permitted to work in the factory until he has been examined and granted a certificate of fitness or a fresh certificate of fitness.

7. Power to make Rules. The State Government may make rules :

(i) prescribing the forms of certificates of fitness to be granted to the young persons and the procedure for their issue;

(ii) prescribing the physical standards to be attained by children and adolescents working in factories;

(iii) regulating the procedure of certifying surgeons and prescribing other duties which the certifying surgeons may be required to perform in connection with the employment of young persons in factories (Section 76).

The provisions relating to the employment of young persons are in addition to, and not in derogation of, the provisions of the Employment of Children Act, 1931 (Section 77).

8. Safety Provisions for Young Persons. (i) Work on or Near Machinery in Motion [Section 22 (2)].

(ii) Employment of young persons on dangerous machines [Section 23 (1)].

(iii) Prohibition of employment near cotton-openers (Section 27).

(iv) Dangerous operation [Section 87 (b)]. No young person shall be employed on any operation carried on in a factory which exposes the young person to a serious risk of bodily injury, poisoning or disease.

EMPLOYMENT OF WOMEN

All the provisions of the Factories Act regarding employment and work of adult male workers apply to adult female worker except the following provisions which apply to adult female workers only :

1. Work on or near Machinery in Motion [Section 22 (2)].

2. Prohibition of Employment near Cotton-Openers (Section 27).

3. Creches (Section 48).

The provisions of Sections 22 (2), 27 and 48 have already been discussed in this Chapter.

4. Working Hours (Sections 51 and 54). A woman shall not be required or allowed to work in a factory for more than 48 hours in any week or 9 hours in any day.

5. Restriction on Employment of Women (Section 66). A woman shall be required or allowed to work in a factory only between the hours of 6 A.M. and 7 P.M. The State Government may, by notification in the Official Gazette in respect of any factory or group or class or description of factories, vary these limits. But no such variation shall authorise the employment of any woman between the hours of 10 P.M. and 5 A.M. Again there shall be no change of shifts in the case of women workers in a factory except after a weekly or any other holiday [Section 66 (1)].

The State Government may make rules providing or the exemption from the restrictions imposed by Section 66 (1) in case of women working in fish-curing or fish canning factories, where the employment of women beyond the specified hours is necessary to prevent damage to, or deterioration in any, raw material [Section 66 (2)]. The rules so make shall remain in force for not more than 3 years at a time [Section 66 (3)].

6. Effect of Certificate of Fitness granted to Female Adolescent [Section 70 (1-A)]. This has already been discussed.

7. Dangerous Operations [Section 87 (b)]. Where the State Government is of opinion that any operation carried on in a factory exposes any person employed in it to a serious risk of bodily injury, poisoning or disease, it may make rules prohibiting or restricting the employment of women in that operation.

ANNUAL LEAVE WITH WAGES

Sections 78 to 84 (Chapter VIII) provide for the grant of a certain period of leave with wages to workmen.

1. Application of Chapter VIII (Section 78)

According to Section 78, the provisions relating to annual leave with wages as contained in Chapter VIII (Sections 78 to 84) of the Act shall not prejudice any rights of workers under any other law, award or agreement (including settlement) or contract of service. When such award, agreement (including settlement) or contract of service provides for a longer annual leave with wages than under the provisions of Section 79 to 82, the worker shall be entitled to such annual leave. But in relation to matters not provided for in such award, agreement or contract of service or matters which are provided for less favourably therein, the provisions of Sections 79 to 82, so far as may be, shall apply [Section 78 (1)]. Further the provisions of Chapter VIII shall not apply to workers in any factory of any railway administered by the Government who are governed by leave rules approved by the Central Government [Section 78 (2)].

2. Rules relating to Annual Leave with Wages

(i) *Leave Entitlement — One Day for Every 20/15 Days of Work performed in Case of Adult/child* : Every worker who has worked for a period of 240 days or more in a factory during a calendar year shall be allowed during the subsequent calendar year leave with wages for a certain number of days. These of leave shall be calculated at the rate of :

(i) if an adult, one day for every 20 days of work performed by him during the previous calendar year;

(ii) if a child, one day for every 15 days of work performed by him during the previous. calendar year [Section 79 (1)].

The leave admissible under the above rule shall be exclusive of all holidays whether occurring during or at either end of the period of leave [Expl. 2 to Section 79 (1)].

(ii) *Computation of Period of 240 Days* : For computing the period of 240 days, the days of lay-off, maternity leave to a female worker not exceeding 12 weeks, and the leave earned in the previous year shall be included in this period of 240 days, but he/she shall not earn leave for these days [Explanation 1 to Section 79 (1)].

A worker who is employed on any day after the first day of January shall be entitled to leave with wages at the rates laid down in Section 79 (1) if he has worked for 2/3rds of the total number of days in the remainder of the calendar year [Section 79 (2)].

(iii) *Discharge, Dismissal, Superannuation, Death or Quitting of Employment* : If a worker is discharged or dismissed from service or quits his employment or is superannuated or dies while in service, during the course of the calendar year, he or his heir or nomince, as the case may be, shall be entitled to wages. These wages shall be in lieu of the quantum of leave to which he was entitled calculated at the rates specified in Section 79 (1). He shall be entitled to these wages even if he had not worked for the entire period specified in Section 79 (1) making him eligible to avail of such leave. The payment of wages shall be made :

(a) where the worker is discharged or dismissed or quits employment, before the expiry of the second working day from the date of such discharge, dismissal or quitting; or

(b) where the worker is superannuated or dies while in service, before the expiry of 2 months from the date of such superannuation or death [Section 79 (2)].

(iv) *Treatment of Fraction of Leave* : In calculating leave period, fraction of leave of half a day or more shall be treated as one full day's leave, and fraction of less than half a day shall be omitted [Section 79 (4)].

(v) *Treatment of Unavailed Leave* : If a worker does not in any one calendar year take the whole of the leave allowed to him, any leave not taken by him shall be added to the leave to be allowed to him in the succeeding calendar year. But the total number of days of leave that may be carried forward to a suceeding year shall not exceed 30 in the case of an adult or 40 in the case of a child. However, annual leave not allowed because of any scheme for leave in operation shall be carried forward without any limit [Section 79 (5)].

(vi) *Application for Leave to be made in Writing Within a Specified Time* : A worker may at any time apply for annual leave in writing to the manager of the factory at least 15 days before the date on which he wishes his leave to begin. In a public utility service the application shall likewise be made at least 30 days before the date on which the worker wishes his leave to begin. But the number of times the leave may be taken during any year shall not exceed 3 [Section 79 (6)].

(vii) *Application for Leave covering a Period of Illness may not be made Within the Specified Time* : If a worker wants to avail himself of the leave with wages due to him to cover a period of illness, he shall be granted such leave even if the application for leave is not made within the time specified. In such a case, advance payment of wages (as admissible under Section 81) shall be made not later than 15 days, or in the case of a public utility service not later than 30 days, from the date of the application for leave [Section 79 (7)].

(viii) *Scheme for the Grant of Leave* : For the purpose of ensuring the continuity of work, the occupier or the manager of the factory, in agreement with the Works Committee (constituted under Section 3 of the Industrial Disputes Act, 1947 in an industrial establishment in which 100 or more workmen are employed), if any, or the representatives of workers, may draw up and lodge with the Chief Inspector a scheme for regulating the grant of leave [Section 79 (8)].

(ix) *Display of Scheme for Grant of Leave* : The scheme shall be displayed at some convenient and conspicuous places in the factory. It shall be in force in the first instance for 12 months, and may be renewed for a further period of 12 months at a time. A Notice of renewal shall be sent to the Chief Inspector before it is renewed [Section 79 (9)].

(x) *Refusal of Leave to be in accordance with Scheme* : An application for leave submitted in proper time shall not be refused, unless refusal is in accordance with the scheme for leave for the time being in operation [Section 79 (10)].

(xi) *Payment of Wages to Worker for Leave Period if he is discharged or if he quits Service* : If a worker being entitled to leave according to the rules is discharged, or if having applied for is refused leave and quits service before he has taken the leave, he shall be paid wages in respect of the leave not taken. The payment shall be made before the expiry of the second working day after discharge or on or before the next pay day in case the worker quits his employment [Section 79 (11)].

(xii) *Unavailed Leave not to be taken into Account while Computing Period of Notice* : The unavailed leave of a worker shall not be taken into consideration in computing the periods of any notice required to be given before discharge of dismissal [Section 79 (12)].

3. Wages during Leave Period (Section 80). (i) For the leave allowed to a worker he shall be entitled to wages at a rate equal to the daily average of his total full time earnings for the days on which he actually worked during the month immediately preceding his leave. The full time earnings shall be exclusive of any overtime and bonus but inclusive of dearness allowance and the case equivalent of the advantage accruing through the concessional sale to the worker of foodgrains and other articles [Section 80 (1)].

(ii) In the case of worker who has not worked on any day during the calendar month immediately preceding his leave, he shall be paid at a rate equal to the daily average of his total full time earnings for the days on which he actually worked during the last calendar month preceding his leave in which he actually worked. These full time earnings shall be exclusive of any overtime wages and bonus but inclusive of dearness allowance and the cash equivalent of the advantage accruing through the concessional sale to the workers of foodgrains and other articles [Previso to Section 80 (1) as added by the Amendment Act of 1987].

(iii) The calculation of cash equivalent of the advantage accruing through the concessional sale to the worker of foodgrains and other articles shall be calculated in the same manner as laid down in Section 59 (4) explained in connection with 'Extra wages for overtime' [Section 80 (2)].

(iv) The State Government may make rules prescribing :

(a) the manner in which the cash equivalent of the advantage accruing through the concessional sale to a worker of foodgrains and other articles shall be computed and

(b) the register that shall be maintained in a factory for the purpose of compliance with the provisions of Section 80 [Section 80 (3)].

4. Other Provisions of Chapter VIII

(i) *Payment in Advance in Certain Cases* (Section 81) : A worker who has been allowed leave for not less than 4 days, in the case of an adult, and 5 days, in the case of a child, shall before his leave begins, be paid the wages due for the period of the leave allowed.

(ii) *Mode of Recovery of Unpaid Wages* (Section 82) : Any sum required to be paid by an employer as wages but not paid by him shall be recoverable as delayed wages under the provisions of the Payment of Wages Act, 1936.

(iii) *Power to make Rules* (Section 83) : The State Government may make rules directing managers of factories to keep registers containing prescribed particulars and requiring the registers to be available for examination by Inspectors.

(iv) *Power to exempt Factories* (Section 84) : The State Government may exempt a factory from the operation of the leave rules if it is satisfied that its own leave rules provide benefits which are not less favourable to the workers than the statutory leave rules.

SPECIAL PROVISIONS

1. Power to apply the Act to Certain Premises (Section 85). The State Government may, by notification in the Official Gazette, declare that all or any of the provisions of the Factories Act shall apply to any place wherein a manufacturing process is carried on with or without the aid of power or is so ordinarily carried on. This provision may be made applicable even where :

(i) the number of persons employed in the place of work is less than 10 if working with the aid of power, and less than 20, if working without the aid of power, or

(ii) the persons working in the place of work are not employed by the owner thereof but are working with the permission of, or under agreement with, such owner.

If the manufacturing process is being carried on by the owner only with the aid of his family, the above provision shall not apply [Section 85 (1)].

After a place is so declared under Section 85 (1), it shall be deemed to be a factory for the purposes of the Act and the owner shall be deemed to be the occupier and any person working therein, a worker [Section 85 (2)].

2. Power to exempt Public Institutions (Section 86). The State Government may exempt, subject to necessary conditions, any workshop or workplace where a manufacturing process is carried on and which is attached to a public institution maintained for the purposes of education, training, research or reformation, from all or any of the provisions of the Factories Act. This shall, however, be subject to a scheme for the regulation of hours of work, intervals for meals and holidays, to be prepared by the person having the control of the institution and to be submitted to the State Government for its approval. If the State Government is satisfied that the provisions of the scheme are not less favourable than the corresponding provisions of this Act, the exemption shall be granted from the provisions of work and holidays.

3. Dangerous Operations (Section 87). A manufacturing process or operation carried on in a factory might expose any person employed in it to a serious risk of bodily injury, poisoning or disease. The State Government may make rules applicable to any such factory or class or description of factories in which the manufacturing process or operation is carried on :

(i) specifying the manufacturing process or operation and declaring it to be dangerous;

(ii) prohibiting or restricting the employment of women, adolescents or children in the manufacturing process or operation;

(iii) providing for the periodical medical examination of persons employed, or seeking to be employed, in the manufacturing process or operation and prohibiting the employment of persons not certified as fit for such employment and requiring the payment by the occupier of the factory of fees for such medical examination;

(iv) Providing for the protection of all persons employed in the manufacturing process or operation or in the vicinity of the places where it is carried on;

(v) prohibiting, restricting or controlling the use of any specified materials or processes in connection with the manufacturing process or operation and

(vi) requiring the provision of additional welfare amenities and sanitary facilities and the supply of protective equipment and clothing, and laying down the standards thereof, having regard to the dangerous nature of the manufacturing process or operation.

4. Power to prohibit Employment on Account of Serious Hazard (Section 87-A as introduced by the Amendment Act of 1987). (i) Sometimes it may appear to the Inspector that conditions in a factory or part thereof are such that they may cause serious hazard by way of injury or death to the persons employed therein or to the general public in the vicinity. In such a case, he may, by order in writing to the occupier of the factory, state the particulars in respect of which he considers the factory or part thereof to be the cause of such serious hazard. He may further prohibit such occupier from employing any person in the factory or any part thereof other than the minimum number of persons necessary to attend to the minimum tasks till the hazard is removed [Section 87-A (1)]. The order so issued by the Inspector shall have effect for a period of 3 days until extended by the Chief Inspector by a subsequent order [Section 87-A (2)].

(ii) Any person aggrieved by an order of the Inspector and the Chief Inspector, as the case may be, shall have the right to appeal to the High Court [Section 87-A (3)].

(iii) Any person whose employment has been affected by an order issued by the Inspector shall be entitled to wages and other benefits. Further it shall be the duty of the occupier to provide alternative employment to the person so affected wherever possible and in the manner prescribed [Section 87-A (4)]. This provision shall however be without prejudice to the rights of the parties under the Industrial Disputes Act, 1947 [Section 87-A (5)].

5. Notice of Certain Accidents (Section 88). (i) Where in any factory an accident occurs which causes death, or which causes any bodily injury by reason of which the person injured is prevented from working for a period of 48 hours or more immediately following the accident, the manager of the factory shall send notice thereof to such authorities, and in such form and within such time, as may be prescribed [Section 88 (1)].

(ii) Where a notice given under Section 88 (1) relates to an accident causing death, the authority to whom the notice is sent shall make an inquiry into the occurrence within 1 month of the receipt of the notice. If such authority is not the Inspector, it shall cause the Inspector to make an inquiry within this period [Section 88 (2)].

6. Notice of Certain Dangerous Occurrences (Section 88-A). Where in a factory any dangerous occurrence of such nature as may be prescribed occurs, whether causing any bodily injury or disability or not, the manager of the factory shall send notice thereof to such authorities, and in such form and within such time, as may be prescribed.

7. Power to direct Inquiry into Cases of Accident or Disease (Section 90). The State Government may appoint a competent person to inquire into the causes of any accident occurring in a factory or into any case where a disease specified in the Third Schedule to the Act has been, or is suspected to have been, contracted in a factory. It may also appoint one or more persons possessing legal or special knowledge to act as assessors in such inquiry [Section 90 (1)]. The person appointed to hold an inquiry under Section 90 shall have the powers of a Civil Court and also of an Inspector under the Act [Section 90 (2)].

The person holding an inquiry under Section 90 shall make a report to the State Government stating the causes of the accident, or as the case may, be disease and any attendent circumstances. He shall also add any observations which he or any of the assessors may think fit to make [Section 90 (3)]. The State Government may, if it thinks fit, cause to be published any report made under Section 90 or any extracts therefrom [Section 90 (4)].

PENALTIES AND PROCEDURE

Sections 92 to 106 (Chapter X) provide for penalties for certain offences and procedural matters,. The Amendment Act of 1987 has considerably enhanced these penalties so that they serve as a deterrent for the commission of offences.

1. General Penalty for Offences (Section 92). (i) If in any factory there is any contravention of any of the provisions of the Act or of any rules made thereunder, the occupier and manager of the factory shall each be guilty of an offence and punishable with imprisonment for a term upto 2 years or with fine upto Rs. 1,00,000 or with both. If the contravention is continued after conviction, they shall be punishable with a further fine which may extend to Rs. 1,000 for each day on which the contravention is so continued. This is subject to other express provisions in the Act and Section 93 (which deals with liability of owner of premises in certain circumstances).

(ii) Where the contravention of any of the provisions of Chapter IV (dealing with 'safety') or any rule made thereunder or under Section 87 (dealing with 'dangerous operations') has resulted in an accident causing death or serious bodily injury, the fine shall not be less then Rs. 25,000 in the case of an accident causing death and Rs. 5,000 in the case of an accident causing serious bodily injury (Proviso to Section 92).

(iii) 'Serious bodily injury' means an injury which involves, or in all probability will involve, the permanent loss of the use of, or permanent injury to, any limb or the permanent loss of, or injury to, sight or hearing or the fracture of any bone. It does not include the fracture of bone or joint (not being fracture of more than one bone or joint) of any phalanges of the hand or foot (Explanation to Section 92).

2. Enhanced Penalty after Conviction (Section 94). (i) If any person who has been convicted of any offence punishable under Section 92 is again guilty of an offence involving a contravention of the same provision, he shall be punishable on a subsequent conviction with imprisonment for a term which may extend to 3 years or with fine which shall not be less then Rs. 10,000 but which may extend to Rs. 2,00,000 or with both. But the Court may for any adequate and special reasons to be mentioned in the judgement, impose a fine of less than Rs. 10,000.

(ii) Where, however, the contravention of any of the provisions of Chapter IV (dealing with 'safety') or any rules made thereunder or under Section 87 (dealing with 'dangerous operations') has resulted in an accident causing death or serious bodily injury, the fine shall not be less than Rs. 35,000 in the case of an accident causing death and Rs. 10,000 in the case of an accident causing serious bodily injury [Section 94 (1)].

(iii) No cognizance shall be taken of any conviction made more than 2 years before the commission of the offence for which the person is subsequently being convicted [Section 94 (2)].

3. Cognizance of Offences (Section 105). (i) No Court shall take cognizance of any offence under this Act except on a complaint by, or with the previous sanction in writing of an Inspector [Section 105 (1)]. Further, no Court below that of a Presidency Magistrate or a Magistrate of the first class shall try any offence punishable under the Act [Section 105 (2)].

(ii) The complaint must be filed within 3 months of the date on which the alleged commission of the offence comes to the knowledge of an Inspector. But where the offence consists of disobeying a written order made by an Inspector, complaint thereof may be made within 6 months of the date on which the offence is alleged to have been committed (Section 106). The 'Explanation' to Section 106 lays down the procedure for the computation of the period of limitation.

4. Appeals (Section 107). The manager of a factory on whom an order in writing by an Inspector has been served under the provisions of this Act or the occupier of the factory may, within 30 days of service of the order, appeal against it to the prescribed authority. Such authority may, subject to rules made in this behalf by the State Government, confirm modify or reverse the order.

5. Display of Notices (Section 108). In addition to the notices required to be displayed in any factory by or under this Act, there shall be displayed in every factory a notice containing such abstracts of this Act and of the rules made thereunder as may be prescribed and also the name and address of the Inspector and the certifying surgeon [Section 108 (1)]. The notices shall be in English and in a language understood by the majority of the workers in the factory. They shall be displayed at some conspicuous and convenient place at or near the main entrance to the factory, and shall be maintained in clean and legible condition [Section 108 (2)]. The Chief Inspector may, by order in writing served on the manager of the factory, require the display of posters relating to the health, safety and welfare of workers [Section 108 (3)].

6. Returns (Section 110). The State Government may make rules requiring owners, occupiers or managers of factories to submit such returns, occasional or periodical, as may in its opinion be required.

7. Power to make Rules and give Directions (Sections 112, 113 and 115). The State Government may make rules providing for any matter which may be considered expedient in order to give effect to the purposes of the Act (Section 112). The Central Government may also give directions to a State Government as to the carrying into execution of the provisions of the Act (Section 113). Section 115 provides for the publication of rules made under the Act in the Official Gazette.

8. Restriction on Disclosure of Information (new Section 118-A as introduced by the Amendment Act of 1987). Every Inspector shall treat as confidential the source of any complaint brought to his notice on the breach of any provision of this Act [Section 118-A (1)]. Further, he shall not, while making any inspection under this Act, disclose to the occupier, manager or his representative that the inspection is made in pursuance of the receipt of a complaint. This rule shall not apply to any case in which the person who has made the complaint has consented to disclose his name [Section 118-A (2)].

QUESTIONS FOR EXERCISE

1. Define the terms factory, occupier, adult, adolescent, young person, worker and manufacturing process, as used in the Factories Act, 1948.
2. Does the Factories Act, 1948 apply to factories belonging to the Central Government?
3. Who are certifying surgeons? What are their duties?

4. What is the procedure of appointment of Inspectors under the Factories Act. 1948. What are their duties and powers?
5. Describe the rules regarding approval, licensing and registration of factories with special reference to notice by occupier as required by the Factories Act, 1948 before starting a factory and occupying the same.
6. Describe the provisions of the Factories Act, 1948 with regard to health, safety and welfare of the workers.
7. Describe provisions in the Factories Act, 1948 for protection against fire and for safety of building and machinery of a factory.
8. What are the provisions of the Factories Act, 1948 with regard to appointment of welfare officers? What are their qualifications and what are their duties?
9. What are the weekly and the daily hours for which an adult worker may be required or allowed to work in a factory?
10. Explain the restrictions imposed by the Factories Act, 1948 on the employment and work of women in a factory.
11. Describe the provisions of the Factories Act, 1948 regarding (a) Extra wages for overtime work, (b) weekly holidays, (c) annual leave with wages.
12. Write a note on provisions relating to hazardous processes as introduced by the Factories (Amendment) Act, 1987.

PRACTICAL PROBLEMS

1. Wives of 3 workmen employed in a Leather factory work in place of their husbands for about half an hour every day after 7 P.M. while the latter take meals brought by them. Discuss if there is a violation of any provision of the Factories Act, 1948. [**Hint** : There is a violation of Section 66 (1)].
2. The services of a woman worker who had completed 4 months' continuous service in a factory were terminated.
   (a) To what leave is she entitled?
   (b) To what leave will she be entitled if she were below 15 years of age?
   [**Hint** : She is entitled to (a) 6 day's (b) 8 day's leave (Section 79 (1)].
3. X is the owner of a concern manufacturing cigars. 20 persons are employed in the concern. Of these 20 employees, one is a graduate for supervising the work and another an apprentice learning work. The remaining 18 are employed not on the time wage system, but on the piece work system. Is the concern a

factory within the meaning of that term under the Factories Act, 1948?

[**Hint** : Yes; (Section 2 (m))].

4. P, an apprentice fitter, was injured while cleaning a dangerous part of a machine which had been manufactured abroad. The machine was unfenced while adjustments were made to it. Is the manager or occupier guilty of an offence?
[**Hint** : Yes; Section 21 (N.B. Mills, India *Vs*. E.S.I. Corpn. A.I.R. (1966) M.P. 324.].

5. X was the owner of a ginning factory. Certain men were engaged in putting the ginned cotton into what are called bojhas and they were engaged for that work not by X but the merchants who owned cotton. X did not show their names in the attendance register of the factory. Are the labour employed by the merchants workers within the meaning of the Factories Act, 1948?
[**Hint** : Yes, as the work performed is incidental to, or connected with the manufacturing process (Local Government *Vs*. Nauserwanji, A.I.R. (1933) Nag. 283)].

PART FOUR

WORKER'S ORGANIZATION

11

Trade Unions

DEFINITION OF TRADE UNION

1. *British Ministry of Labour* — "Trade Unions are all Organisations of employees including those salaried and professional workers as well as those of manual wage earners which are known to include among their functions that of negotiating with their employers with the object of regulating conditions of employment."

2. *Dale Yoder* — "Trade Union is the continuous and long period workers' Organisation which is meant for attainment of specific objectives to protect the interests of its members and for the improvement of labour relations."

3. *V.V. Giri* — "A Trade Union is such as Organisation which in created voluntarily on the basis of collective strength to secure the interests of workers."

4. *Laster* — "A Trade Union is an Association of employees designed primarily to maintain or improve the conditions of employment of its members."

5. *Edwin B. Flippo* — "A Trade Union is the Workers' Organisation which is established by their collective activities to the welfare of the members in social, economic and potential interests and to keep them secured and for improvement in it."

6. *G.D.H. Cole* — "A Trade Union mean an Association of workers in one or more occupations, as Association carried on mainly for the purpose of protecting and advancing the members' economic interests in connection with their daily work."

7. *Webb* — "A Trade Union is a continuous association of wage earners for the purpose of maintaining or improving the conditions of their working force."

8. *Cunnison* — "Trade Union is a monopolistic combination of wage earners who stand to the employers in a relation of dependence for the sale of their labour and even for its production; and that the general purpose of the Association is in view of that dependence to strengthen their power to bargain with the employers."

Thus, A Labour Union or Trade Union is an Organisation of workers to promote, product and improve, through collective, action the social, economic and political interests of its member. The workers form an association in order to protect and safeguard their economic interests and put up a united resistance against exploitation by the industrialists. The most outstanding feature of the trade unions is their own accord. Generally, all workers in a particular occupations are the members of the Trade Union representing their occupation. But there is no element of compulsion in membership. If a worker so desires he can stay away from the Trade Union.

CHARACTERISTICS OF TRADE UNION

1. It is continuing long-term association of workers. They are not temporary or causal association.

2. It may be an association either of the employers or employees or of independent workers.

3. It is essentially "a co-operative labour marketing association". It is an association of workers who are engaged in securing economic benefits (sometimes social, political and cultural benefits/interests) for their members.

OBJECTIVES OF TRADE UNIONS

1. To increase the Co-operative Feeling. In sophisticated modern industrial complexes, thousands of workers are engaged simultaneously. However, the modern industrial system is so complex that all jobs are highly specialized. As a consequence of extreme departmentalization and division of work there is growth of individualism in modern industry. The relations between workers are ceasing to be personal and are becoming increasingly impersonal and formal. There is no common or uniting thread or unifying bond between workers. Even in one industry there is no homogeneity among workers, they hail from different regions, speak different tongues and profess different religions. Under these circumstances the first and foremost task of the trade unions is to promote friendliness among workers and bind them in the thread of fellowship and brotherhood. The Trade Unions provide a forum for the workers to come together and know each other. All common problems are discussed in one form. Besides discussing problems connected with jobs, the Trade Unions also provide opportunity of play, relaxation and entertainment to workers. Thus, Trade Unions promote intimacy of relations among workers; make them sweet, personal and informal.

2. To secure Facilities for Workers. The majority of industrialists are indifferent to the comforts and needs of the workers. They pay no attention to making the working conditions healthy and hygienic, to mental and physical relaxation of the workers. They are interested only in getting maximum work from the workers like toilet facility, canteen etc. Under these circumstances trade unions agitate for the provisions of various facilities and see to it that these are provided for.

3. To establish Contract among Workers and Employers. The industrial complexes today have grown into giants. A single unit may employ hundreds of workers. Under these circumstances the line between employers, high managerial cadre and employees gets broken down.

Many a time workers may not have seen even the face of their employer. Under these conditions the workers are not in a position to express their grievances before their employers nor do the employers have any means to know the difficulties being faced by their employees. The Trade Unions play the important role of bringing to the notice of employers the grievances and difficulties of the employees. The Trade Unions also try to arrange face to face meeting between employers and employees. Thus, better relations are established between employers and employees through the medium of Trade Unions.

4. To work for the Progress of Employees. The urban life is much different from the rural life. Most of the workers hail from villages; but after finding jobs in cities they have no residences in the cities. In cities they need a good bit of money for establishing themselves. The Trade Unions try to improve the economic conditions of workers and remove their hardships and handicaps. For increase in their wages, the unions represent their case before the employers and also try to get adequate bonus for the workers. The unions also try to get overtime wages to the workers.

5. To safeguard the Interests of Workers. Under ordinary conditions the employers tend to exploit the workers to the maximum. They care nothing for the employees; they do not give them any paid leaves and if a worker goes on leave the wages for the period of leave are deducted from the monthly wage bill of the workers. Besides, workers are denied all chances of promotion. For a very long period the workers have to work on the same post. In many industries the workers are not made permanent even after a long period of service. They are removed from services summarily. The Trade Unions try to protect the workers from all such eventualities. They try to secure to workers the benefits of leave, permanency and promotion. The Trade Unions see to it that the workers under their aegis are not shunted out summarily and that they receive all the benefits due to them.

6. To provide for Labour Welfare. In India the economic condition of the industrial workers are not too good. The labour class is backward in every respect. The standard of living is very low. The majority of workers are illiterate or semi-liberate. Moreover, they have large families and their condition is therefore much worse. They live in slums and cat coarse food only. It is the task of trade unions to promote the social and economic welfare of the labourers. The Trade Unions try to get them housing facilities and also try to arrange for the education of the children of workers. The Trade Unions also try to protect workers from evil habits.

FUNCTIONS OF TRADE UNIONS

Mr. Broughton has classified the functions of trade unions into three categories : (1) Inter-mural activities, (2) Extra-mural activities and (3) Political activities.

1. Inter-mural Activities. These include those activities of the trade unions which are carried on within the four walls of the orgainsation for the welfare of the members. These activities also include the efforts of the union which improve the employment and working conditions within the organization. Such activities are bargaining with the employer for better wages and working conditions and for workers participation in management, providing labour welfare activities, getting share in the profits of the organisation. Collective bargaining, group discussions, gherao and strikes are some of the tools which help the Trade Unions in getting their functions performed.

2. Extra-mural Activities. Extra-mural activities are those which are performed outside the compound of the organisation for the general welfare of their members. Their main object is to seek their cooperation and help them in time of crisis. These include the provisions of sanitary houses, fair-price shops, library and reading rooms, entertainment etc. Trade Unions provide facilities for the education of workers and their children and medical facilities etc. Such functions are also known as 'Fraternal activities or functions'. These activities very much depend upon the availability of funds.

3. Political Activities. In today's world of democracy, Trade Unions play a very important role in the politics of the country. They send their representatives to the Legislative Assembly and Parliament through general elections so that they may safeguard their own interest.

CONDITIONS TO MAKE TRADE UNIONS USEFUL

1. Compulsory Membership. The mainstay of a trade union is its orgainsational. In order to fortify and consolidate an oragnisation, it is essential that a trade union should have maximum membership. A Trade Union is an organisation of industrial workers. In order to make Trade Unions forceful instruments of labour welfare, it is essential that the workers should compulsorily become its members. It must be borne in mind in this connexion that a nominal membership is not enough. In order to render a trade union useful all workers should be actively associated with the work of the trade union. Every worker should consider the trade union as his or her own organisation and work relentlessly for its success.

2. Strong Economic Base. A trade needs not only members but money for its successful functioning. A Trade Union must have a strong economic base. The Trade Unions need large funds to support their members in emergency and during protracted strikes and lockouts. The Trade Unions have to support their members in the event of accident, disablement or in the event of suspension of workers by the employers. The Trade Unions have no special means of collecting funds. It is necessary, therefore, that each member must make his contribution regularly. The membership fee can be determined after taking various factors into account.

3. Freedom from External Pressure. The Trade Unions must function as independent organizations; they should not be under any external pressure or control. The various political parties try to bring trade unions under their domain by extending various baits. These political parties are not genuinely interested in workers' welfare; they have their own axes to grind. Besides, the pressure of political parties, trade unions should also safeguard themselves against and other type of pressure.

4. Spirit of Unity and Sacrifice. The true basis of Trade Union is the spirit of unity and sacrifice in its members. It is on the strenght of unity that Trade Unions are able to function. Besides general problems, the members of a Trade Union also have personal problems. For the redress of personal problems, unity among workers is most essential. Besides unity, the spirit of sacrifice is also needed. The money collected from all members may be very largely spent on few workers. Without a spirit of sacrifice such a action may not be feasible.

5. Capable Leadership. Capable leaderships a *sine qua non* for the success and usefulness of the trade unions. The average worker in India is still illiterate. He is innocent of the complexities of urban life and the clever tricks of employers to exploit him. Therefore, it is very necessary that a group of such simple fellows should have capable and selfless leadership. Some trade union leaders are quite selfish and they ae dangerous to the well being of workers. Instead of giving workers proper guidance these leaders use them for their narrow selfish ends. Thus, it is very necessary that the leadership of trade unions should be in the hands of selfless workers and persons genially interested in the welfare of workers. Besides that, it is also very necessary that the leadership of workers should be in the hands of workers and not professionals. Only a worker is capable in understanding fully the problems of workers; a professional has no first-hand knowledge of their difficulties. Above all, a labour leader should be fully conversant with labour laws and bye-laws.

6. Practical Outlook. The main task of Trade Unions is to defend the interest of labour and to promote their economic and social welfare. But while trying to achieve these laudable aims it should also be borne in mind that these aims can be achieved only in the context of overall industrial prosperity. Therefore, the economic and monetary conditions prevailing in the industry have to be taken into account while trying to achieve economic propriety and the social well-being of workers. Thus, a Trade Union should adopt a practical and pragmatic attitude to all problems. Only if the demands are practical and relative to actual conditions can these be met; unreasonable demands will create unnecessary friction, disharmony and hardship to all concerned. The Trade Unions cannot afford to be wholly oblivious of the interest of the industrialists. The employers are entitled to legitimate profits and gain. Besides, it must aslo be borne in mind as to what sort of economic and social conditions are being faced by the society at any particular time. For example, during war the workers should not demand more wages nor should they press for reduction of workload. At times there is international economic depression. Under these conditions the demand of higher wages will be most unrealistic. In short, Trade Unions should relate their demands to prevalent conditions and not make extravagant and unrealistic demands.

7. Democratic Outlook. The success of Trade Union requires demoratic structure. By democratic structure what is meant is that in all crucial matters the opinion of each and every members of the trade union should be taken into account. This has another purpose.

The worker in a vast industrial complex comes to look upon himself as a non-entity and feels sense of humiliation, whereas by exercising the privilege of vote in trade union affairs etc., he develops a sense of dignity and feels his importance. This feeling helps to keep up his morale. The leaders of Trade Unions should also be democratically chosen by workers themselves.

8. Constructice Outlook. The Trade Union try to have the demands of workers fulfilled and this is their real aim. But it is essential that the trade unions should adopt constructive outlook for achieving this goal. Indeed the workers need not deem their industrialist bosses to be enemies but should try to settle their problems by mutual consolations in an amicable way. Some Trade Union leaders incite the workers, poison their minds against employers and instigate them to violence and subversion. This negative attitude is not desirable. Indeed the Trade Unions should adopt a policy which is mutually beneficial. As a matter of fact supervision does not pay. It is harmful for all concerned parties as well as for the whole society.

9. Freedom from Policies. The utility of Trade Unions is greatly undermined by outside political interference. At times Trade Union leaders forget their true aims and indulge in politics. Such leaders deliver no benefit to workers, indeed they harm their interest. Thus, Trade Unions have limited resources and these should not be frittered away in politicising.

10. Aim of Welfare. The welfare of workers should be the primary aim of Trade Unions. They should refrain from all such activities as are detrimental to the welfare of workers. The Trade Unions should spend their money on projects which are likely to contribute to the workers' welfare and help to raise their standard of living. Besides, they could provide for education and entertainment of workers.

QUESTIONS FOR EXERCISE

1. Define Trade Union and explain its characteristics and objectives.
2. What are the functions of Trade Unions? What condition are required to make them useful?

12

The Trade Unions Act, 1926

The honour of organizing labour in India goes to M.S.S. Bengali. Mr. Bengali made first yeoman effort in 1875 to reform the deplorable conditions prevailing among the Indian labour. He also drew the attention of authorities to the pitiable situation of the labour. However, the efforts of Mr. Bengali did not bear much fruit and there was no substantial improvement in the lot of Indian labour.

In India the first Industries Act was promulgated in 1881 by Government of India. In 1881, Mr. Narayan-Meghji Lokhande made renewed efforts for reform in the conditions of Indian labour. Mr. Lokhande summoned a summit conference of workers engaged in mills in Bombay Presidency. In this conference the essential demands of labour were considered and a number of resolutions were passed. The major demand of this conference was that the workers should be granted a weekly holiday and given half an hour rest every day. Besides it was also insisted that workers suffering accidental injuries should be adequately compensated. The efforts of this conference bore some healthy fruits. Some industrialists accepted some of the above demands. As a consequence of success achieved by the conference Mr. Lokhande felt encouraged and he established a Trade Union in Bombay. He christened this organization "Bombay Mill Hands Association". He also helped publication of a labour magazine. This magazine was christened "Deenbandhu". Thus, Mr. Lokhande stood by the working class and did a great deal to improve their lot. But after the death of Mr. Lokhande, the momentum of the work being done by him was lost. Afterwards Railway employees organized themselves into a union.

In 1905 British Government, as a result of the diplomacy divided Bengal in two parts. The partition of Bengal was stoutly opposed by workers and social reformers. As a result of this protest a wave of awakening swept the working classes and they got organized. After the partition of Bengal and till 1909 a number of strikes on various issues were organized. In 1908 an eminent national leader Shri Lokmanya

Tilak was imprisoned for six years. As a protest against this injustice a very big strike was organized. In this period a number of Trade Unions came into being. In Calcutta in 1905, the workers of printing presses organized themselves into a Trade Union. In Bombay in 1907, postal workers formed a Trade Union. A Labour Welfare Association was established in Bombay in 1910. This association did a number of good things for workers.

MODERN HISTORY OF TRADE UNION

Modern history of labour movement in India dates from First World War. During war a wave of awakening swept the labour; they became conscious of their importance, role and worth. They also realized that they were entitled to certain rights and privileges. There were various causes of this awakening. Firstly, as a result of war there were radical changes in the industrial system and economic conditions. Secondly, many national leaders devoted particular attention to working classes. As a result of the efforts made by Lokmanya Tilak, Annie Besant and Gandhi, the working classes began to get organized. The non-cooperation movement launched by Gandhi deserves special mention in this connection. As a result of the efforts made by Gandhiji, Ahmedabad Textile Labour Association was established. During these days a branch of International Labour Organization was established. After this, regular conferences of I.L.O. were started being held in India.

In 1920, Indian National Trade Union Congress was established. With the establishment of this Trade Union the labour movement in India received tremendous fillip. A special step towards progress was made in 1923. In 1923, the then Government passed Indian Trade Union Act. With the passage of this Act, the Trade Unions greatly benefited. According to this Act all registered Trade Unions were granted constitutional recognition. The organization of Trade Unions underwent great change in 1926. In 1926, the leadership of Trade Unions went over to communists. The communists made radical changes in the policies and organization of Trade Unions and as a consequence of this the Trade Union divided itself into two. The workers owing allegiance to old leadership had peaceful and constructive outlook, whereas those owing allegiance to communists, had radical outlook. Owing to difference of outlook the two Trade Unions were virtually always at loggerheads. The mutual strife between unions was advantageous to the employers.

The mutual strife among trade unions went on increasing. In 1929, Indian National Trade Union Congress held its 10th session in Nagpur. This session was presided over by an eminent social reformer

Pandit Jawaharlal Nehru. Subsequent to this session, some trade unions severed their connexion with the parent body. The unions which separated themselves from INTUC formed their own all India body under the name All India Trade Union Federation. Thee internecine struggle between Trade Unions did not limit itself upto here only. As a result of the mutual strife in 1931 a new All India Trade Union under the label All India Red Trade Union Congress came into being.

The mutual bickering and strife among Trade Unions proved advantageous to employers and hurt the interests of workers. At Length in 1934, this mutual strife ended. In this year a grand session of Indian Trade Union Congress took place. This session was presided over by Pandit Harinath Shastri. In this session an agreement was reached between All India Red Trade Union Congress and Trade Union Congress. According to this agreement, All India Red Trade Union Congress was abolished. Subsequently in 1938 Trade Union Federation was also merged in Indian National Trade Union Congress. The credit for this agreement is due to a former President of India Shri V.V. Giri. Thus, once again in 1940 a united body of Trade Union was established. However, this mutual amity among unions proved to be short-lived and the Second World War brought to surface once again mutual dissensions and disagreements. Indian National Trade Union Congress opposed the war and condemned the Government. However, leaders like M.N. Roy were opposed to this attitude and as a consequence, rift developed among leaders of INTUC. As a sequel to this rift 'Indian Trade Union Labour Federation' came into existence. This was headed by M.N. Roy. For a long time two parallel labour unions continued to function. The dissensions and conflicts among communists and Congressmen persisted and ultimately due to the efforts of Gulzarilal Nanda and Sardar Patel Indian National Trade Union Congress was established. An official survey in 1948 revealed that the membership of Indian National Trade Union Congress was 9, 73, 179 and that of All India Trade Union 8, 15, 011. As a result of this survey Indian National Trade Union Congress was declared the representative union of Indian labour. Subsequently Communists also set up an all India Trade Union. This Trade Union was labelled Hind Mazdoor Sabha. This Trade Union of Communists did not also escape the courage of rifts and dissensions and in 1949 it also split up into two groups. As a result of this split a new Trade Union came into being and this was named United Trade Union Congress. This Trade Union was headed by Professor K.T. Shah. In 1955, Jan Sangh also established a labour organization. The Trade Union under the aegis of Jan Sangh was known as 'Bhartiya Mazdoor Sangh'. Its headquarter was in Bhopal. Bhartiya Mazdoor Sangh was not a popular trade union. Another trade union has been established by Socialist Party and this is known as Hind Mazdoor Panchayat.

Thus, it is clear that there are four All India Unions functioning in India at the moment. All India Trade Union Congress is wholly dominated by communists. According to the leaders of this union all industries must be nationalized. They support all types of freedom and facility for workers. The second Indian National Trade Union Congress is under the influence of Congress Party. This Trade Union has conciliatory attitude and wants to settle problems peacefully and by mutual negotiations. It also believes in the Government launched Five Year Plans. It also supports the idea of partnership of workers in industry. 'The third important Trade Union is 'Hind Mazdoor Sabha' which is under the influence of Socialist Party. This Trade Union also favours nationalization. The fourth union is United Trade Union Congress. This union is not directly connected with any party but holds radical views. 'The aim of this union is to establish government of workers and peasants.

In India, present the number of labour unions and their membership attached with Central Labour Organisation are as under :

TRADE UNION IN INDIA

Name of Trade Union	No. of Attached Trade Unions	No. of Members (in lakhs)
1. Indian National Trade Union Congress (INTUC)	3,457	35.09
2. Hind Mazdoor Sabha (HMS)	1,725	18.80
3. United Trade Union Congress (UTUC-LS)	154	12.39
4. All India Trade Union Congress (AITUC)	1,366	10.64
5. Centre of Indian Trade Unions (CITU)	1,737	10.33
6. National Labour Organisation (NLO)	249	4.05
7. National Front of Indian Trade Unions (NFITU)	166	5.27
8. United Trade Union Congress (UTUC)	618	6.08
9. Trade Union Congress Committee (TUCC)	182	2.72

	Name of Trade Union	No. of Attached Trade Unions	No. of Members (in lakhs)
10.	Trade Union Co-ordination Committee (TUCC)	182	2.72
11.	Bhartiya Mazdoor Sabha (BMS)	1,725	18.80

OBSTACLES IN THE PROGRESS OF TRADE UNIONISM IN INDIA

Sufficient time has elapsed since the founding of Trade Unions in India. But unlike Western countries, the Indian trade unions have not made the expected progress. They suffer from a number of *lacunas*. They have not developed on proper lines. There are various reasons for this. Certain conditions must be met if there is to be a proper growth of Trade Unions. In Indian industries all these conditions are not fully met. 'There are various types of obstacles in the development of India Labour Unions. Chiefly these fall into two categories : internal and external difficulties. The internal difficulties are related to labour and the external difficulties pertain to industrialists, intermediaries and official laws. Following discussion will make the nature of these two types of difficulties clear.

(A) INTERNAL OBSTACLES

Indian labour has certain traits peculiar to it. Some of these traits have provide to be obstacles in the way of the growth of Labour Unions. Mainly, following traits of labour prove to be hindrances in the way of Labour Union's development and growth :

1. Majority of Indian Labour is Illiterate. For any organization it is vitally important whether its members are educated or not. The educated members are an asset and the illiterate members a liability to the organization. Education broadens the outlook of individuals. An educated person understands what is beneficial and what is harmful to him. But the majority of Indian labour is illiterate. The illiteracy of labour is a hindrance in the growth of Labour Unions. It is difficult to keep the illiterate labour disciplined. Besides, illiterate workers are not fully conscious of their duties. They fall easy prey to the machinations of opposite groups. Without any proper reason they go on strike and indulge in subversion. They do not understand the true role and function of Trade Unions.

2. Migratory Habit. The majority of Indian labour hails from rural areas. The families of most of them reside in villages. Under these circumstances workers do not reside permanently in cities. As and when they get leaves or holidays they go to there wives and children. Thus, they are unable to participate regularly in the confabulations and discussions of Trade Unions. A number of workers do not enroll themselves as members of Trade Unions for this very reason. They are under the impression that if they become members of Trade Unions they cannot easily go to their villages. Even if they become members of unions they rush back home in the event of strikes and lock outs. On account of this habit of workers trade unionism in India does not work properly.

3. Heterogeneous Character. From the above discussion it is plain that Indian labour has a tendency to migrate from place to place. In every big industrial centre one can find workers coming from almost all regions of India. These workers are of very heterogeneous character. They differ *inter se* in regard to language, religion, habits of food and dress. On account of wide heterogeneity of the workers, a sense of unity cannot easily take root among them. But for the success of trade unions the trait of unity is of paramount importance. Many workers even today practise untouchability. Thus, it is plain that the heterogeneous character of Indian labour proves to be a stumbling block in the progress and development of Indian Trade Union Movement.

4. Low Economic Standards. The economic condition of Indian labour is not good. 'The average Indian worker's earnings are so low that he can barely meet the expenses of his family with his wages. On account of low wages he is usually under debt. On accounting their poverty the workers are unable to take active part in trade union activity. Due to poor economic conditions they are unable to bear the strain of strikes and lock outs. 'Thus, it is clear that the poverty of workers come in the way of the growth and development of Trade Unions.

5. Mutual Strife. In India there are numerous Trade Unions functioning independently. Each of these Trade Unions is under the influence of one or other political party. The political parties are usually at cross purposes and pursuing contradictory policies. The political parties misuse Trade Unions to further their own political ends. This tendency foments dissension and strife among trade unions. The mutual strife among trade unions weakens them. If there is unity among labour all over India the labour organizations can work effectively and need not pursue contradictory and mutually harmful ends. Due to mutual dissension among trade unions each agitation is supported by some and opposed by others. This results in half-hearted action or utter failure. Obviously, mutual strife is a big impediment in the way of the development of Trade Union activity in India.

6. Lack of Able Leadership. The majority of Indian workers are illiterate and ignorant. None of these ailliterate workers has the courage to take up the leadership of trade unions in his hands. Besides not possessing courage, these persons lack the ability and capacity for leadership. Under these circumstances outsiders are usually the leaders of Indian Trade Unions. Generally, social reformers, lawyers or politicians hold these post. These persons are professional, well-qualified and clever people. 'They are well- informed about legal intricacies. However, these persons are as a rule selfish and self-seeking. They have no intimate or first-hand knowledge of labour problems. They are therefore indifferent to the true interests of labour. There are instances when these persons have been found to have worked in collusion with industrialists and to have been receiving regularly money from them. These persons do not let any real protest against industrialists build up. As and when there is agitation they cleverly sabotage it.

7. Unemployment Problem. The problems of unemployment in India is getting worse every day. 'The workers have to toil hard in order to find a job. Once a person finds some job he is most reluctant to leave it. This is so because finding alternative job is both uncertain and hazardous. An average Indian worker labours under the impression that by joining trade unions he is putting his job in danger. He is afraid he may be shunted out of job or his promotion stayed. Influenced by this fear psychosis the Indian worker does not participate actively in trade union activity. This indifference obviously is an obstacle in the way of the progress of Trade Union Movement.

(B) EXTERNAL OBSTACLES

Besides internal impediments, there are certain external obstacles which impede and thwart the growth of trade unionism in India. The more important of these obstacles are concerned with the role of intemediaries, recruitment of workers, the industrialists management boards and labour and industrial laws. In the absence of active co-operation among various factors no trade union movement can make much progress. In the following lines these will be discussed in detail :

1. Opposition and Non-Co-operation of Intermediaries. Even at present the recruitment of labour in industry is not direct but is in the hands of intermediaries. The intermediaries are mostly the agents of the industrialists. They receive money from industrialists. These intermediaries are ever opposed to and unreconciled with the growth of trade unions. This is quite understandable because once trade unions become strong the role and importance of these intermediaries will be finished. That is why they are ever conspiring against workers and eager to eavesdrop on worker's conferences and pass on all information to the industrialists. Thus, it is evident that the opposition and non-information to the industrialists. Thus, it is evident that the opposition and non-cooperation of intermediaries is an obstacle to the growth of Trade Union activity.

2. Opposition and Non-Co-operation of Industrialists. The Indian industrialists deem trade unions their enemies. They are of the view that the growth of Trade Unions is not in consonance with their interests. Therefore, they try to undermine and sabotage all efforts designed to strengthen trade unions. They try to wean the workers from Trade Unions by bribing their leaders. At times the industrialists try to win over professional leaders of Trade Unions by giving them huge bribes.

3. Lack of Legal Support. There is not enough support to workers by governmental laws and machinery. There are no adequate provisions to safeguard the interests of workers. In the event of strike there is not much protection of workers by laws. The industrialists are better placed to take advantage of law. Therefore, the growth of Trade Unions is impeded.

The Trade Unions Act, 1926

The law relating to the registration of trade unions and certain other matters is contained in the Trade Unions Act, 1926.

Objectives of the Act

Act was passed to regulate :

1. To regulate the conditions governing the registration of Trade Unions;

2. To regulate obligations imposed upon a registered Trade Union and

3. To Regulate rights and liabilities of registered Trade Unions.

The Act came into force on 1st June, 1927 [Section 1 (3)].

Scope and Coverage

The Act applies to registered Trade Unions and specifies the mode of their registration. It extends to the whole of India [Section 1(2)]. It was extended to Jammu and Kashmir by the Central Labour Laws (extension to Jammu and Kashmir) Act, 1970.

DEFINITIONS

1. Appropriate Government (Section 2). In relation to Trade Unions whose objects are not confined to one State, the 'Appropriate Government' means the Central Government. In relation to other

Trade Unions, the, appropriate Government' means the State Government (Introductory part of Section 2).

2. Executive [Section 2 (a)]. 'Executive' means the body, by whatever name called, to which the management of the affairs of a Trade Union is entrusted.

3. Trade Dispute [Section 2 (g)]. It means any dispute :

(i) between employers and workmen, or

(ii) between workmen and workmen, or

(iii) between employers and employers, which is connected with (a) the employment or non-employment, or (b) the terms of employment, or (c) the conditions of labour, of any person.

'Workmen' means all persons employed in trade or industry whether or not in the employment of the employer with whom the trade dispute arises.

4. Trade Union [Section 2 (h)). It means any combination, whether temporary or permanent, formed :

(i) primarily for the purpose of regulating the relations,

(a) between workmen and employers, or

(b) between workmen and workmen, or

(c) between employers and employers, or

(ii) for imposing restrictive conditions on the conduct of any trade or business.

It includes any federation of 2 or more Trade Unions.

5. Registered Trade Union [Section 2 (e)]. It means a Trade Union registered under the Act.

AGREEMENTS NOT AFFECTED BY THE ACT

(1) any agreement between partners as to their own business;

(2) any agreement between an employer and those employed by him as to such employment; or

(3) any agreement in consideration of the sale of the goodwill of a business or of instruction in any profession, trade or handicraft (Proviso to Section 2).

Acts not to apply to registered trade unions (Section 14).

(1) The Societies Registration Act 1860;

(2) The Co-operative Societies Act 1912; and

(3) The Companies Act, 1956.

The registration of any trade union under these Acts is void.

APPOINTMENT OF REGISTRARS

A State Government appoints a person to be the Registrar of Trade Unions for the State [Section 3(1)]. It may also appoint as many Additional and Deputy Registrars of Trade Unions as it thinks fit for the purposes of exercising and discharging the powers and functions of the Registrar. Deputy Registrars have to act under the superintendence and control of the Registrar. The State Government also defines the local limits within which they shall exercise and discharge the powers and functions so specified [Section 3 (2)].

Where an Additional or Deputy Registrar exercises and discharges the powers and functions of a Registrar in an area within which the registered office of a Trade Union is situated, the Additional or Deputy Registrar is deemed to be the Registrar in relation to the Trade Union for the Act. [Section 3 (3)].

REGISTRATION OF TRADE UNIONS

1. Mode of Registration (Section 4)

(i) *Application for Registration* : Any 7 or more members of a Trade Union may, by subscribing their names to the rules of the Trade Union and by otherwise complying with the provisions of the Act with respect to registration, apply for its registration [Section 4 (1)].

(ii) *Applicants ceasing to be Members or dissociating not to affect Application unless Their Number is more than Half* : At any time after the date of the application, but before the registration of the Trade Union, some of the applicants who made the application may cease to be members of the Trade Union or may give notice in writing to the Registrar dissociating themselves from the application. In such a case, the application shall not be deemed to have become invalid merely by reason of this fact. But if the number of applicants ceasing to be members or dissociating themselves from the application exceeds half of the total number of persons who made the application, the application shall be deemed to have become invalid [Section 4 (2)].

2. Application for Registration to Registrar (Section 5)

Application for registration of a Trade Union as to be made to the Registrar of Trade Unions. It must be accompanied by a copy of its rules and a statement of the following particulars, *viz.*,

(i) the names, occupations and addresses of the members making the application;

(ii) the name of the Trade Union and the address of its head office; and the titles, names, ages, addresses and occupations of the officers of the Trade Union [Section 5 (1)].

Where a Trade Union has been in existence for more than 1 year before the making of an application for its registration. A general statement of its assets and liabilities prepared in the prescribed form has also to be delivered to the Registrar, together with the application [Section 5 (2)].

3. Rules of Trade Union (Section 6)

A Trade Union is entitled to registration only if its executive is constituted in accordance with the provisions of the Act and Its rules provide for the following matters, namely;

(i) the name of the trade union;

(ii) the whole of its objects;

(iii) the whole of the purposes for which the general funds of the Trade Union shall be applicable under Section 15;

(iv) the maintenance of a list of the members of the Trade Union and adequate facilities for the inspection thereof by the office-bearers and members of the Trade Union;

(v) the admission of ordinary members who shall be persons actually engaged or employed in the industry with which the Trade Union is connected, and also the admission of the number of honorary or temporary office-bearers to form the executive of the Trade Union;

(vi) the payment of a subscription by the members of the Trade Union which shall be not less than 25 paise per month per member;

(vii) the conditions under which any members shall be entitled to any benefit assured by the rules and conditions under which fines may be imposed on the members;

(viii) the manner in which the rules shall be amended, varied or rescinded;

(ix) the manner in which the members of the executive and other office-bearers of the Trade Union shall be appointed and removed;

(x) the safe custody of the funds of the Trade Union, and annual audit of the accounts thereof, and facilities for the inspection of the account books by the office-bearers and members of the Trade Union and

(xi) the manner in which the Trade Union may be dissolved.

4. Power to call for Further Particulars and to require Alteration of Name (Section 7)

(i) *Compliance* : The Registrar may call for further information for the purpose of satisfying himself that an application for registration complies with the provisions of Section 5, or that the Trade Union is entitled to registration under Section 6. He may refuse to register the Trade Union until such information is supplied [Section 7 (1)].

(ii) *Alteration* : If the name under which a Trade Union is proposed to be registered is identical with that by which any other existing Trade Union has been registered or, in the opinion of the Registrar, so nearly resembles such name as to be likely to deceive the public or the members of either Trade Union, the Registrar shall require the persons applying for registration to alter the name of the Trade Union stated in the application. He shall refuse to register the Trade Union until such alteration has been made [Section 7 (2)].

5. Registration (Section 8)

The Registrar, on being satisfied that the Trade Union has compiled with all the requirements of this Act in regard to registration, shall register the Trade Union. He shall register the Trade Union by entering in a register, to be maintained in such form as may be prescribed, the particulars relating to the Trade Union contained in the statement accompanying the application.

6. Certificate of Registration (Section 9)

The Registrar, on registering a Trade Union under Section 8, shall issue a certificate of registration in the prescribed form. The certificate shall be conclusive evidence that the Trade Union has been duly registered under the Act.

7. Characteristics of Registered Trade Union on Incorporation (Section 13)

(i) It becomes a body corporate by the name under which it is registered, and becomes a legal entity distinct from the members of which it is composed.

(ii) It has perpetual succession and a common seal.

(iii) It has the power to acquire and hold both movable and immovable properties.

(iv) It has the power to contract.

(v) It can by the name under which it is registered sue and be sued.

8. Change of Names (Sections 23, 25 and 26)

(i) Procedure. Any registered Trade Union may, with the consent of not less than 2/3rds of total number of its members, change its name (Section 23). Notice in writing of the change signed by the Secretary and by 7 members of the Trade Union shall be sent to the Registrar [Section 25 (1)]. If the proposed name is not identical with that of any existing Trade Union. The Registrar shall register the change of name in the register referred to in Section 8 [Section 25 (2)]. The Registrar shall, if he is satisfied that the provisions of the Act in respect of change of name have been complied with, register the change of name in the register referred to in Section 8, and the change of name shall have effect from the date of such registration [Section 25 (3)].

(ii) *Impact* : The change in the name does not affect any rights or obligations of the Trade Union or render defective any legal proceeding by or against the Trade Union [Section 26 (1)].

9. Registered Office (Section 12). All communications and notices to a registered Trade Union may be addressed to its registered office. Notice of any change in the address of the head office shall be given within 14 days of such change to the Registrar in writing, and the changed address shall be recorded in the register maintained by the Registrar under Section 8.

10. Who may become Members (Section 21). (i) *Age* : Any person who has attained the age of 15 years may be a member of a registered Trade Union. This is subject to any rules of the Trade Union to the contrary. Any such member, subject to the rules of the Trade Union, may enjoy all the rights of a member and execute all instruments and give all acquittances necessary to be executed or given under the rules (Section 21). But he cannot be an office-bearer of the Trade Union until he attains the age of 18 years [Section 21-A (1)(i)].

(ii) *Can every employee become member of a trade union*? : It is only persons engaged in trade or business (which includes an industry) who can form a Trade Union or become members of a Trade Union. As such persons employed in a Raj Bhawan for domestic and other duties cannot form a Trade Union [Rangaswamy *Vs*. Registrar of Trade Unions, (1981) 1 L.L.J. 599]. Likewise the Government servants engaged in the task of sovereign and regal functions are not entitled to the registration of a Trade Union [Tamil Nadu Non-Gazetted Officers Union, Madras *Vs*. Registrar of Trade Unions, Madras, (1972) 1 L.L.J. 153].

CANCELLATION OF REGISTRATION AND APPEAL

1. Cancellation of Registration (Section 10)

A certificate of registration of a Trade Union may be withdrawn or cancelled by the Registrar :

(i) on the application of the Trade Union to be verified in the prescribed manner; or

(ii) if the Registrar is satisfied that the certificate has been obtained by fraud or mistake; or

(iii) if the Registrar is satisfied that the Trade Union has ceased (a) to exist, or (b) wilfully contravened any provisions of the Act, or (c) allowed any rule to continue in force, which is inconsistent with any such provisions, or (d) rescinded any rule which ought to be there.

In cases (ii) and (iii) the Registrar has to give to the Trade Union not less than 2 months' previous notice in writing specifying the ground on which it is proposed to withdraw or cancel the certificate of registration. No such notice is necessary in case (i).

2. Appeal (Section 11)

(i) *Procedure* : If the registration of a Trade Union is refused or if a certificate of registration is withdrawn or cancelled, any person aggrieved or the Trade Union may appeal to the Court within the prescribed period. The proceedings by way of appeal must be started within 60 days of the date on which the Registrar passed the order against which appeal is made (Rule 10, Central Trade Union Regulations, 1938). Where the head office of a Trade Union is situated within the limits of a Presidency Town, the appeal lies to the High Court. Where the head office is situated in any other area, the appeal lies to such Court, not inferior to the Court of an additional or assistant judge or a principal Civil Court of original jurisdiction, as the appropriate Government may appoint in this behalf for that area [Section 11(1)].

(ii) *Action of the Court* : The Appellate Court may dismiss the appeal, or order the Registrar to register the union and to issue a certificate of registration, or set aside the order for withdrawal or cancellation of the certificate, as the case may be. The Registrar shall comply with such order of the Court [Section 11(2)].

(iii) *Powers of Court* : For the purpose of an appeal under Section 11(1) an Appellate Court shall follow the same procedure and shall have the same powers as it follows and has when trying a suit under the Code of Civil Procedure, 1908. It may direct by whom the costs of the appeal shall be paid and such costs shall be recovered as if they had been awarded in a suit under the said Code [Section 11(3)].

RIGHTS AND PRIVILEGES OF A REGISTERED TRADE UNION

The following are the rights and privileges of a registered Trade Union :

1. Body corporate (Section 13). Every Registered Trade Union is a body corporate by the name under which it is registered and has perpetual succession and a common seal with power to acquire and hold both movable and immovable property and to contract and can by the said name sue and be sued.

2. Separate Fund for Political Purposes (Section 16). A registered Trade Union may constitute a separate fund, from contributions separately levied for or made to that fund. From which payments may be made for the promotion of the civic and political interests of its members [Section 16 (1)].

3. Immunity from Punishment for Criminal Conspiracy (Section 17). An office-bearer or member of a registered Trade Union shall not be liable to punishment under Section 120-8 (2) of the Indian Penal Code, 1860 in respect of any agreement made between the members for the purpose of furthering any such object of the Trade Union on which general funds may be spent.

Where, for example, a strike is accompanied by violence, assault, intimidation, threat etc., this exemption is not available [Jay Engineering Works *Vs.* Workmen, A.I.R. (1968) Cal. 407]. Likewise a union leader is not entitled to claim immunity from punishment for breach of discipline [Burn & Co. *Vs.* Their Workmen, A.I.R (1959) S.C. 529].

4. Imnuinity from Civil Suits (Section 18). A suit or other legal proceeding shall not be maintainable in any Civil Court against any Trade Union or any office-bearer or member thereof in respect of any act done in contemplation or furtherance of a trade dispute to which a member of the trade union is a party. This protection is available only on the ground that such act induces some other persons to break contract of employment, or that it is in interference with the trade, business or employment of some other person or with the right of some other person to dispose of his capital or his labour as he wills [Section 18 (1)]. The union, its office-bearer and members shall, however, be liable for acts which are not covered by Section 18 (1), *e.g.*, acts of violence or vandalism or any act of deliberate trespass [Daimia Cement Ltd. *Vs.* Narain Das, A.I.R. (1939) Sind 256].

A registered Trade Union is not liable in any suit or other legal proceedings in any Civil Court in respect of any tortious act done in contemplation or furtherance of a trade dispute by an agent of the Trade Union if it is proved that such person acted without the knowledge of, or contrary to the express instructions given by, the executive of the Trade Union [Section 18 (2)].

5. Enforceability of Agreements (Section 19). Notwithstanding anything contained in any other law for the time being in force, an agreement between the members of a registered Trade Union shall not be void or voidable merely by reason of the fact that any of the objects of the agreement is in restraint of trade.

6. Right to inspect Books of Trade Union (Section 20). 'The account books of a registered Trade Union and the list of members thereof is open to inspection by an office-bearer or member of the Trade Union. The inspection may be done at such time as may be provided for in the rules of the Trade Union. The object of conferring this right on office-bearers and members is that they satisfy themselves as to the genuineness of members and of the accounts of the union.

7. Right of Minors to be Members (Section 21). Subject to any rules of the Trade Union to the contrary, any person who has attained the age of 15 years may be a member of a registered Trade Union and enjoy all the rights of a member.

DUTIES AND LIABILITIES OF A REGISTERED TRADE UNION

The Trade Unions Act imposes the following duties and liabilities on a registered Trade Union :

1. Change of Registered Office (Section 12). If any change in the address of the head office of a Trade Union takes place, notice of change must be given to the Registrar in writing.

2. Objects on which General Funds may be spent (Section 15). 'The general funds, of a registered Trade Union shall be spent only on the following objects, namely :

(i) the payment of salaries, allowances and expenses to office-bearers of the Trade Union;

(ii) the payment of expenses for the administration of the Trade Union, including audit of the accounts of the general funds of the Trade Union;

(iii) the expenses in prosecution or defence of any legal proceeding to which the Trade Union or any member thereof is a party, undertaken for the purpose of securing or protecting any rights of the Trade Union;

(iv) the conduct of trade disputes on behalf of the Trade Union or any members thereof;

(v) the compensation of members for loss arising out of trade disputes;

(vi) allowances to members or their dependents on account of death, old age, sickness, accidents or unemployment of such members;

(vii) the issue of, or the undertaking of liability under, policies of assurance on the lives of members, or under policies insuring members against sickness, accident or unemployment;

(viii) the provision of educational, social, or religious benefits for members (including the payment of the expenses of funeral or religious ceremonies for deceased members) or for the dependents of members;

(ix) the upkeep of a periodical published mainly for the purpose of discussing questions affecting employees or workmen as such;

(x) the payment of contributions to any cause intended to benefit workmen in general. The expenditure in respect of such contributions in any financial year shall not at any time during that year be in excess of 1/4th of the combined total of the gross income which has up to that time accrued to the general funds of the Trade Union during that year and of the balance at the credit of those funds at the commencement of that year and

(xi) subject to any conditions contained in the notification, any other object notified by the appropriate Government in the Official Gazette.

If the union funds are spent on any objects other than those enumerated in Section 15, the expenditure will be unlawful and *ultra vires* the Act. The union can be restrained by injunction from applying its funds for any such object.

3. Constitution of a Fund for Political Purposes (Section 16). A registered Trade Union may constitute a separate fund from which payments may be made for the promotion of the civic and political interests of its members [Section 16 (1)]. Such fund can be used in furtherance of the following objects, *viz.*,

(i) the payment of any expenses incurred by a candidate or prospective candidate for election as a member of any legislative body constituted under the Constitution or of any local authority; or

(ii) the holding of any meeting or the distribution of any literature or documents in support of any such candidate or prospective candidate, or

(iii) the maintenance of any person who is a member of any legislative body constituted under the Constitution or for any local authority; or

(iv) the registration of electors or the election of a candidate for any legislative body constituted under the Constitution or of any local authority; or

(v) the holding of political meetings of any kind, or the distribution of political literature or political documents of any kind [Section 16 (2)].

Expenditure for political purposes is in no case permitted out of the general funds. Not only this, even interest on investments of general fund will have to be credited to the general fund.

The conditions for the creation of a political fund :

(i) Such fund can be created only from contributions separately levied or made to that fund [Section 16 (1)].

(ii) Members must not be compelled to contribute to the fund.

(iii) A member who does not contribute to the fund must not be excluded from any benefits of the Trade Union, or placed under any disability or disadvantage, directly or indirectly, as compared with other members of the Trade Union (except in relation to control or management of the political fund).

(iv) Contribution to the political fund must not be made a condition for admission to the trade union [Section 16 (3)].

4. Proportion of Officers to be connected with the Industry (Section 22). Not less than one-half of the total number of the office-bearers of every registered Trade Union must be persons actually engaged or employed in an industry with which the Trade Union is connected. The other half of the office bearers may be social or political workers. The idea behind this rule is that persons actually engaged or employed in the industry may not have enough courage to form a Trade Union for fear of reprisal from the employers.

The appropriate Government may, however, by special or general order, exempt a Trade Union from the application of this provision.

5. Returns (Section 28). Every registered Trade Union shall send annually to the Registrar a general statement, audited in the prescribed manner, of all receipts and expenditure during the year ending on the 31st day of December. It shall also send a statement of assets and liabilities on that date [Section 28 (1)1. Together with the general statement it shall send a statement showing all changes of office-bearers made by the Trade Union during the year, and a copy of the rules of the Trade Union corrected up to the date of the despatch to the Registrar [Section 28 (2)]. A copy of every alteration made in the rules of the registered Trade Union shall be sent to the Registrar within 15 days of the making of the alteration [Section 28 (3)].

For the purpose of examining the documents and statements sent to Registrar, the Registrar or any officer authorised by him may at all reasonable times inspect the certificate of registration, account books, registers, and other documents relating to a Trade Union, at its registered office, or may require their production at a place which shall not be at a distance of more than 10 miles (16 kilometres) from the registered office of a Trade Union [Section 28 (4)].

6. Disqualifications of Office-bearers of Trade Union (Section 21 -A). A person shall be disqualified for being chosen as, and for being, a member of the executive or any other office-bearer of a registered Trade Union if :

(i) he has not attained the age of 18 years;

(ii) he has been convicted by a Court in India of any offence involving moral turpitude and sentenced to imprisonment [Section 21-A (1)].

In case (ii), if a period of 5 years has elapsed since his release, the disqualifications are removed [Section 21-A (2)].

AMALGAMATION OF TRADE UNIONS (Sections 24 to 26)

1. Amalgamation. Any 2 or more registered Trade Unions may become amalgamated together as one Trade Union with or without dissolution or division of the funds of such Trade Unions. The amalgamation shall take place only when votes of at least one-half of the members of each Trade Union entitled to vote are recorded, and that at least 60 per cent of the votes recorded are in favour of the proposal of amalgamation (Section 24).

2. Notice of Amalgamation. Notice in writing of every amalgamation, signed by the Secretary and by 7 members of each and every Trade Union which is a party thereto, shall be sent to the Registrar. If the head office of the amalgamated Trade Union is situated in a different State. Such notice shall be sent to the Registrar of such State also [Section 25 (1)]. If the Registrar of the State in which the registered head office of the amalgamated Trade Union is situated is satisfied that all necessary formalities have been complied with, he may register the Trade Union and the amalgamation shall have effect from the date of such registration [Section 25 (4)].

3. Effect of Amalgamation. An amalgamation of 2 or more registered Trade Unions shall not prejudice any right of any such Trade Unions or any right of a creditor of any of them [Section 26 (2)].

DISSOLUTION OF TRADE UNION

1. When a Trade Union is dissolved, notice of the dissolution signed by 7 members and by the Secretary of the Trade Union shall be sent to the Registrar within 14 days of the dissolution. If the Registrar is satisfied that the dissolution has been effected in accordance with the rules of the Trade Union, he shall register the fact of dissolution. The dissolution shall take effect from the date of such registration [Section 27 (1)).

2. Where the dissolution of a registered Trade Union has been registered and the rules of the Trade Union do not provide for the distribution of funds of the Trade Union on dissolution, the Registrar shall divide the funds amongst the members in such manner as may be prescribed [Section 27 (2)].

REGULATIONS

1. Power to make Regulations (Section 29)

The appropriate Government may make regulations for the purpose of carrying into effect the provisions of the Act [Section 29 (1)].

In particular and without prejudice to the generality of the foregoing power, such regulations may provide for all or any of the following matters, namely :

(i) the manner in which Trade Unions and the rules of Trade Unions be registered and the fees payable on registration;

(ii) the transfer of registration in the case of any registered Trade Union which has changed its head office from one State to another;

(iii) the manner in which, and the qualifications of persons by whom, the accounts of registered Trade Unions or of any class of such unions shall be audited;

(iv) the conditions subject to which inspection of documents kept by Registrars shall be allowed and the fees which shall be chargeable in respect of such inspections and

(v) any matter which is to be or may be prescribed [Section 29 (2)].

2. Publication of Regulations (Section 30)

(i) *Condition* : The power of the appropriate Government to make regulations conferred by Section 29 is subject to the condition of the regulations being made after previous publication [Section 30 (1)]. The regulations so made shall be published in the Official Gazette.

(ii) *Date* : The date to be specified in accordance with Section 23 (3) of the General Clauses Act 1897, as that after which a draft of regulations proposed to be made will be taken into consideration shall not be less than 3 months from the date on which the draft of the proposed regulations was published for general information [Section 30 (2)].

(iii) *Regulations* : The regulations after publication in the Official Gazette shall have effect as if enacted in this Act [Section 30(3)].

PENALTIES

1. Failure to submit Returns (Section 31). If default is made on the part of any registered Trade Union in giving any notice or sending any statement or other document as required by or under any provision of this Act, every office-bearer or other person bound by the rules of the Trade Union to give or send the same, shall be punishable with fine which may extend to Rs. 5. It there is no such officer or person, every member of the executive of the Trade Union shall be punishable with fine which may extend to Rs. 5. In the case of continuing default, the fine may extend to an additional fine which may extend to Rs. 5 for each week after the flat during which the default continues [Section 31 (1)].

The information or statements required to be submitted by a registered Trade Union shall include :

(i) Notice of change in the address of the head office of the Trade Union (Section 12);

(ii) Notice of change of name on amalgamation (Section 25);

(iii) Notice of dissolution (Section 27);

(iv) Returns (Section 28).

Further any person who wilfully makes, or causes to be made, any false entry in, or any emission from, the general statement required by Section 28 or from any copy of rules or of alterations of rules sent to the Registrar under Section 28 shall be punishable with fine which may extend to Re. 500 [Section 31(2)].

2. Supplying False Information regarding Trade Unions (Section 32). Sometimes a person, with intent to deceive, gives to any member of a registered Trade Union, or to any person intending or applying to become a member of such Trade Union, any document purporting to be a copy :

(i) of the rules of the Trade Union, or

(ii) of any alterations to the same,

which he knows, or has reason to believe, is not a correct copy of such rules or alterations as are for the time being in force.

Such a person shall be punishable with fine which may extend to Rs. 200. Likewise, any person who, with intent to deceive, gives a copy of any rules of an unregistered Trade Union to any person on the pretence that such rules are the rules of a registered Trade Union, shall be punishable with fine which may extend to Rs. 200.

3. Cognizance of Offences (Section 33). No Court inferior to that of a Presidency Magistrate or a Magistrate of the First Class shall try any offence under this Act (Section 33(1)]. Further no Court shall take cognizance of any offence under the Act, unless complaint thereof has been made by, or with the previous sanction of the Registrar. In the case of an offence of supplying false information regarding the Trade Union the complaint may be made by the aggrieved person within 6 months of the date on which the offence is alleged to have been committed [Section 33 (3)].

QUESTIONS FOR EXERCISE

1. Define the following terms as used in the Trade Unions Act, 1926 :

   (a) Trade Union, (b) Trade dispute, (c) Registered Trade Union.
2. How are Trade Unions registered and certificates of registration thereof issued under the Trade Unions Act, 1926? Can a minor be admitted as a member of a Trade Union?
3. State the rules regarding change of name of a Trade Union.
4. When can the registration of a Trade Union be cancelled or withdrawn? is amalgamation of 2 or more trade Unions possible?
5. Describe the privileges of a registered Trade Union.
6. Write a note on the amalgamation of Trade Unions.
7. When and for what purposes may a Trade Union create a political fund?
8. State the objects on which general funds of a Trade Union may be spent.
9. State the penalty for supplying false information regarding a Trade Union.
10. What are the provisions relating to dissolution of a Trade Union under the Trade Unions Act, 1926.

13

The Industrial Disputes Act, 1947

According to Industrial Dispute Act 1947, Industrial disputes is "any dispute or difference between employers and employers, between employer & workman, between workman & workman, which is connected with the employment or non employment or the terms of employment or with the conditions of labour, of any person."

CHARACTERISTICS OF INDUSTRIAL DISPUTES

1. Collective Dispute. The dispute must be between (i) Employers and employers, (ii) Employers and workman, (iii) Workmen and workmen.

Thus, collective disputes are industrial disputes. Unless it is espoused by a trade union or by an appreciating number of workmen. Where the dispute is between an individual workman and his employer it is an individual dispute and not industrial dispute.

2. Connected with Various Condition. The dispute must be "connected with the employment or non-employment or the terms of employment or with the conditions of labour of any person."

3. Differences. A dispute is a kind of some real or substantial difference which may engender industrial peace if not resolved. It is not essential for the workman to show that they had made the demand before the management earlier and it is rejected by the management. The dispute may exist even if the demand was not made before the management but is raised now by the government either expressly or implied.

Thus, industrial dispute is unrest in labour which expresses itself in many ways and forms. The most striking feature of the labour unrest expressed itself in the forms of strikes or stoppage of work. As a result of strike the factories are closed down and this prove harmful both to employees and employers. In order to prevent such colossal waste the government tries to prevent or minimize the strikes. A strike by workers is followed by lock out by the industrialists. Both strike and lock out are manifestations of industrial conflict and tension between the employer and employees. Besides strikes, the unrest among labour may manifest itself in demonstrations, taking out processions, inserting support of politicians etc. Many political parties today are vying with each other to gain domination over labour movement and capture the control of trade unions.

CONSEQUENCES OF INDUSTRIAL DISPUTES

1. Unrest. As we have already mentioned, industrial conflicts and disputes lead to widespread unrest in social life and also disruption of political harmony and peace.

2. Economic Loss. The industrial disputes most obviously injure the economic interest of both the employees and employers. This effect is direct and palpable. Both indirectly and in a subtle way these also prove economically harmful to nation as a whole. Everyone is ultimately affected.

3. Economic Depression. The industrial disputes are not only harmful to the industry involved but lead to all-round economic depression. A closure of one industry lead to the reduction of demand of goods of other industries or trades. For example, closure of textile industry would lead to drastic reduction in the demand of cotton.

4. Workers' Hardships. The majority of workers in India do not earn enough to be able to save something for the rainy days. They are hand to mouth, if nor worse. Therefore, strikes and lock outs put unbearable burden on them and they are reduced to the level of beggars.

5. Threat to Social Security and Public Peace. If industrial disputes spread in an epidemic form they pose threat to public peace.

If the tension among workers and employers mounts and takes serious form, the workers are liable to become violent or indulge in sabotage. This may compel the employer to take the help of police force and this may still further aggravate the tension which may manifest itself in the form of rioting, looting and arson. This surely disturbs the public peace. If a strike becomes a prestige issue and is long drawn, the workers may face starvation. This may compel them to beggary and other social crimes.

CAUSES OF INDUSTRIAL DISPUTES

1. Low Wages. In India, the remuneration paid to workers for their work is not adequate to meet their expenses. They can either provide for the education of their children nor can they feed them properly. Their living conditions are deplorable. Their, future is uncertain and a deep sense of insecurity pervades their life. With the death of the earning member the dependents are reduced to penury and compelled to take to beggary, prostitution and other social evils. The low wages are the main reason of discontent among the workers. It is this discontent which ultimately expresses itself in the form of industrial disputes and tensions.

2. Rising Prices. If we review the statistics regarding the wages of workers in India we find that in most states the wages have doubled. For example, in 1954, the average annual income of workers in Andhra Pradesh was Rs.595 which in the year 1964 rose to Rs. 1,097. However, the doubling of income has brought no relief to the workers; because whereas the wages have gone up by 200 per cent, the prices have risen 400 per cent. Thus, the real income of the workers has in fact dropped sharply. After the Second World War, the prices of commodities have been steadily rising, eroding the real earning of the workers. Therefore, this inflationary spiral has made the workers poorer still. This obviously produces tension and conflict among workers.

3. Absence of Link with D.A. and Price Rise. The various trade unions in India have been clamouring for 100 per cent neutralisation of prices rise by corresponding increase in the dearness allowance. This, however, has not happened in all industries. This is a great source of conflict and tension between workers and their employers.

4. Unsatisfactory Working Conditions. Another cause of industrial disputes is the fact that the working conditions in most of the factories are unhygienic and poor in respect of lighting and ventilation. This tells upon the health of the workers. They are mostly suffering from some or the other chronic ailment. Being ill and unhealthy they are depressed and irritable. This makes them permanently discontented.

5. Demand for Leave with Pay. Like workers every where the industrial workers, too, need holiday from work from time to time. Therefore, Trade Unions press for a permanent provision of regular leaves with pay. This is also a source of contention among workers and employers.

6. Resistance to Misconduct of Officers. Today there is sufficient awakening among the workers and they are very conscious of self-respect and preserve it jealously. Therefore, any slight or insult by officers provokes them. Such incidents many at time ignite fire of conflict and tension which takes the form of gheraos etc.

7. Demand for Adequate Bonus. The political leaders and Trade Unionists have inspired the workers to think and believe that they are partners in mills and factories and that they are fully entitled to share the profits earned by the factory as a result of their labour. Though in many industries bonus is being paid now, but the amount or percentage of bonus is a source of frequent disputes among workers and employers.

8. Demand for Re-instatement. At times the employers arbitrarily retrench many workers and this naturally is resisted by the affected workers. Besides, other workers are made to feel insecure. Therefore, the workers resist such moves. They stand united and-agitate for the reinstatement of the retrenched colleagues.

9. Non-recognition of Trade Unions. Sometimes employers refuse to recognise the Trade Unions in their factories. This too becomes a source of contention and conflict and may result in strikes etc.

10. Retrenchment Due to Sophisticated Machinery. In modern industries many new and sophisticated machines are installed. These machines are labour saving. Naturally, therefore, as a result of these there is retrenchment of workers. Recently there was great hue and cry in the Life Insurance Corporation of India due to installation of computers.

11. Political Causes. A major cause of industrial disputes is political machinations. Now-a-days various political parties in India vie with each other to gain sympathy and support of workers and for this reason go out of way to support all types of agitations and even foment discontent among them.

12. Misconduct of Intermediates. In many industries there is no direct contact between the employer and the workers. The workers are recruited through intermediaries or brokers. These brokers usually subject workers to various kinds of humiliation and exploitation. In resentment to these foul tactics the workers start agitations and launch other forms of protests.

The foregoing discussion of the causes of industrial disputes in India makes it clear that the problem of labour unrest is quite complex. 'The worker is a human being and as a human being he feels discontented and frustrated if his day-to-day needs are not met properly. If the workers are given adequate wages, there is improvement of working conditions. If brokers and political agents are eliminated the chances of conflict and tensions among workers and employers will be greatly minimized.

THE INDUSTRIAL DISPUTES ACT, 1947

Historical Review

1. The first Enactment about the Settlement of Industrial Disputes. Employers' and Workmen's (Disputes) Act, 1860 weighed much against the workers and was replaced.

2. Trade Disputes Act, 1929. It contained special provisions regarding strikes in public utility services and general strikes affecting the community as a whole. Its main purpose, however, was to provide a conciliation machinery to bring about peaceful settlement of industrial disputes. In this regard the Whitely Commission made the perceptive observation that the attempt to deal with unrest must begin rather with the creation of an atmosphere unfavourable to disputes than with machinery for their settlement.

3. The Industrial Disputes Act, 1947. It was passed to remove certain shortcomings found in the working of the Trade Disputes Act of 1929. The Act came into force on the first day of April, 1947 [Section 1(3)]. It introduced Works Committees and Industrial Tribunals, new institutions for the prevention and settlement of industrial disputes. It seeks to reorient the administration of the conciliation machinery. Under the Act conciliation has been made compulsory in all disputes in public utility services and optional in all other industrial establishments.

A. Objectives was of the Act

(1) to secure industrial peace :

(i) by preventing and settling Industrial disputes between the employers and workmen.

(ii) by securing and preserving amity and good relations between the employers and workmen through an internal Works Committee and

(iii) by promoting good relations through an external machinery of conciliation. Courts of Inquiry, Labour Courts, Industrial Tribunals and National Tribunals.

(2) to ameliorate the condition of workmen in industry :

(i) by redressal of grievances of workmen through a statutory machinery and

(ii) by providing job security [S.N. Rai *Vs*. Vishwanath Lal, A.I.R. (1960) Pat. 10].

B. Extent of the Act

The Act extends to the whole of the India [Section 1 (2)]. It applies to all industries whether they be carried on by private owners or by the Government [Western India Automobile Assn. *Vs*. Industrial Tribunal, Bombay, A.I.R. (1949) F.C. 111].

C. Amendment

The Act has been amended from time to time. The latest amendment to the Act was made in August, 1984.

DEFINITION OF INDUSTRY

1. Amended Definition. The Amendment Act of 1982 has re-defined the term 'industry' in the light of the observations of the

Supreme Court in the case of Bangalore Water Supply & Sewerage Board, etc. *Vs*. A. Rajappa, (1978) Lab. I.C. 467. The definition has now been made wider and more specific.

According to new Section 2 (j) as substituted by the Amendment Act of 1982, 'Industry' means any systematic activity carried on by co-operation between an employer and his workmen. The workmen may be employed by the employer directly or by or through any agency, including a contractor. The employment should, however, be for the production, supply or distribution of goods or services with a view to satisfy human wants or wishes (not being wants or wishes which are merely spiritual or religious in nature). It makes no difference whether or not :

(i) any capital has been invested for the purpose of carrying on the activity referred to above 11 or

(ii) such activity is carried on with a motive to make any gain or profit.

2. What is included in the Term 'Industry'?

(i) any activity of the Dock Labour Board established under Section 5-A of the Dock Workers (Regulations of Employment) Act, 1948;

(ii) any activity relating to the promotion of sales or business or both carried on by an establishment.

3. What is not included in the Term 'Industry'?

(i) any agricultural operation except where such agricultural operation is carried on in an integrated manner with any other systematic activity and such other activity is the predominant one; or

'Agricultural operation' does not include any activity carried on in a plantation as defined in Section 2 (1) of the Plantations Labour Act, 1951.

(ii) hospitals or dispensaries; or

(iii) educational, scientific, research or training institutions; or

(iv) institutions owned or managed by organisations wholly or substantially engaged in any charitable, social or philanthropic service; or

(v) khadi or village industries; or

According to new clause (kka) as introduced in Section 2 by the Amendment Act of 1982, 'khadi' has the meaning assigned to it in Section 2 (d) of the Khadi and Village Industries Commission Act, 1956.

(vi) any activity of the Government relatable to the sovereign functions of the Government including all the activities carried on by the departments of the Central Government dealing with defence research, atomic energy and space; or

(vii) any domestic service; or

(viii) any activity, being a profession practised by an individual or body of individuals, if the number of persons employed in relation to such profession is less than 10; or

(ix) any activity, being an activity carried on by a co-operative society or a club or any other like body of individuals. If the number of persons employed in relation to such activity is less than 10.

4. Definition of Industry before Amendment in 1962

The definition of the term 'industry' has been amended by the Amendment Act of 1982 but the amendment has not yet been brought into force. Prior to amendment in 1982, the definition of the term 'industry (which still continues to be effective) was as follows :

'Industry' means any business, trade, undertaking, manufacture or calling of employees and includes any calling, service, employment, handicraft, or industrial occupation or avocation of workmen.'

WHAT IS AN INDUSTRIAL DISPUTE? [Section 2 (k)]

1. Meaning. 'Industrial dispute' means any dispute or difference between

(i) employers and employers,

(ii) employers and workmen, or

(iii) workmen and workmen, which is connected with (a) the employment or non-employment, (b) the terms of employment, or (c) the conditions of labour of any person.

2. Real and Substantial Difference. The term industrial dispute connotes a real and substantial difference having some element of persistency and continuity till resolved and is likely. if not resolved, to endanger the industrial peace of the undertaking or the community. When parties are at variance and the dispute or difference is connected with employment or non-employment or the terms of employment or with the conditions of labour, there comes into existence an industrial dispute [Sharnbhu Nath Goyal *Vs.* Bank of Baroda, (1978) 2 B.C.C. 353]. The expression 'terms of employment' would ordinarily include only the contractual terms and conditions but those terms which are understood and applied by the parties in practice or habitually or by common consent without ever being incorporated in the contract are also included [Workmen *Vs.* Hindustan Lever Ltd, (1984) 1 S.C.C. 392].

3. Three Ingredients of Industrial Dispute. In the ordinary language an industrial dispute is implied to mean a dispute between the workmen and the management. In Standard Vacuum Refining Co. of India Ltd. *Vs.* Their Workmen, A.I.R. (1960) S.C. 948, it was held that a dispute as to whether the system of engaging contract labour prevailing in certain sections of an industrial concern should be discontinued and the contractors' laborers should be made 'workmen' of the company is an 'industrial dispute' if it is taken up and sponsored by the regular workmen of the concern. It was observed in this case :

The definition of 'Industrial dispute' in Section 2(k) of the Industrial Disputes Act, 1947 has three ingredients, and if all three ingredients are satisfied. The dispute raised is an industrial dispute which could validly be referred under Section 10 to a Tribunal for adjudication. These three ingredients are :

(i) there should be real and substantial dispute or difference;

(ii) the dispute or difference should be between employer and his workmen and

(iii) the dispute or difference must be connected with the employment or non-employment or terms of employment, or with the conditions of labour of any person.

4. Limitations of Definition. The definition of 'industrial dispute' contains two limitations :

First, the adjective 'Industrial' relates the dispute to an industry as defined in the Act and

Secondly, the definition expressly states that not disputes and differences of all sorts but only those which bear upon the relationship of employers and workmen and the terms of employment or non-employment and the conditions of labour are contemplated.

5. Test of Industrial Dispute. (i) A dispute is an 'industrial dispute' only when it arises in any activity which is an 'industry' as defined in Section 2(j) of the Act [D.N. Banerji *Vs.* P.R. Mukkherjee, A.I.R. (1953) S.C. 58]

(ii) The real test whether a dispute is an industrial dispute or not is whether the majority or a large number of workmen are involved in the dispute. An individual dispute between an employer and one of his workmen is by itself not an industrial dispute which can be referred to under Section 10. But such dispute may become an industrial dispute, provided that the cause of the particular workman concerned is taken up by a majority of workmen in the particular industrial establishment or by any union of such workmen [Express Newspapers (Pvt.). Ltd. *Vs.* First Labour Court, A.I.R. (1959) Cal. 265.

(iii) it makes no difference even if the union which takes up the cause of the dismissed workman itself comes into existence after the date of dismissal and the dismissed workman joins the union thereafter; the dispute in such a case would be a valid industrial dispute [Workmen of Jamadoba Colliery of Tata Iron & Steel Co. *Vs*. Jamadoba Colliery of Tata Iron & Steel Co., (1967) 2 L.L.J. 633].

(iv) But where the cause of a workman is espoused by a union which has absolutely nothing to do with the establishment from which the workman comes, it is not an industrial dispute [Motor & Machinery Mfrs. Ltd. *Vs*. Industrial Tribunal. (1963) 1 L.L.J. 222].

INDIVIDUAL AND COLLECTIVE DISPUTES

The industrial disputes may be (1) individual disputes, or (2) collective disputes.

1. Industrial Disputes. Section 2-A provides that where any employer discharges, dismisses, retrenches or otherwise terminates the services of an individual workman any dispute or difference between that workman and his employer connected with, or arising out of, such discharge, dismissal, retrenchment or termination shall be deemed to be an industrial dispute even if no other workman nor any union of workmen is a party to the dispute.

2. Collective Dispute. A Collective dispute may relate to any of the following matters :

(i) Wages, bonus, profit-sharing, gratuity, compensatory and other allowances.

(ii) Hours of work, leave with wages, holidays.

(iii) Rules of discipline, retrenchment of workmen, closure of establishment, rationalftsation.

All collective disputes are industrial disputes.

DEFINITIONS

1. Appropriate Government [Section 2 (a)]. 'Appropriate Government' means the Central Government in relation to any Industrial dispute concerning :

(1) any industry carried on (i) by or under the authority of the Central Government, or (ii) by a railway company, or (iii) concerning any such controlled industry as may be specified in this behalf by the Central Government

(2) (i) a Dock Labour Board established under Section 5-A of the Dock Workers (Regulation of Employment) Act, 1948, or

(ii) the Industrial Finance Corporation of India established under Section 3 of the, Industrial Finance Corporation Act, 1,948, or

(iii) the Employees' State Insurance Corporation established under Section 3 of the Employees' State Insurance Act, 1948, or

(iv) the Board of Trustees constituted under Section 3-A of the Coal Mines Provident Fund and Miscellaneous Provisions Act, 1948, or

(v) the Central Board of Trustees and State Boards of Trustees constituted under Section 5-A and Section 5-B. respectively, of the Employees' Provident Funds and Miscellaneous Provisions Act, 1952, or

(vi) the 'Indian Airlines' and 'Air India' Corporations established Tender Section 3 of the Air Corporations Act, 1952, or

(vii) the Life Insurance Corporation of India established under Section 3 of the Life Insurance Corporation Act, 1956, or

(viii) the Oil and Natural Gas Commission established under Section 3 of the Oil and Natural Gas Commission Act, 1959, or

(ix) the Deposit Insurance and Credit Guarantee Corporation established under Section 3 of the Deposit Insurance and Credit Guarantee Corporation Act, 1961, or

(x) the Central Warehousing Corporation established under Section 3 of the Warehousing Corporations Act, 1962, or

(xi) the Unit Trust of India established under Section 3 of the Unit Trust of India Act, 1963, or

(xii) the Food Corporation of India established under Section 3, or a Board of Management established for 2 or more contiguous States under Section 16 of the Food Corporation Act, 1964, or

(xiii) the International Airports Authority of India constituted under Section 3 of the International Airports Authority of India Act. 1971, or

(xiv) a Regional Rural Bank established under Section 3 of the Regional Rural Banks Act, 1976, or

(xv) the Export Credit and Guarantee Corporation Limited, or

(xvi) the Industrial Reconstruction Bank of India, or

(xvii) the Banking Service Commission established under Section 3 of the Banking Service Commission Act, 1975, or

(xviii) a banking or an insurance company, or

(xix) a mine, an oilfield, a Cantonment Board, or a major port.

In relation to any other industrial dispute, the 'appropriate Government' means the State Government. In case of a Union Territory, there is no difference between the State Government and the Central

Government [National Bldgs. Construction Corpn. Ltd., New Delhi *Vs*. M.K. Jain, (1981) Lab. I.C. 62].

2. Average Pay [Section 2 (aaa)]. It means the average of the wages payable to a workman :

(i) in the case of a monthly paid workman, in the 3 complete calendar months,

(ii) in the case of a weekly paid workman, in the 4 complete weeks and

(iii) in the case of a daily paid workman, in the 12 full working days.

This period of 3 months, 4 weeks and 12 working days must precede the date on which the average pay becomes payable to the workman, provided he had worked during this period as the case may be. Where such calculation cannot be made. The average pay shall be calculated as the average of the wages payable to the workman during the period he actually worked.

3. Award [Section 2 (b)]. It means an interim or a final determination of any industrial dispute or of any question relating thereto by any Labour Court, Industrial Tribunal or National Tribunal. It also includes an arbitration award made under Section 10-A.

4. Board [Section 2 (c)]. 'Board' means a Board of Conciliation constituted under the Act.

5. Closure [Section 2 (cc)]. It means the permanent closing down of a place of employment or part thereof.

6. Conciliation Officer [Section 2 (d)]. 'Conciliation officer' means a conciliation officer appointed under the Act.

7. Conciliation Proceeding [Section 2 (e)]. It means any proceeding held by a conciliation officer or Board of Conciliation under the Act.

8. Controlled Industry [Section 2 (ee)]. It means any industry the control of which by the Union has been declared by any Central Act to be expedient in the public interest.

9. Court [Section 2 (f)]. It means a Court of Inquiry constituted under the Act.

10. Employer [Section 2 (g)]. 'Employer' in relation to an industry carried on by or under the authority of any department of the Central Government or a State Government means the authority prescribed in this behalf. Where no authority is prescribed, the 'employer' means the head of the department carrying on the industry. But in relation to an industry carried on by or on behalf of a local authority, 'employer' means the chief executive officer of the authority.

This definition of 'employer' is neither exhaustive nor conclusive. It extends to all industrial undertakings and not merely to those run by Governments or local authorities [Bombay Province *Vs*. Western India Automobile Assn., A.I.R (1949) Bom. 1411.

In Sholapur Spg. & Wvg. Co. *Vs*. Maruf, (1058) 2 L.L.J. 123, it was held that the term 'employee includes, among others, an agent of an employer, general manager, director and occupier of a mill.

11. Executive and Office Bearer in Relation to a Trade Union [Section 2 (gg) and Section 2 (lll)]. 'Executive' in relation to a Trade Union means the body, by whatever name called. To which the management of the affairs of the Trade Union is entrusted [Section 2 (gg)].'Office bearer', in relation to a Trade Union, includes any member of the executive thereof, but does not include an auditor [Section, 2(lll)].

12. Independent Person [Section 2 (4)]. A person shall be deemed to be 'independent' for the purpose of his appointment as the Chairman or other member of Board of Conciliation, Court of Inquiry or Industrial Tribunal if he is unconnected with the industrial dispute referred to such Board of Conciliation, Court of Inquiry or Industrial Tribunal or with any industry directly affected by such dispute. No person shall cease to be independent by reason only of the fact that he is a shareholder of an incorporated company which is connected with, or likely to be affected by, such industrial dispute; but in such a case, he shall disclose to the appropriate Government the nature and extent of the shares held by him in such company.

13. Industrial Establishment or Undertaking [Section 2 (ka)]. It means an establishment or undertaking in which industry is carried on. Sometimes several activities may be carried on in an establishment or undertaking and only one or some of such activities is or are an industry or industries.

(i) in such a case if any unit of such establishment or undertaking carrying on any activity, being an industry, is severable from the other unit or units of such establishment or undertaking, such unit shall be deemed to be a separate industrial establishment or undertaking.

(ii) If the predominant activity or each of the predominant activities carried on in such establishment or undertaking or any unit thereof is an industry and the other activity or each of the other activities carried on in such establishment or undertaking or unit thereof is not *severable* from and is, for the purpose of carrying on, or aiding the carrying on of, such predominant activity or activities, the entire establishment or undertaking or, as the cage may be, unit thereof shall be deemed to be an industrial establishment or undertaking.

14. Labour Court (Section. 2 (kkb)]. It means a Labour Court constituted under Section 7.

15. Lay-off [Section 2(kkk). (i) *Causes*. 'Lay-off' means the failure, refusal or inability of an employer to give employment to a workman (a) whose name is borne on the muster-rolls of his industrial establishment, and (b) who has not been retrenched. The failure, refusal, or Inability to give employment may be due to :

(a) shortage of coal, power or raw materials, or

(b) the accumulation of stocks, or

(c) the breakdown of machinery, or

(d) natural calamity or for any other connected reasons.

(i) *Essentials of lay off* : (a) There must be failure or refusal or inability of the employer to continue employees in his employment.

(b) The employees laid off must be on the muster-rolls of the establishment on the day of lay-off.

(c) The failure, refusal or inability to give employment may be due to shortage of raw materials or accumulation of stocks or breakdown of machinery or natural calamity or some other reason.

(d) The employees must not have been retrenched.

16. Lock-out [Section 2 (i)]. (i) *Meaning* : It means the temporary closing of a place of employment, or the suspension of work, or the refusal by an employer to continue to employ any number of persons employed by him. The word 'temporary' was added to the definition by the Amendment Act of 1982.

(ii) *Essentials of a Lock-out* : (a) There is a temporary closing of the place of employment, or suspension or withholding of the work by the employer in some form.

(b) 'Mere is an element of demands for which the place of employment is locked-out or closed.

(c) There is an intention to re-employ the workers if they accept the demands.

(iii) *Lock-out is Employer's Weapon* : In Kairbetta Estate *Vs*. Rajamanickam, A.I.R. (1960) S.C. 893, the Supreme Court observed :

"Lock-out can be described as the antithesis of a strike. Just as a strike is a weapon available to the employees for enforcing their industrial demands, a lock-out is a weapon available to the employer to persuade by a coercive process the employees to see his point of view to accept his demands."

In a tussle between employees and an employer whereas 'strike' is the weapon of the employees, 'lock-out' is the corresponding weapon in the armoury of the employer. If the employer shuts down his place of business as a means of reprisal or as an instrument of coercion or as a mode of exerting pressure on the employees, or, generally speaking, when his act is what may be called an act of belligerency, there would be a lock-out [Sri Ramachandran Spg. Mills *Vs.* State of Madras, A.I.R. (1956) Mad. 2411.

(iv) *Difference between Lock-out and Lay-offs* : (a) Under lock-out the employer refuses to give employment because of closing of a place of employment or suspension of work. Under lay-off the employer refuses to give employment because of shortage of coal, power or raw materials or the accumulation of stocks or the breakdown of machinery or natural calamity or for any other reason to give employment.

(b) Lock-out is resorted to by the employer to coerce or pressurise the workmen to accept his demands; lay-off is for trade reasons beyond the control of the employer.

(c) Lock-out is due to an industrial dispute and continues during the period of dispute . Lay-off is not concerned with a dispute with the workmen.

(v) *Difference between Lock-out and Closure* : Lock-out and closure of a business are often confused. This is because cessation of work is common to both.

(a) Closure is a fundamental right and if it is not a lock-out, the workers cannot grudge [J.K. Hosiery Factory *Vs.* Labour Appellate Tribunal, A.I.R (1956) All. 498]. The State cannot compel an employer to carry on his business because several employees may be thrown out of employment if it is closed. The grounds for closure of a business may be actual loss or apprehended loss. It may also be disinclination to run the risk of running the business [Indian Metal & Metallurgical Corpn. *Vs.* Industrial Tribunal, Madras, 3 F. J.R. 420, High Court, Madras]. The Points of difference between a lock-out and closure are as follows :

(b) In the case of lock-out it is only the place of business which is closed (and not the business itself), while in the case of closure of a business not only the place of business but the business itself is closed [Express Newspapers (Pvt.) Ltd. *Vs.* Their Workmen, A.I.R. (1963) S.C. 569]. The closure of a business indicates the final and irrevocable termination of the business itself. Lock-out, on the other hand, indicates the closure of the place of business or the place of employment and not the closure of the business itself.

(c) Lock-out is a weapon of coercion in the hands of employer; closure is generally for trade reasons.

(d) In closure there is severance of employment relationship whereas in lock-out there is no severance but only suspension of such relationship.

(e) A lock-out is caused by the existence or apprehension of an industrial dispute whereas a closure need not be in consequence of an industrial dispute.

17. National Tribunal [Section. 2 (ll)]. It means a National Industrial tribunal constituted under Section 7-B.

18. Public Utility Service [Section 2(n)]. It means :

(i) any railway service or any transport service for the carriage of passengers or goods by air;

(ii) any service in, or in connection with the working of any major port or dock;

(iii) any section of an industrial establishment, on the working of which the safety of the establishment or the workmen employed therein depends;

(iv) any postal, telegraph, or telephone service;

(v) any industry which supplies power, light or water to the public;

(vi) any system of public conservancy or sanitation;

(vii) any industry specified in the First Schedule.

The appropriate Government may, if satisfied that public emergency or interest so requires, by notiftcation in the Official Gazette, declare any industry specified in the First Schedule to be a public utility service for the purposes of the industrial disputes Act for such period as may be specified in the notification. The period so specified shall not, in the first instance, exceed 6 months. But it may, by a like notification, be extended from time to time by any period not exceeding 6 months at any time if in the opinion of the appropriate Government, public emergency or public interest requires such extension. The First Schedule is reproduced below.

THE FIRST SCHEDULE

[See Section 2 (n) (vi)]

Industries which may be declared to be Public Utility Services under Section 2(n)(vi)

1. Transport (other than railways) for the carriage of passengers or goods by land or water.

2. Banking.
3. Cement.
4. Coal.
5. Cotton textiles.
6. Foodstuffs.
7. Iron and steel.
8. Defence establishments.
9. Service in hospitals and dispensaries.
10. Fire Brigade Service.
11. India Government Mints.
12. India Security Press.
13. Copper mining.
14. Lead mining.
15. Zinc mining.
16. Iron ore mining.
17. Service in any oilfield.
18. Service in uranium industry.
19. Pyrites mining industry.
20. Security Paper Mill, Hoshangabad
21. Service in Bank Note Press, Dewas
22. Phosphorite mining.
23. Magnesite mining.
24. Currency Note Press.
25. Manufacture or production of mineral oil (crude oil), motor and aviation spirit, diesel oil, Kerosene oil, fuel oil, diverse hydrocarbon oils and their blends including synthethic fuels, lubricating oils and the like.
26. Service in the International Airports Aurthority of India.

19. Retrenchment [Section 2(oo)]. (i) *Meaning* : It means "to end, conclude, or cease". The term as used in the Industrial Disputes Act means the termination by the employer of the service of a workman for any reason whatsoever, otherwise than as punishment inflicted by way of disciplinary action [Ramachandra Vittuji Kothare *Vs*. Industrial Court, Nagpur, (1985) Lab. I.C. 1787 (Bomb.)].

(ii) 'Retrenchment' does not include :

(a) voluntary retirement of the workman; or

(b) retirement of the workman on reaching the age of superannuation if the contract of employment between the employer and the workman concerned contains a stipulation in that behalf; or

(c) termination of the service of the workman as a result of the non-renewal of the contract of employment between the employer and the workman concerned on its expiry or of such contract being terminated under a stipulation in that behalf contained therein; or

(d) termination of the service of a workman on the ground of continued ill health.

(iii) *Difference between Retrenchment and Closure* : The important points of difference between 'retrenchment' and 'closure' may be enumerated as follows :

(a) Retrenchment is the termination by the employer of the service of a workman for any reason whatsoever, otherwise than as punishment inflicted by way of disciplinary action. It affects only some of the workmen. Closure, on the other hand, means closing down of the business for trade reasons and it affects all the workmen.

(b) In case of retrenchment the services of workmen are terminated on account of surplus labour while in case of closure it is on account of total closure of work by an employer.

(c) In retrenchment the trade or business remains uninterrupted as it continues; while in closure the business itself is discontinued.

(d) The compensation payable to a workman on retrenchment either an account of surplus labour or closure, shall be equivalent to 15 days' average pay for every completed year of continuous service or any part thereof in excess of 6 months. Retrenchment as a result of *bona fide* closure of business does not entail any compensation beyond average pay for 3 months.

(iv) *Difference between Lock-out and Retrenchment* : (a) Lock-out is temporary retrenchment is permanent. Retrenchment results in complete severance of industrial relationship between an employer and an employee while lock-out keeps this relationship alive even during the cessation of work. The former results in severance of relationship between the employer and the employee while the latter amounts to only suspension of this relationship.

(b) Lock-out is with a motive to coerce the workmen to accept the demands of the employer; retrenchment is resorted to dispense with surplus labour.

(c) Lock-out is due to and during an industrial dispute , there is no such dispute in case of retrenchment.

20. Settlement [Section 2(p)]. It means :

(i) a settlement arrived at in the course of conciliation proceedings (which may be held by a Conciliation Officer or Board of Conciliation), and includes

(ii) a written agreement between the employer and workmen arrived at otherwise than in the course of conciliation proceeding where such agreement has been signed by the parties thereto in such manner as may be prescribed and a copy thereof has been sent to an officer authorized in this behalf by the appropriate Government and the Conciliation Officer.

21. Strike [Section 2(q)]. It means -

(i) a cessation of work by a body of persons employed in any industry acting in combination, or

(ii) a concerted refusal of any number of persons who are or have been so employed to continue to work or to accept employment, or

(iii) refusal under a common understanding of any number of such persons to continue to work or to accept employment.

22. Trade Union [Section 2(qq)]. It means a Trade Union registered under the Trade Unions Act, 1926.

23. Tribunal (Section 2(r)]. It means an Industrial Tribunal constituted under Section 7-A and includes an Industrial Tribunal constituted before the 10th day of March, 1957 under this Act.

24. Unfair Labour Practice [Section 2 (ra)]. It means any of the practices specified in the Fifth Schedule (introduced by the Amendment Act of 1982) which declares certain labour practices as unfair on the part of employers and their Trade Unions and on the part of workmen and their Trade Unions. The Amendment Act of 1982 prohibits commission of any unfair labour practice by employers and workmen (Section 25-T as introduced by the Amendment Act of 1982). The person committing any unfair labour practice is punishable with imprisonment up to 6 months and fine up to Rs. 1.000 or with both (Section 25-U as introduced by the Amendment Act of 1982). The Fifth Schedule to the Act is reproduced below :

THE FIFTH SCHEDULE
(See Section 2(ra)]

Unfair Labour Practices

I. On the part of Employers and Trade Unions of Employers

1. To interfere with, restrain from, or coerce, workmen in the exercise of their right to organise, form, join or assist a Trade Union or to engage in concerted activities for the purposes of collective bargaining or other mutual aid or protection, that is to say :

(a) threatening workmen with discharge or dismissal, if they join a Trade Union;

(b) threatening a lock-out or closure, if a Trade Union is organised;

(c) granting wage increase to workmen at crucial periods of Trade Union organization, with a view to undermining the efforts of the Trade Union at organlsation.

2. To dominate, interfere with or contribute support, financial or otherwise, to and Trade Union, that is to say :

(a) an employer taking an active interest In organisms a Trade Union of his workmen and

(b) an employer showing partiality or granting favour to one of several Trade Unions attempting to organise his workmen or to Its members, where such a Trade Union is not a recognised Trade Union.

3. To establish employer-sponsored Trade Unions of workmen.

4. To encourage or discourage membership in any Trade Union by discriminating against any workman, that is to say :

(a) discharging or punishing a workman, because he urged other workmen to join or organise a Trade Union;

(b) discharging or dismissing a workman for taking part in any strike (not being a strike which is deemed to be an illegal strike under this Act);

(c) changing seniority rating of workmen because of Trade Union activities;

(d) refusing to promote workmen to higher posts on account of their Trade Union activities;

(e) giving unmerited promotions to certain workmen with a view to creating discord amongst other workmen, or to undermine the strength of their Trade Union;

(f) discharging office-bearers or active members of the Trade union on account of their Trade Union activities.

5. To discharge or dismiss workmen :

(a) by way of victimisation;

(b) not in good faith, but in the colourable exercise of the employer's rights;

(c) by falsely implicating a workman in a criminal case on false evidence or on concocted evidence;

(d) for patently false reasons;

(e) on untrue or trumped up allegations of absence without leave;

(f) in utter disregard of the principles of natural justice in the conduct of domestic inquiry or with undue haste;

(g) for misconduct of a minor or technical character, without having any regard to the nature of the particular misconduct or the past record or service of the workman, thereby leading to a disproportionate punishment.

6. To abolish the work of a regular nature being done by workmen, and to give such work to contractors as a measure of breaking a strike.

7. To transfer a workman *mala fide* from one place to another, under the guise of following management policy.

8. To insist upon Individual workmen, who are on a legal strike to sign a good conduct bond, as a pre-condition to allowing them to resume work.

9. To show favouritism or partiality to one set of workers regardless of merit.

10. To employ workmen as '*badlis*', casuals or temporaries and to continue them as such for years with the object of depriving them of the status and privileges of permanent workmen.

11. To discharge or discriminate against any workman for filing charges or testifying against an employer in any inquiry or proceeding relating to any industrial dispute.

12. To recruit workmen during a strike which is not an illegal strike.

13. Failure to implement award, settlement or agreement.

14. To indulge in acts of force or violence.

15. To refuse to bargain collectively, in good faith with the recognised Trade Unions.

16. Proposing or continuing a lock-out deemed to be illegal under this Act.

II. On the Part of Workmen and Trade Unions of Workmen

1. To advise or actively support or instigate any strike deemed be illegal under this act.

2. To coerce workmen in the exercise of their right to self-organisation or to join a Trade Union or refrain from joining any Trade Union, that is to say :

(a) for a Trade Union or its members to picketing in such a manner that non-striking workmen are physically debarred from entering the work places;

(b) to indulge in acts of force or violence or to hold out threats of intimidation in connection with a strike against non-striking workmen or against managerial staff.

3. For a recognised union to refuse to bargain collectively in good faith with the employer.

4. To indulge in coercive activities against certification of a bargaining representative.

5. To stage, encourage or instigate such forms of coercive actions as wilful 'go show', squatting on the work premises after working hours or 'gherao' of any of the members of the managerial or other staff.

6. To stage demonstrations at the residences of the employers or the managerial staff members.

7. To incite or indulge in wilful damage to employer's property connected with the industry.

8. To indulge in acts of force or violence or to hold out threats of intimidation against any workman with a view to prevent him from attending work.

The following have been held to be unfair labour practices :

(a) The termination of the service of a daily wage labourer on his passing matriculation examination, where the terms and conditions of appointment contained no such stipulation. This is an unfair trade practice by way of victimisation [H.D. Singh *Vs*. Reserve Bank of India, (1985) 4 S.C.C. 2011.

(b) Offering work on rotation basis to-workmen treating them as *badli* workers and continuing them as such for years together (H.D.Singh *Vs*. Reserve Bank of India, *supra*).

(c) Issuance of repeated orders of appointment and termination with a view to bypass the provisions of Section 25-B (which defines continuous service) [Ferozpur Central Co-op. Bank *Vs*. Labour Court, (1986) 1 L.L.N. 20 (P. & H.)].

25. Wages [Section 2 (rr)]. (i) *Meaning* : 'Wages' means all remuneration capable of being expressed in terms of money, which would, if the terms of employment, express or implied, were fulfilled, be payable to a workman in respect of his employment or of work done in such employment.

(ii) *What is included in Wages*? :

(a) such allowances (including dearness allowance) as the workman is for the time being entitled to;

(b) the value of any house accommodation, or of supply of light, water, medical attendance or other amenity or of any service or of any concessionsal supply of foodgrains or other articles;

(c) any travelling concession;

(d) any commission payable on the promotion of sales or business or both. This Clause has been added by the Amendment Act of 1982.

(iii) *What is not included in wages?* :

(a) any bonus;

(b) any contribution paid or payable by the employer to any pension fund or provident fund or for the benefit of the workmen under any law for the time being in force;

(c) any gratuity payable on the termination of his service.

26. Workman [Section 2 (s)]. (i) *Meaning* : 'Workman' means any person (including an apprentice) employed in any industry to do any manual, unskilled, skilled, technical operational, clerical or supervisory work for hire or reward. His terms of employment may be express or implied. For the purposes of any proceeding under this Act in relation to an industrial dispute, 'workman' includes any person who has been dismissed, discharged or retrenched in connection with, or as a consequence of, that dispute, or whose dismissal, discharge or retrenchment has led to that dispute.

(ii) *Persons who are not Workmen* : 'Workman' does not include any such person —

(a) who is subject to the Air Force Act. 1950, or the Army Act, 1950, or the Navy Act, 1957; or

(b) who is employed in the police service or as an officer or other employee of a prison; or

(c) who is employed mainly in a managerial or administrative capacity; or

(d) who being employed in a supervisory capacity, draws wages exceeding Rs. 1,600 per mensem (the limit has been 'raised from Rs. 500 to Rs. 1,600 by the Amendment Act of 1982) or exercises, either by the nature of the duties attached to the office or by reason of the powers vested in him, functions mainly of a managerial nature.

REFERENCE OF CERTAIN INDIVIDUAL DISPUTES TO GRIEVANCE SETTLEMENT AUTHORITIES

(Chapter 11-B. Section 9-C as introduced by the Amendment Act of 1982)

The employer in relation to every industrial establishment in which 50 or more workmen are employed or have been employed on any day in the preceding 12 months shall provide for a Grievance Settlement Authority for the settlement of industrial disputes connected with an individual workman employed in the establishment. The provision of such a Grievance Settlement Authority shall be in accordance with the rules made in that behalf under the Act [Section 9-C(1)].

Where an industrial dispute connected with an individual workman arises in an establishment referred to above. A workman or any Trade Union of workmen of which such workman is a member may refer such dispute to the Grievance Settlement Authority for settlement [Section 9-C (2)]. The Grievance Settlement Authority shall follow such procedure and complete its proceedings within such period as may be prescribed [Section 9-C(3)].

Section 9-C specifically provides that no reference shall be made under Chapter III (which deals with reference of disputes to Boards of Conciliation, Courts of Inquiry or Industrial Tribunals) with respect to any dispute referred to above unless :

(a) such dispute has been referred to the Grievance Settlement Authority concerned and

(b) the decision of the Grievance Settlement Authority is not acceptable to any of the parks to the dispute [Section 9-C (4)].

PROCEDURE FOR SETTLEMENT OF INDUSTRIAL DISPUTES AND AUTHORITIES UNDER THE ACT

(Chapter 11, Sections 3 to 9)

The Industrial disputes Act intends, by making various provisions, the prevention and settlement of industrial disputes. The Act, in Its Preamble, has also emphasized this point by saying that the Act is 'for the investigation and settlement of industrial disputes'.

'Me Act provides an elaborate and effective machinery for bringing about industrial peace by setting up various authorities for the investigation and settlement of industrial disputes. These authorities are :

1. Works Committees (Section 3).
2. Conciliation Officers (Section 4).
3. Boards of Conciliation (Section 5).
4. Courts of Inquiry (Section 6).
5. Labour Courts (Section 7).
6. Industrial Tribunals (Section 7-A).
7. National Tribunals (Section 7-B).

The Act provides for the following modes of settlement of disputes under the Act :

1. Voluntary settlement and conciliation,
2. Adjudication and
3. Arbitration.

Conciliation. The authorities that make use of conciliation as a method of settlement of industrial disputes are :

1. Works Committees,

The Act encourages voluntary settlement of disputes through the Works Committees whose object is to remove causes of friction between the employers and workmen in the day-to-day working of establishments and to promote measures for securing amity and good relations between them.

Industrial peace will be most enduring where it is founded on voluntary settlement.

2. Conciliation Officers,

3. Boards of Conciliation and

4. Courts of Inquiry which may be constituted for inquiring into any matter appearing to be connected with or relevant to an Industrial dispute.

Adjudication. The aforesaid authorities endeavour to compose any industrial difference of opinion or settle the industrial dispute before it may be adjudicated upon by :

1. Labour Courts,
2. Industrial Tribunals and
3. National Tribunal.

Voluntary Reference. Section 10-A makes provision for voluntary reference of disputes to arbitration.

The various authorities which constitute the machinery for the prevention and settlement of industrial disputes are discussed below :

CONCILIATION MACHINERY

Works Committees, Conciliation Officers, Boards of Conciliation, and Courts of Inquiry constitute the conciliation machinery for settlement of industrial disputes. They can only promote settlement of industrial disputes or inquire into them but cannot make any awards which are binding on the parties.

1. Works Committees (Section 3)

In the case of any industrial establishment in which 100 or more workmen are employed or have been employed on any day in the preceding 12 months, the appropriate Government may, by general or special order, require the employer to constitute a Works Committee. The Committee shall consist of representatives of employers and workmen engaged in the establishment. The number of representatives of workmen on the Committee shall not be less than the number of representatives of the, employer. 'The representatives of the workmen shall be chosen in the prescribed manner from among the workmen engaged in the establishment and in consultation with their Trade Union, if any, registered under the Trade Unions Act, 1926 [Section 3 (1)].

Powers and Duties. It shall be the duty of the Works Committee to :

(i) promote measures for securing and preserving amity and good-relations between the employers and workmen and, to that end,

(ii) comment upon matters of their common interest or concern and

(iii) endeavour to compose any material difference of opinion in respect of such matters [Section 3 (2)]. These matters are so wide-ranging as to include welfare of workers, supervision of recreational facilities and creches and hospitals, their training, wages, hours of work, bonus, gratuity, holidays with pay, and working conditions including discipline, promotions, and transfers, etc.

2. Conciliation Officers (Section 4)

The appropriate Government may, by notification in the Official Gazette, appoint such number of persons as it thinks fit to be Conciliation Officers. The duty of the Conciliation Officers shall be to mediate in and promote the settlement of industrial disputes [Section 4 (1)].

1. Appointment. A Conciliation Officer may be appointed for a specified area or for specified industries in a specified area or for one or more specified industries He may be appointed either permanently or for a limited period [Section 4 (2)]. He shall be deemed to be a public servant within the meaning of Section 21 of the Indian Penal Code, 1860 [Section 11 (6)].

2. Duties (Section 12). (a) *To hold Conciliation Proceedings* : Where any industrial dispute exists or is apprehended, the Conciliation Officer may hold conciliation proceedings. Where the dispute relates to a public utility service and a notice under Section 22 has been given, he shall hold conciliation proceedings in the prescribed manner [Section 12 (1)].

(b) *To investigate the Dispute* : The Conciliation Officer shall, for the purpose of bringing about a settlement of the dispute, without delay. Investigate the dispute and all matters affecting the merits and the right settlement thereof. He may do all such things as he thinks fit for the purpose of inducing the parties to come to a fair and amicable settlement of the dispute [Section 12 (2)). But he has no authority to make a final decision.

(c) *To send a Report and Memorandum of Settlement to Appropriate Government* : If a settlement of the dispute is arrived at in the course of the conciliation proceedings, the Conciliation Officer shall send a report thereof to the appropriate Government or an officer authorised in this behalf by the appropriate Government. He shall also send a memorandum of the settlement signed by the parties to the dispute to the appropriate Government [Section 12 (3)].

(d) *To send a full Report to the Appropriate Government setting forth the Steps taken by Him in Case no Settlement is arrived at* : If no such settlement is arrived at, the Conciliation Officer shall as soon as after the close of the investigation, send to the appropriate Government a full report setting forth the steps taken by him for ascertaining the facts and circumstances relating to the dispute and for bringing about a settlement thereof The report shall be accompanied with a full statement of such facts and circumstances, and the reasons on account of which, in his opinion, a settlement could not be arrived at [Section 12 (4)].

Time for the Submission of the Report : The report by the Conciliation Officer shall be submitted within 14 days of the commencement of the conciliation proceedings or within such shorter period as may be fixed by the appropriate Government [Section 12 (6)].

Further Reference by the Appropriate Government : *if no reference is made, reasons to be communicated to the parties.* If, on a consideration of the report referred to in Section 12 (4). The appropriate Government is satisfied that there is a case for reference to a Board of Conciliation, Labour Court, Industrial Tribunal or National Tribunal, it may make such reference. Where the appropriate Government does not make such a reference, it shall record and communicate to the parties concerned its reasons therefor [Section 12 (5)].

3. Powers. (a) *Power to enter Premises* : A Conciliation Officer may for the purpose of inquiry into any existing or apprehended industrial dispute, after giving reasonable notice, enter the premises occupied by the establishment to which the dispute relates [Section 11 (2)].

(b) *Power to call for and inspect Documents* : He may call for and inspect if any document which he has ground for considering to be relevant to the industrial dispute or to be necessary for the purpose of verifying the implementation of any award or carrying out any other duty imposed on him under the Act. For these purposes, he shall have the same powers as are vested in a Civil Court under the Code of Civil Procedure, 1908 in aspect of compelling the production of documents [Section 11(4)].

3. Boards of Conciliation (Section 5)

1. Appointment and Constitution. The appropriate Government may as occasion arises, by notification in the Official Gazette constitute, a Board of Conciliation (hereinafter called the Board) for promoting the settlement of an industrial dispute [Section 5 (1)].

The Board shall consist of a chairman and 2 or 4 other members, as the appropriate Government thinks fit [Section 5 (2)]. The chairman shall be an independent person [For the definition of 'independent person'. Refer to Section 2(i)]. The other members shall be persons appointed in equal number to represent the parties to the dispute. A person appointed to represent a party shall be appointed on the recommendation of that party [Section 5 (3)]. But if any party fails to make a recommendation within the prescribed period, the appropriate Government shall appoint such persons as it thinks fit to represent that party [Proviso to Section 5 (3)].

A Board, having the prescribed quorum, may act, notwithstanding the absence of the chairman or any of its members or any vacancy in its number [Section 5 (4)]. But if the appropriate Government notifies the Board that the services of the chairman or any other member have ceased to be available, the Board shall not act until a new chairman or member, as the case may be, has been appointed [Proviso to Section 5 (4)].

2. Reference of Dispute. Where the appropriate Government is of opinion that any industrial dispute exists or is apprehended, it may at any time, by order in writing, refer the dispute to a Board of Conciliation for promoting a settlement thereof [Section 10(1)(a)].

Where the parties to an industrial dispute apply in the prescribed manner, whether jointly or separately, for a reference of the dispute to a Board, the appropriate Government, if satisfied that the persons applying represent the majority of each party, shall make the reference Accordingly [Section 10 (2)].

3. Prohibition of Strike or Lock-out. Where an industrial dispute has been referred to a Board under Section 10, the appropriate Government may by order prohibit the continuance of any strike or lock-out in connection with such dispute which may be in distance on the date of the reference [Section 10 (3)].

4. Duties (Section 13). (a) *To bring about a Settlement of the Dispute* : Where a dispute has been referred to a Board of Conciliation, it shall be the duty of the Board to endeavour to bring about a settlement of the same. It shall, without delay, investigate the dispute and all matters affecting the merits and the right settlement thereof. It may also do all such things as it thinks fit for the purpose of inducing the parties to come to a fair and amicable settlement of the dispute [Section 13 (1)].

(b) *To send a Report and Memorandum of Settlement to the Appropriate Government* : If a settlement of the dispute is arrived in the course of conciliation proceedings, the Board shall send a report thereof to the appropriate Government together with a memorandum of the settlement, signed by the parties to the dispute [Section 13 (2)).

(c) *To send a Full Report to the Appropriate Government setting forth the Steps taken by the Board in Case no Settlement is arrived at* : If no such settlement is arrived at, the Board shall, as soon as practicable after the close of the investigation, send to the appropriate Government a full report setting forth the proceedings and steps taken by the Board for, ascertaining the facts and the circumstances relating to the dispute and for bringing about a settlement thereof. The report shall be accompanied with a full statement of such facts and circumstances, its findings thereon, the reasons on account of which, in its opinion, a settlement could not be arrived at and its recommendations for the determination of the dispute [Section 13 (3)].

(d) *To communicate Reasons to the Parties if no Further Reference made* : If on the receipt of a report in respect of a dispute relating to a public utility service, the appropriate Government does not make a reference to a Labour Court, Industrial Tribunal or National Tribunal under Section 10, it shall record and communicate to the parties concerned its reasons therefor [Section 13 (4)].

(e) *To Submit Report within 2 Months* : The Board shall submit its report within 2 months of the date on which the dispute was referred to it or within such shorter period as may be fixed by the appropriate Government [Section 13 (5)]. The appropriate Government may, from time to time, extend the time for the submission of the report by such further periods not exceeding 2 months in the aggregate. The time for the submission of the report may also be extended by, such period as may be agreed on in writing by all the parties to the dispute.

(f) *Report of the Board to be in Writing and to be signed and its Publication* : The report of the Board shall be in writing and shall be signed by all the members of the Board. A member of the Board may record any minute of dissent from a report together with the minute of dissent recorded therewith shall be published by the appropriate Government within 30 days from the receipt thereof [Section 17(1)].

The duty of a Court is to abide by the principle of fairplay and justice [Hindustan Steel Ltd. *Vs*. State of Orissa, A.I.R. (1968) Ori. 345].

5. Powers. (i) *Power to enter Premises* : A member of a Court may for the purpose of inquiry into an existing or apprehended industrial dispute, after giving reasonable notice, enter the premises occupied by any establishment to which the dispute relates [Section 11 (2)].

(ii) *Powers of Civil Court* : A Court shall have the same powers as are vested in a Civil Court under the Code of Civil Procedure 1908, when trying a suit in respect of the following matters, namely :

(a) enforcing the attendance of any person and examining him on oath;

(b) compelling the production of documents and material objects;

(c) issuing commissions for the examination of witnesses;

(d) in respect of such other matters as may be prescribed.

Every inquiry or investigation by a Court shall be deemed to be a judicial proceeding within the meaning of Sections 193 and 228 of the Indian Penal Code, 1860 [Section 11(3)].

A Court may, if it so thinks fit, appoint one or more persons having special knowledge of the matter under consideration as assessor or assessors to advise it in the proceeding before it [Section 11(5)].

ADJUDICATION MACHINERY

Sections 7 to 9 pertain to the constitution of adjudication authorities under the Act. These authorities are :

1. Labour Courts (Section 7)

Appointment and constitution. The appropriate Government may, by notification in the Official Gazette, constitute one or more Labour Courts for adjudication of industrial disputes relating to any matters specified in the Second Schedule (reproduced below). These Courts shall also perform such other functions as may be assigned to them [Section 7 (1)].

THE SECOND SCHEDULE
(See Section 7)

1. LABOUR COURTS

A. Matters within the Jurisdiction of Labour Courts

1. The propriety or legality of an order passed by an employer under the standing orders;

2. The application and interpretation of standing orders;

3. Discharge or dismissal of workmen including reinstatement or grant of relief to workmen wrongfully dismissed;

4. Withdrawal of any customary concession or privilege;

5. Illegality or otherwise of a strike or lock-out and

6. All matters other than those specified in the Third Schedule.

A Labour Court shall consist of one person only to be appointed by the appropriate Government [Section 7 (2)].

B. Rules about Labour Court

2. Qualifications. A person shall not be qualified for appointment as the presiding officer of a Labour Court, unless :

(i) he is, or has been a Judge of a High Court, or

(ii) he has, for a period of not less than 3 years, been a District Judge or an Additional District Judge; or

(iii) he has held any judicial office in India for not less than 7 years; or

(iv) he has been the presiding officer of a Labour Court constituted under any Provincial Act for not less than 5 years [Section 7 (3)].

The presiding officer of a Labour Court shall be deemed to he a public servant within the meaning of Section 21 of the Indian Penal Code, 1860 [Section 11 (6)].

2. Disqualifications. Section 7-C provides that no person shall be appointed to, or continue in, the office of the presiding officer of a Labour Court, if (a) he is not an independent person; or (b) he has attained the age of 65 years.

3. Reference of Disputes. Where the appropriate Government is of opinion that any industrial dispute exists or is apprehended, it may at any time, by order in writing, refer the dispute or any matter appearing to be connected with or relevant to, the dispute to a Labour Court for adjudication. The matter must however relate to any matter specified in the Second Schedule [Section 10 (1) (c)]. Where the dispute relates to any matter specified in the Third Schedule and is not likely to affect more than 100 workmen, the appropriate Government may, if it so thinks fit, make the reference to a Labour Court [Proviso 1 to Section 10 (1)].

Subject to any rules that may be made in this behalf, a Labour Court shall follow such procedure as it may think fit [Section 11(1)].

4. Duties. (i) *To adjudicate upon Industrial Disputes relating to Matters Specified in the Second Schedule* : It is the duty of a Labour Court to adjudicate upon the industrial disputes relating to any matter specified in the Second Schedule and to perform such other functions assigned to fit [Section 7 (1)].

(ii) *To give Award within the Specified Period* : Where an industrial dispute has been referred to a Labour Court for adjudication, it shall hold its proceedings expeditiously and shall, within the period specified in the order referring such industrial dispute, submit its award to the appropriate Government (Section 15). The period may be extended under proviso 2 to Section 10 (2-A).

(iii) Award to be in writing and signed and its publication. The award of a Labor Court shall be in writing and shall be signed by its presiding officer [Section 16 (2)]. It shall, within a period of 30 days from the date of its receipt by the appropriate Government, be published in such manner as the appropriate Government thinks fit [Section 17 (1)].

4. Powers. (i) *Power to enter Premises* : The presiding officer of a Labour Court may for the purpose of inquiry into an existing or apprehended industrial dispute enter the premises occupied by any establishment to which the dispute relates. He must however give a prior reasonable notice [Section 11 (2)].

(ii) *Powers of Civil Court* : Labour Court shall have the same powers as are vested in a Civil Court under the Code of Civil Procedure 1908, when trying a suit in respect of the following matters, namely :

(a) enforcing the attendance of any person and examining him on oath;

(b) compelling the production of documents and material objects;

(c) issuing commissions for the examination of witnesses;

(d) in respect of such other matters as may be prescribed.

Every inquiry or investigation by a Labour Court shall be deemed to be a judicial proceeding within the meaning of Sections 193, and 228 of the Indian Penal Code, 1860 [Section 11 (3)].

When the parties to an industrial dispute apply in the prescribed manner, whether jointly or separatel, for a reference of the dispute to the Labour Court, the appropriate Government, if satisfied that the persons applying represent the majority of each party, shall make the reference accordingly [Section 10 (2)].

5. Prohibition of Strike or Lack-out. Where an industrial dispute has been referred to a Labour Court, the appropriate Government may by order prohibit the continuance of any strike or lock-out in connection with such dispute which may be in existence on the date of the reference [Section 10 (3)].

6. Jurisdiction. Where in an order referring an industrial dispute to a Labour Court under Section 10 or in a subsequent order, the appropriate Government has specified the points of dispute for adjudication, the Labour Court shall confine its jurisdiction to those points and matters incidental thereto [Section 10(4)].

7. Inclusion of Other Parties. (i) *Opinion of Appropriate Govt.* : Where a dispute concerning any establishment or establishments has been, or is to be, referred to a Labour Court, under Section 10, the appropriate Government may be of opinion, whether on an application made to it in this behalf or otherwise, that the dispute is of such a nature that any other establishment, group or class of establishments of a similar nature is likely to be interested in, or affected by, such dispute. In such a case, the appropriate Government may, at the time of making the reference or at any time thereafter but before the submission of the award, include in that reference such establishment, group or class of establishments, whether or not at the time of such inclusion any dispute exists or is apprehended in that establishment, group or class of establishments [Section 10 (5)].

(ii) *Costs of the Proceeding* : Subject to any rules made under this Act, the costs of, and incidental to any, proceeding before a Labour Court shall be in the discretion of the Labour Court. It shall have full power to determine by and to whom and to what extent and subject to what conditions, if any, such costs are to be paid. It shall also have the power to give all the necessary directions for the purposes aforesaid. These costs may, on application made to the appropriate Government by the person entitled, be recovered by that Government in the same manner as an arrear of land revenue [Section 11 (7)].

(iii) *Labour Court deemed to be a Civil Court* : Every Labour Court shall be deemed to be a Civil Court for the purposes of Sections 345, 346 and 348 of the Code of Criminal Procedure, 1973 [Section 11(8)].

2. INDUSTRIAL TRIBUNAL (Section 7-A)

Appointment and Constitution. The appropriate Government may, by notification in the Official Gazette, constitute one or more Industrial Tribunals (hereinafter called the Tribunal) for the adjudication of industrial disputes relating to any matter, whether specified in the Second Schedule or the Third Schedule (reproduced below) and for performing such other functions as may be assigned to them under this Art [Section 7-A (1)].

THE THIRD SCHEDULE
(See Section 7-A)

A. Matters within the Jurisdiction of Industrial Tribunal

1. Wages, including the period and mode of payment;

2. Compensatory and other allowances;

3. Hours of work and rest intervals;

4. Leave with wages and holidays;

5. Bonus, profit sharing, provident fund and gratuity;

6. Shift working otherwise than in accordance with standing orders;

7. Classification by grades;

8. Rules of discipline;

9. Rationalisation;

10. Retrenchment of workmen and closure of establishment;

11. Any other matter that may be prescribed.

The Tribunal shall consist of one person only, to be appointed by the appropriate Government [Section 7-A(2)].

B. Rules about Tribunal

1. Qualifications. A person shall not be qualified for appointment as the presiding officer of the Tribunal, unless :

(i) he is, or has been a Judge of a Hiigh Court; or

(ii) he has, for a period of not less than 3 years, been a District Judge or an Additional District Judge [Section 7-A(3)].

The presiding officer of a Tribunal shall be deemed to be a public servant within the meaning of Section 21 of the Indian Penal Code, 1860 [Section 11 (6)].

The appropriate Government may, if it so thinks fit, appoint 2 persons as assessors to advise the Tribunal in the proceedings before it [Section 7-A (4)1.

2. Disqualifications. No person shall be appointed to or continue in the office of the presiding officer of a Tribunal, if (a) he is not an independent person; or (b) he has attained the age of 65 years (Section 7-C).

3. Reference of Disputes. (i) *Govt. opinion* : Where the appropriate Government is of opinion that any industrial dispute exists or is apprehended, it may at any time, by order in writing, refer the dispute or any matter appearing to be connected with, or relevant to the dispute, whether it relates to any matter specified in the Second Schedule or the Third Schedule, to a Tribunal for adjudication (Section 10(l)(d)].

Where the parties to an industrial dispute apply in the prescribed manner, whether jointly or separately, for a reference of the dispute to a Tribunal, the appropriate Government, if satisfied that the persons applying represent the majority of each party, shall make the reference accordingly [Section 10 (2)].

(ii) *Procedure of Tribunal* : Subject to any rules that may be made in this in this behalf, a Tribunal shall follow such procedure as it may think fit [Section 11(1)].

4. Prohibition of Strike or Lock-out. Where an industrial dispute has been referred to a Tribunal, the appropriate Government may by order prohibit the continuance of any strike or lock-out in connection with such dispute which may be in distance on the date of the reference [Section 10 (3)].

5. Jurisdiction. Where in an order referring an industrial dispute to a Tribunal under Section 10, or in a subsequent order, the appropriate Government has specified the points of dispute for adjudication, the Tribunal shall confine its jurisdiction to those points and matters incidental thereto [Section 10 (4)].

6. Inclusion of Other Parties. Where a dispute concerning any establishment or establishments has been, or is to be, referred to a Tribunal under Section 10, the appropriate Government may be of opinion, whether on an application made to it in this behalf or otherwise, that the dispute is of such a nature that any other establishment, group or class of establishments of a similar nature is likely to be interested in, or affected by, such dispute. In such a case, the appropriate Government may, at the time of making the reference or at any time thereafter but before the submission of the award, include in that reference such establishment, group or class of establishments, whether or not at the time of such inclusion any dispute exists or is apprehended in that establishment, group or class of establishments [Section 10 (5)].

7. Duties. Where an industrial dispute has been referred to a Tribunal for adjudication, it shall hold its proceedings expeditiously and shall, within the period specified in the order referring such industrial dispute, submit its award to the appropriate Government (Section 15). The period may be extended under Proviso 2 to Section 10 (2-A).

Award to be in writing and signed and its Publication : The award of a Tribunal shall be in writing and shall be signed by its presiding officer [Section 16 (2)]. It shall, within a period of 30 days from the date of its receipt by the appropriate Government, be published in such manner as the appropriate Government may think fit [Section 17 (1)].

8. Powers. (i) *Power to enter Premises* : The presiding officer of a Tribunal may for the purpose of inquiry into an existing or apprehended industrial dispute, after giving reasonable notice, enter the premises occupied by any establishment to which the dispute relates (Section 11(2)].

(ii) *Powers of Civil Court* : A Tribunal shall have the same powers as are vested in a Civil Court under the Code of Civil Procedure, 1908, when trying a suit in respect of the following matters, namely :

(a) enforcing the attendance of any person and examining him on oath;

(b) compelling the production of documents and material objects;

(c) issuing commissions for the examination of witnesses;

(d) in respect of such other matters as may he prescribed.

Every inquiry or investigation by a Tribunal shall be deemed to be a judicial proceeding within the meaning of Sections 193 and 228 of the Indian Penal Code. 1860 [Section 11(3)].

(iii) *Power to appoint Assessors* : It may, if it so thinks fit, appoint one or more persons having special knowledge of the matter under consideration as assessors to advise it in the proceeding before it [Section 11(5)].

(iv) *Power to award Costs* : Subject to any rules made under this Act, the costs of, and incidental to, any proceeding before a Tribunal shall be in the discretion of the Tribunal. The Tribunal shall have full power to determine by and to whom and to what extent and subject to what conditions, if any, such costs are to be paid. It shall also have the power to give all the necessary directions for the purposes aforesaid. These costs may, on applicable made to the appropriate Government by the person entitled, be recovered by that Government in the same manner as an arrear of land revenue [Section 11(7)].

Every Tribunal shall be deemed to be a Civil Court for the purposes of Sections 345, 346 and 348 of the Code of Criminal Procedure, 1973 [Section 11(8)].

3. NATIONAL TRIBUNAL (Section 7-B)

1. Appointment and Constitution. The Central Government may, by notification in the Official Gazette, constitute one or more 'National,, Industrial Tribunals for the adjudication of industrial disputes which, in the opinion of the Central Government, involve questions of nationals importance or are of such a nature that industrial establishments situated in more than one State are likely to be interested in, or affected by, such disputes (Section 7-B (1)].

A National Tribunal shall consist of one person only to be appointed by the Central Government [Section 7-B (2)].

2. Qualifications. A person shall not be qualified for appointment as the presiding officer of a National Tribunal unless he is, or has been, a Judge of a High Court [Section 7-B (3)].

The Central Government may, if it so thinks fit, appoint 2 persons as assessors to advise the National Tribunal in the proceeding before it [Section 7-B (4)].

The presiding officer of a National Tribunal shall be deemed to be a public servant within the meaning of Section 21 of the Indian Penal Code, 1860 [Section 11 (6)].

3. Disqualification. No person shall be appointed to, or continue in, the office of the presiding officer of a National Tribunal, if (a) he is not an independent person; or (b) he has attained the age of 65 years (Section 7-C).

4. Reference of Disputes. Sometimes the Central Government may be of opinion that any industrial dispute exists or is apprehended and the dispute involves any question of national importance or is of such a nature that industrial establishments situated in more than one State are likely to be interested in, or affected by, such dispute and the dispute should be adjudicated by a National Tribunal. In such a case the Central Government may, whether or not it is the appropriate Government in relation to that dispute, at any time, by order in writing, refer the dispute or any matter appearing to be connected with or relevant to, the dispute, whether it relates to any matter specified in the Second Schedule or the Third Schedule, to a National Tribunal for adjudication [Section 10 (I-A)].

Where the parties to an industrial dispute apply in the prescribed manner, whether jointly or separately, for a reference of the dispute to a National Tribunal, the appropriate Government, if satisfied that persons applying represent the minority of each party, shall make the reference accordingly [Section 10 (2)].

Subject to any rules that may be made in this behalf, a National Tribunal shall follow such procedure as it may think fit [Section 11(1)].

Jurisdiction of Labour Court and Industrial Tribunal to cease on a Reference made to National Tribunal : Where any reference has been made under Section 10 (I-A) to a National Tribunal, then notwithstanding anything contained in the Act, no Labour Court or Tribunal shall have jurisdiction to adjudicate upon any matter which is under adjudication before the National Tribunal.

If the matter under adjudication before the National Tribunal is pending in a proceeding before a Labour Court or Industrial Tribunal, the proceeding before the Labour Court or the Industrial Tribunal, as the case may be, in so far as it relates to such matter, shall be deemed to have been quashed on such reference to the National Tribunal. Further it shall not be lawful for the appropriate Government to refer the matter under adjudication before the National Tribunal, to any Labour Court or Industrial Tribunal for adjudication during the pendency of the proceeding in relation to such matter before the National Tribunal [Section 10 (6)].

'Labour Court' or 'Tribunal' in Section 10 (6) includes any Court or Tribunal or other authority constituted under any law relating to investigation and settlement of industrial disputes in force in any State [Explanation to Section 10 (6)].

5. Prohibition of Strike or Lock-out. Where an industrial dispute has been referred to a National Tribunal under Section 10, the appropriate Government may by order prohibit the continuance of any strike or lock out in connection with such dispute which may be in existence on the date of the reference [Section 10 (3)].

6. Jurisdiction. Where in an order referring an industrial dispute to a National Tribunal under Section 10 or in a subsequent order, the appropriate Government has specified the points of dispute for adjudication, the National Tribunal shall confine its adjudication to those points and matters incidental thereto [Section 10 (4)].

7. Inclusion of Other Parties. Where a dispute concerning any establishment or establishments has been, or is to be, referred to a National Tribunal under Section 10, the appropriate Government may be of opinion that the dispute is of such a nature that any other establishment, group or class of establishments of a similar nature is likely to be interested in, or affected by, such dispute. In such a case, the appropriate Government may, at the time of making the reference, or at any time thereafter but before the submission of the award, include in that reference such establishment, group or class of establishments, whether or not at the time of such inclusion any dispute exists or is apprehended in that establishment. Group or class of establishments [Section 10 (5)].

Duties. Where an industrial dispute has been referred to a National Tribunal for adjudication, it shall hold its proceedings expeditiously. Further, it shall, within the period specified in the order referring such industrial dispute, submit its award to the appropriate Government (Section 15). The period may be extended under Proviso 2 to Section 10 (2-A).

Award to be in writing and signed and its Publication : The award shall be in writing and shall be signed by the presiding officer of the National Tribunal [Section 16 (2)]. It shall, within a period of 30 days from the date of its receipt by the appropriate Government, be published in such manner as the appropriate Government thinks fit [Section 17 (1)].

8. Powers. (i) *Power to enter Premises* : The presiding officer of a National Tribunal may for the purpose of inquiry into any existing or apprehended industrial dispute, after giving reasonable notice, enter the premises occupied by any establishment to which the dispute relates [Section 11(2)].

(ii) *Powers of Civil Court* : A National Tribunal shall have the same powers as are vested in a Civil Court under the Code of Civil Procedure, 1908, when trying a suit, in respect of the following matters, namely;

(a) enforcing the attendance of any person and examining him on oath;

(b) compelling the production of documents and material objects;

(c) issuing commissions for the examination of witnessess;

(d) in respect of such other matters as may be prescribed.

Every inquiry or investigation by a National Tribunal shall be deemed to a judicial proceeding within the meaning of Sections 193 an 2 of the Indian Penal Code, 1860 [Section 11(3)].

(iii) *Power to appoint Assessors.* The National Tribunal may, if it so thinks fit, appoint one or more persons having special knowledge of the matter under consideration as assessor or assessors to advise it in the proceeding before it [Section 11(5)].

(iv) *Power to award Costs.* Subject to any rules made under this Act, the costs of, and incidental to, any proceeding before a National Tribunal shall be in the discretion of the National Tribunal. Further the National Tribunal shall have full power to determine by and to whom and to what extent and subject to what conditions, such costs are to be paid. It shall also have the power to give all necessary directions for the purposes aforesaid. These costs may, on application made to the appropriate Government by the person entitled, be recovered by the Government in the same manner as an arrear of land revenue [Section 11 (7)].

Every National Tribunal shall be deemed to be a Civil Court for the purposes of Sections 345, 346 and 348 of, the Code of Criminal Procedure, 1973 [Section 11 (8)].

PROCEDURE, POWERS AND DUTIES OF AUTHORITIES
(Chapter IV, Sections 11 to 21)

1. Procedure [Section 11(1)]

Subject to any rules that may be made in this behalf, an arbitrator (appointed under Section 10-A), a Board of Conciliation (appointed under Section 5), a Court of Inquiry (appointed under Section 6), a Labour Court (appointed under Section 7), an Industrial Tribunal (appointed under Section 7- A), or a National Tribunal (appointed under Section 7-B) shall follow such procedure as the arbitrator or other authority concerned may think fit.

2. Power and Duties of Authorities

3. Powers of Labour Courts, Industrial Tribunals and National Tribunals to give appropriate Relief in Case of Discharge or Dismissal of Workmen (Section 11-A)

Where an industrial dispute relating to the discharge or dismissal of a workman has been referred to a Labour Court, Industrial Tribunal or National Tribunal for adjudication and, in the course of adjudication proceedings, the Labour Court, Industrial Tribunal or National Tribunal, as the case may be, is satisfied that the order of discharge or dismissal was not justified, it may, by its ward, set aside the order of discharge or dismissal. It may also direct reinstatement of the workman on such terms and conditions, if any, as it thinks fit, or give such other relief to the workman including the award of any lesser punishment in lieu of discharge or dismissal as the circumstances of the case may require (Section 11-A). The Labour Court or the Tribunal has to be satisfied that even though the misconduct is proved and a penalty has to be imposed, the extreme penalty of dismissal or discharge was not justified in the facts and circumstances of the case, meaning thereby that the punishment was either disproportionately heavy or excessive. In order to avoid the charge of vindictiveness, justice, equity and fair play demand that punishment must always be commensurate with the gravity of the offence charged [Rama Kant Mishra *Vs.* State of U.P., (1982) 3 S.C.C. 346].

4. Filling of Vacancies (Section 8)

If, for any reason, a vacancy (other than a temporary absence) occurs in the office of :

(a) the presiding officer of (i) a Labour Court, (ii) an Industrial Tribunal, or (iii) a National Tribunal,

(b) the Chairman or any other member of (i) a Board of Conciliation, or (ii) a Court of Inquiry, then, in the case of a National Tribunal, the Central Government and, in any other case, the appropriate Government, shall appoint another person in accordance with the provisions of the Act to fill the vacancy and the proceeding may be continued before the Labour Court, Industrial Tribunal, National Tribunal, Board of Conciliation or Court of Inquiry, an the case may be, fare the stage at which the vacancy is filled.

NOTICE OF CHANGE IN CONDITIONS OF SERVICE

(Chapter II-A. Sections 9-A and 9-B)

1. Meaning of Conditions of Service. The expression 'conditions of service' means the terms of employment between the employer and the employees governed by :

(a) the contract between the employer and the employee,

(b) the statute law,

(c) the decisions of the Courts,

(d) the standing order and

(e) the customs and usages of trade.

'Conditions of service' of employees in industrial establishments must be precisely defined. The necessity of regulating changes in conditions of service arises because changes are inevitable. If these changes are not regulated, they are bound to become a major source of industrial strike.

2. Notice of change (Section 9-A)

According to Section 9-A, no employer, who proposes to effect any change in the conditions of service applicable to any workman in respect of any matter specified in the Fourth Schedule (reproduced on next page) shall effect such change :

(a) without giving to the workmen likely to be affected by such change a notice in the prescribed manner of the nature of the change proposed to be effected; or

(b) within 21 days of giving such notice (Section 9-A).

No notice required : According to Proviso to Section 9-A no notice shall be required for effecting any change in conditions of service :

(a) where the change is effected in presence of any settlement or award; or

(b) where the workmen likely to be affected by the change are persons to whom the Fundamental and Supplementary Rules, Civil Services (Classification, Control and Appeal) Rules, Civil Services

(Temporary Service) Rules, Revised Leave Rules, Civil Service Regulations, Civilians in Defence Services (Classification, Control and Appeal) Rules or the Indian Railway Establishment Code or any other rules or regulations that may be notified in this behalf by the appropriate Government in the Official Gazette, apply.

THE FOURTH SCHEDUL
(See Section 9-A)

1. Conditions of Service for Change of which Notice is to he given

(i) Wages, including the period and mode of payment;

(ii) Contribution paid, or payable by the employer to any provident fund or pension fund or for the benefit of the workmen under any law for the time being in force;

(iii) Compensatory and other allowances;

(iv) Hours of work and rest intervals;

(v) Leave with wages and holidays;

(vi) Starting, alteration or discontinuance of shift working otherwise standing orders;

(vii) Classification by grades;

(viii) Withdrawal of any customary concession or privilege or change in usage;

(ix) Introduction of new rules of discipline, or alteration of existing rules, except in so far as they are provided in standing orders;

(x) Rationalisation, standardisation or improvement of plant or technique which is likely to lead to retrenchment of workmen and

(xi) Any increase or reduction (other than casual) in the number of persons employed or to be employed in any occupation or process or department or shift, not occasioned by circumstances over which the employer has no control.

Section 9-A is mandatory [Navbharat Hindi Daily *Vs.* Sharamik Sangh, (1984) 2 L.L.J. 132 (Bom.)].

2. Power of Government to exempt (Section 9-B)

The appropriate Government has the power to direct, by notification in the Official Gazette, that the provisions of Section 9-A shall not apply or shall apply subject to such conditions as may be specified in the notification to any class of industrial establishments or to any class of workmen employed in any industrial establishment. The appropriate Government shall do so (a) if it is of opinion that the application of the provisions of Section 9-A shall affect the employers so prejudicially that such application may cause serious repercussion on the industry concerned, or (b) if it is necessary in public interest.

REFERENCE OF DISPUTES TO BOARDS. COURTS OR TRIBUNALS AND VOLUNTARY REFERENCE

(Chapter III, Sections 10 and 10-A)

1. Reference of Disptues to Boards, Courts or Tribunals (Section 10)

(i) *The Appropriate Government may make a Reference in Case a Dispute exists in Non-Public Utility Service* : Section 10 provides that where the appropriate Government is of opinion that any industrial dispute exists or is apprehended, it may at any time, by order in writing :

(a) refer the dispute to a Board of Conciliation for promoting a settlement thereof, or

(b) refer any matter appearing to be connected with or relevant to the dispute to a Court of Inquiry for inquiry; or

(c) refer the dispute or any matter appearing to be connected with, or relevant to the dispute, where it relates to any matter specified in the Second Schedule, to a Labour Court for adjudication, or

(d) refer the dispute or any matter appearing to be connected with, or relevant to the dispute, where it relates to any matter specified in the Second Schedule or the Third Schedule, to an Industrial Tribunal for adjudication [Section 10 (1)].

Where the dispute relates to any matter specified in the Third Schedule and is not likely to affect more than 100 workmen, the appropriate Government may, if it so thinks fit, make the reference to a Labour Court under Clause (e) proviso 1 to Section 10 (1)].

(ii) *The Appropriate Government shall make a Reference in Case a Dispute relates to Public Utility Service* : Where the dispute relates to a public utility service and a notice under Section 22 has been given, the appropriate Government shall make a reference under Section 10 (1) notwithstanding that any other proceeding under this Act in respect of the dispute may have convinced. But if the appropriate Government considers that the notice has been frivolously or vexatiously given or that it would be inexpedient so to do, it may not make a reference under Section 10 (1) [Proviso 2 to Section 10(1)].

Where the dispute in relation to which the Central Government is the appropriate Government, it shall be competent for that Government to refer the dispute to a Labour Court or an Industrial Tribunal, as the case may be, constituted by the State Government [Proviso 3 to Section 10 (1)]

2. Reference to a National Tribunal. Where the Central Government is of opinion that :

(i) any industrial dispute exists, or

(it) is apprehended, or

(iii) the dispute involves any question of national importance, or

(iv) is of such a nature that industrial establishments situated in more than one State are likely to be interested in, or affected by, such dispute and

(v) that the dispute should be adjudicated by a National Tribunal,

then, the Central Government may, at any time, by order in writing, refer the dispute to a National Tribunal for adjudication. It makes no difference whether the Central Government is the appropriate Government in relation to (that matter or not. The Central Government may also refer to the National Tribunal for adjudication any matter appearing to be connected with, or relevant, to the dispute whether it relates to any matter specified in the Second Schedule or the Third Schedule, for adjudication (Section 10 (1-A)].

3. Persons Applying to represent Majority. Where the parties to an industrial dispute apply in the prescribed manner, whether jointly or separately, for a reference of the dispute to a Board of Conciliation, Court of Inquiry, Labour Court, industrial Tribunal or National Tribunal, the appropriate Government shall make the reference accordingly. It shall however do so if it is satisfied that the persons applying represent the majority [Section 10 (2)].

4. Period for Submission of the Award. (i) *Specification of Period* : An order referring an industrial dispute to a Labour Court, Industrial Tribunal under Section 10 shall specify the period within which such Labour Court, Industrial Tribunal or National Tribunal shall submit its award on such dispute to the appropriate Government [Section 10 (2-A) as introduced by the Amendment Act of 1982]. Where such industrial dispute is connected with an individual workman, period specified for the submission of the award shall not exceed 3 months [Proviso 1 to Section 10 (2-A)].

(ii) *Extension of Period* : The parties to an Industrial dispute may apply in the prescribed manner, whether jointly or separately, to the Labour Court, Industrial Tribunal or National Tribunal for extension of the period specified for the submission of the award or for any other reason. If the presiding officer of such Labour Court., Industrial Tribunal or National Tribunal considers it necessary or expedient to extend such period, he may for reasons to be recorded in writing extend such period by such further period as he may think fit (Proviso 2 to Section 10 (2-A)].

(iii) *Computation of the Period of Submission of the Award* : In computing the period specified for the submission of the award, the period, if any, for which the proceedings before the Labour Court, Industrial Tribunal or National Tribunal had been stayed by any injunction or order of a Civil Court shall be scheduled [Proviso 3 to Section 10 (2-A)]. Further no proceedings before a Labour Court, Industrial Tribunal or National Tribunal shall lapse merely on the ground that any period specified for the submission of the award had expired without such proceedings being completed (Proviso 4 to Section 10 (2-A)].

5. Prohibition of Strikes and Lock-outs. Where an industrial dispute has been referred to a Board of Conciliation, Labour Court. Industrial Tribunal or National Tribunal under Section 10, the appropriate Government may by order prohibit the continuance of any strike or lock-out in connection with such dispute which may be in existence on the date of the reference [Section 10 (3)].

6. Jurisdiction. Where in an order referring an industrial dispute to a Labour Court, Industrial Tribunal, or National Tribunal under Section 10 or in a subsequent order, the appropriate Government has specified the points of dispute for adjudication, the Labour Court or the Industrial Tribunal or the National Tribunal, as the case may be, shall confine its adjudication to those points and matters incidental thereto [Section 10 (4)].

VOLUNTARY REFERENCE OF DISPUTES TO ARBITRATION (Section 10-A)

1. Reference. Where any industrial dispute exists or is apprehended and the employer and the workmen agree to refer the dispute to arbitration, they may by a written agreement refer the dispute to arbitration. They can however do so at any time before the dispute has been referred under Section 10 to a Labour Court or Industrial Tribunal or National Tribunal. The reference shall in such a case be to such person or persons (including the presiding officer of a Labour Court or Industrial Tribunal or National Tribunal) as an arbitrator or arbitrators as may, be specified in the arbitration agreement [Section 10-A (1)].

2. Umpire. Where an arbitration agreement provides for a reference of the dispute to an even number of arbitrators, the agreement shall provide for the appointment of another person as umpire. The umpire shall enter upon the reference, if the arbitrators are equally divided in their opinion, and the award of the umpire shall prevail and shall be deemed to be the arbitration award, for the purposes of this Act [Section 10-A (1-A)].

3. Form of Agreement. An arbitration agreement shall be in such form and shall be signed by the parties thereto in such manner as may be prescribed [Section 10-A (2)].

A copy of the arbitration agreement shall be forwarded to the appropriate Government and the Conciliation Officer. The appropriate Government shall, within 1 month from the date of the receipt of such copy, publish the same in the official Gazette [Section 10-A (3)].

4. Proceedings. Where an industrial dispute has been referred to arbitration and the appropriate Government is satisfied that the persons making the reference represent the majority of each party, the appropriate Government may, within 1 month from the date of the receipt of a copy of the arbitration agreement, issue a notification in such manner as may be prescribed. When any such notification is issued, the employers and workmen who are not parties to the arbitration agreement but are concerned in the dispute, shall be given an opportunity of presenting their case before the arbitrator or arbitrators [Section 10-A(3-A)].

5. Award. The arbitrator or arbitrators shall investigate the dispute and submit to the appropriate Government the arbitration award signed by the arbitrator or all the arbitrators, as the case may be [Section 10-A (4)].

6. Prohibition of Strike or Lock-out. Where an industrial dispute has been referred to arbitration and a notification has been issued under Section 10-A (3-A), the appropriate Government may, by order, prohibit the continuance of any strike or lock-out in connection with such dispute which may be in distance on the date of the reference [Section 10-A (4-A)].

7. Arbitration Act, 1940 not to apply. Nothing in the Arbitration Act, 1940 shall apply to arbitrations under Section 10-A [Section 10-A (5)].

AWARD AND SETTLEMENT

The meaning of the terms 'award' and 'settlement' has already been explained while discussing the definitions of various terms used In the Act.

1. Form of Report or Award (Section 16)

The report of a Board of Conciliation or Court of Inquiry shall be in writing and shall be signed by all the members of the Board or Court, as the case may be [Section 16 (1)]. A member of the Board or Court can, however, record a minute of dissent from a report or from any recommendation made therein [Proviso to Section 16 (1)].

The award of a Labour Court or Industrial Tribunal or National Tribunal shall be in writing and shall be signed by its presiding officer [Section 16 (2)].

2. Publication of Reports and Awards (Section 17)

(i) Every report of a Board of Conciliation or Court of Inquiry together with any minute of dissent recorded therewith,

(ii) every arbitration award,

(iii) every award of a Labour Court, Industrial Tribunal or National Tribunal,

shall, within a period of 30 days from the date of its receipt by the appropriate Government, be published in such manner and the appropriate Government thinks fit [Section 17 (1)].

Subject to the provisions of Section 17-A, the award published under Section 17 (1) shall be final and shall not be called in question by any Court in any manner whatsoever [Section 17 (2)].

3. Commencement of Award (Section 17-A)

(i) *Award to become Enforceable on Expiry of 30 Days from its Publication* : An award (including an arbitration award) shall become enforceable on the expiry of 30 days from the date of its publication under Section 17 [Section 17-A (1)]. But

(a) the appropriate Government may if it is of opinion, in any case where the award has been given by a Labour Court or an Industrial Tribunal in relation to an industrial dispute to which it is a party; or

(b) the Central Government may if it is of opinion, in any case where the award has been given by a National Tribunal, by notification in the Official Gazette,

declare that the award shall not become enforceable on the expiry of the said period of 30 days. The appropriate Government, or as the case may be, the Central Government, shall do so if it is expedient on public grounds affecting :

(a) national economy,

(b) or social justice to give effect to the whole or any part of the award [Proviso to Section 17-A (1)].

(ii) *Rejection or Modification of Award within 90 Days* : Where any declaration has been made in relation to an award under the Proviso to Section 17-A (1), the Appropriate Government or the Central Government may within 90 days from the date of publication of the award under Section 17, make an order rejecting or modifying the award. In such a case, it shall, on the first available opportunity, lay the award together with a copy of the order :

(a) before the Legislature of the State, if the order has been made by a State Government, or

(b) before Parliament, if the order has been made by the Central Government [Section 17-A (2)].

Where any award as rejected or modified by an order is laid before the Legislature of a State or before Parliament, it shall become enforceable on the expiry of 15 days from the date on which it is so laid. Where no order is made rejecting or modifying the award in pursuance of declaration, the award shall become enforceable on the expiry of the period of 90 days from the day of the publication of the award [Section 17-A (3)].

Subject to the above provisions regarding the enforceability of an award, the award shall come into operation with effect from such date as may be specified therein. Where no date is so specified, the award shall come into operation on the expiry of 30 days from the date of its publication [Section 17-A (4)].

4. Payment of full Wages pending Proceedings (Section 17-B)

When in any case, a Labour Court, Industrial Tribunal or National Tribunal by its award directs reinstatment of any workman, the employer may prefer any proceedings against such award in a High Court or the Supreme Court. But during the period of pendency of such proceedings the employer shall be liable to pay such workman full wages last drawn by him. The wages shall be inclusive of any maintenance allowance admissible to the workman if :

(i) he had not been employed in any establishment during the period of pendency of the proceedings and

(ii) an affidavit by such workman had been filed to that effect in the Court in which the proceedings are pending (Section 17-B).

Where however it is proved to the satisfaction of the High Court or the Supreme Court that such workman had been employed and had been receiving adequate remuneration during the period of pendency of the proceedings or part thereof, the Court shall order that no wages shall be payable for such period or part, as the case may be (Proviso to Section 17-B).

5. Persons on Whom Settlements and Awards are binding (Section 18).

(i) A settlement arrived at by agreement between the employer and workmen otherwise than in the course of conciliation proceedings is binding on the parties to the agreement [Section 18 (1)].

(ii) An arbitration award which has become enforceable is binding on the parties to the agreement who referred the dispute to arbitration [Section 18 (2)]. This is however subject to the provision contained in Section 18 (3).

(iii) A settlement arrived at in the course of conciliation proceedings or an arbitration award (in a case where a notification has been issued under Section 10-A (3-A) or an award of a Labour Court, Industrial Tribunal or National Tribunal which has become enforceable, shall be binding :

(a) on all parties to the dispute;

(b) on all other parties summoned to appear in the proceedings as parties to the dispute, unless the Board of Conciliation, arbitrator, labour Court, Industrial Tribunal, or National Tribunal, as the case may be, records the opinion that they were so summoned without proper cause;

(c) where a party referred to in Clause (a) or Clause (b) is an employer, or his heirs, successors or assigns in respect of the establishment to which the dispute relates;

(d) where a party referred to in Clause (a) or Clause (b) is composed of workmen, or all persons who were employed in the establishment or part of the establishment, as the case may be, to which the dispute relates on the date of the dispute and all persons who subsequently become employed in the establishment or part of the establishment [Section 18(3)].

(6) Period of Operation of Settlement (Section 19). A settlement arrived at in the course of conciliation proceedings before a Conciliation Officer or a Board of Conciliation shall come into operation :

(a) on such date as is agreed upon by the parties to the dispute and

(b) if no date is agreed upon, on the date on which the memorandum of the settlement is signed by the parties to the dispute [Section 19 (1)].

Settlement Binding for Period Agreed upon or for 6 Months : Such settlement shall be binding for such period as is agreed upon by the parties. If no such period is agreed upon, the settlement shall be binding for a period of 6 months from the date on which the memorandum of settlement is signed by the parties to the dispute. It shall continue to be binding until a party gives notice in writing to terminate the settlement. The settlement ceases to be binding on the expiry of 2 months from such notice of termination given by one of the parties to the other party or parties to the settlement [Section 19 (2)].

A notice given under Section 19 (2) shall have no effect unless it is given by a party representing the majority of persons bound by the settlement [Section 19(7)].

(7) Period of Operation of Award (Section 19). An award shall, subject to the provisions of Section 19, remain in operation for a period of 1 year from the date on which the award becomes enforceable [Section 19 (3)]. But the appropriate Government may reduce the said period and fix such period as it thinks fit [Proviso 1 to Section 19 (3)]. Again the appropriate Government may, before the expiry of the said period, extend the period of operation by any period not exceeding 1 year at a time as it thinks fit. But the total period of operation of any award shall not exceed 3 years from the date on which it came into operation [Proviso 2 to Section 19 (3)].

The provisions of Section 19 (3) shall not, however, apply to any award which by its nature, terms or other circumstances does not impose, after it has been given effect to, any continuing obligation on the parties bound by the award [Section 19 (5)].

(i) *Shortening of Period of Operation of Award on a Material Change in the Circumstances* : Where there is a material change in the circumstances on which an award is based, the appropriate Government may refer the award or a part of it :

(a) to a Labour Court, if the award was that of a Labour Court, or

(b) to a Tribunal, if the award was that of a Tribunal or of National Tribunal for decision whether the period of operation should not, by reason of change, be shortened.

The appropriate Government may refer the award of its own motion or on the application of any party bound by the award. The decision of the Labour Court or the Tribunal, as the case may be, on such reference shall be final [Section 19(4)].

(ii) *Award to continue to be Binding until the Expiry of 2 Months from the Date of Notice of its Termination by a Party* : The award shall continue after the expiry of the period of operation till a party bound by the award gives notice to the other party or parties intimating its intention to terminate the contract. The award ceases to be binding on the expiry of 2 months from such notice [Section 19 (6)]. The notice shall not have effect unless it is given by a party representing the majority of persons bound by the award [Section 19 (7)].

(8) Penalty for Breach of Settlement or Award (Section 29)

Any person who commits a breach of any term of any settlement or award, which is binding on him, shall be punishable with imprisonment for a term which may extend to 6 months, or with fine, or with both.

Where the breach is a continuing one, he shall be punishable with a further fine which may extend to Rs. 200 for every day during which the breach continues after the conviction for the first offence. Further the Court trying the offence may, if it fines the offender, direct that the whole or any part of the fines realised from him shall be paid, by way of compensation, to any person who, in its opinion, has been injured by such breach.

(9) Commencement and Conclusion of Proceedings (Section 20)

(i) *Commencement of Proceedings* : A conciliation proceeding shall be deemed to have commenced on the date on which a notice of strike or lock-out under Section 22 is received by the Conciliation Officer or on the date of the order referring the dispute to a Board of Conciliation, as the case may be [Section 20 (1)].

(ii) *Conclusion of Proceedings* : A conciliation proceeding shall be deemed to have concluded :

(a) where a settlement to arrived at, when a memorandum of the settlement is signed by the parties to the dispute;

(b) where no settlement is arrived at, when the report of the Conciliation Officer is received by the appropriate Government or when the report of the Board of Conciliation is published under Section 17, as the case may be; or

(c) when the reference is made to a Court of Inquiry, Labour Court, Industrial Tribunal or National Tribunal, during the pendency of conciliation proceedings [Section 20 (2)].

(iii) *Arbitration and Adjudication Proceedings* : Proceedings before an Arbitrator or before a Labour Court, Industrial Tribunal or National Tribunal shall be deemed to have commenced on the date of reference of the dispute for arbitration or adjudication, as the case may be, and such proceedings shall be deemed to have concluded on the date on which the award becomes unforceable under Section 17-A [Section 20(3)].

STRIKES AND LOCK-OUTS

(Chapter V, Sections 22 to 25]

The meaning of the terms 'strike' and 'lock-out' has already been explained. Certain types of strikes and lock-outs are prohibited by the Industrial Disputes Act.

1. Prohibition of Strikes and Lock-outs (Sections 22 and 23)

(i) Strike in a Public Utility Service [Section 22 (1)]. No person employed in a public utility service shall go on strike in breach of contract :

(a) without giving to the employer notice of strike, within 6 weeks before striking; or

(b) within 14 days of giving such notice; or

(c) before the expiry of the date of strike specified in any such notice as aforesaid; or

(d) during the pendency of any conciliation proceedings before a Conciliation Officer and 7 days after the conclusion of such proceedings.

A strike notice is valid only for 6 weeks.

Clause (b) ensures that there is enough prior warning before the workmen actually go on strike.

(ii) Lock-out in a Public Utility Service [Section 22 (2)]. No employer carrying on any public utility service shall lock-out any of his workmen :

(a) without giving them notice of lock-out, within 6 weeks before locking-out; or

(b) within 14 days of giving such notice; or

(c) before the expiry of the date of lock-out specified in any such notice as aforesaid; or

(d) during the pendency of any conciliation proceedings before a Conciliation Officer and 7 days after the conclusion of such proceedings.

A lock-out notice is valid only for 6 weeks.

Clause (b) ensures that there is enough prior warning.

The notice of lock-out shall be given in such manner as may be prescribed [Section 22(5)].

Rules about Notice

(a) *Notice of Lock-out or Strike not Necessary in Certain Cases* : The notice of lock-out or strike shall not be necessary where there is already in existence a strike, or as the case may be, lock-out in the public utility service. But the employer shall send intimation of such lock-out or strike on the day on which it is declared, to such authority as may be specified by the appropriate Government either generally or for a particular area or for a particular class of public utility services [Section 22 (3)].

(b) *Intimation of Notices of Strike or Lock-out to be given within 5 days* : If on any day an employer receives from any person employed by him any notices of strike or gives to any persons employed by him any notices of lock-out, he shall within 5 days thereof report to the appropriate Government or to such authority as that Government may prescribe the number of such notices received or given on that day [Section 22 (6)].

(iii) Strike and Lock-out in an Industrial Establishment (Section 23). No workman who is employed in any industrial establishment shall go on strike in breach of contract and no employer of any such workman shall declare a lock-out :

(a) during the pendency of conciliation proceedings before a Board of Conciliation and 7 days after the conclusion of such proceedings;

It is only a conciliation proceeding before a Board of Conciliation which is referred to in this Clause. A conciliation proceeding before a Conciliation Officer is no bar to a strike or lock-out under Section 23.

(b) during the pendency of proceedings before a Labour Court, Industrial Tribunal or National Tribunal and 2 months after the conclusion of such proceedings;

(c) during the pendency of arbitration proceedings before an arbitrator and 2 months after the conclusion of such proceedings where a notification has been issued under Section 10-A (3-A); or

(d) during any period in which a settlement or award is in operation in respect of any of the matters covered by the settlement or award.

The underlying reason behind Sections 22 and 23 is that where a dispute has been referred to conciliation or adjudication, a strike or lock-out, in furtherance thereof, is both unnecessary and inexpedient.

(iv) Illegal Strikes and Lock-outs (Section 24). A strike or a lock-out shall be illegal if :

(i) it is commenced or declared in contravention of Section 22 or Section 23 or

(ii) it is continued in contravention of an order made under Section 10 (3) or Section 10-A (4-A).

Where a strike or a lock-out in pursuance of an industrial dispute has already commenced and is in existence at the time of the reference of the dispute to a Board of Conciliation, a Labour Court, Industrial Tribunal or National Tribunal, the continuance of such strike or lock-out shall not he deemed to be illegal provided such strike or lock-out was not at its commencement in contravention of the provisions of this Act or the continuance thereof was not prohibited under Section 10 (3) or Section 10-A (4-A) [Section 24 (2)].

A lock-out declared in consequence of an illegal strike or a strike declared in consequence of an illegal lock-out shall not be deemed to be illegal [Section 24 (3)).

Prohibition of Financial Aid to Illegal Strikes and Lock-outs (*Section 25*) : No person shall knowingly expend or apply any money in direct furtherance or support of any illegal strike or lock-out.

(v) Penalties regarding Strikes and Lock-outs. (i) *Penalty for Illegal Strikes* [Section 26 (1)] : Any workman who commences, continues or otherwise acts in furtherance of a strike which is illegal, shall be punishable with imprisonment for a term which may extend to 1 month, or with fine which may extend to Rs. 50, or with both.

(ii) *Penalty for Illegal Lock-out* (Section 26 (2)] : Any employer who commences, continues or otherwise acts in furtherance of a lock-out which is illegal, shall be punishable with imprisonment for a term which may extend to 6 months, or with fine which may extend to Rs. 1,000, or with both.

(iii) *Penalty for Instigation, etc.* (Section 27) : Any person who instigates or incites others to take part in or otherwise acts in furtherance of, a strike or lock-out which is illegal, shall be punishable with imprisonment for a term, which may extend to 6 months, or with fine which may extend to Rs. 1,000 or with both.

(iv) *Penalty for giving Financial Aid for Illegal Strikes and Lock-out* (Section 28) : Any person who knowingly expends or applies any money in' direct furtherance or support of any illegal strike or lock-out shall be punishable with an imprisonment for a term which may extend to 6 months, or with fine which may extend to Rs. 1,000 or with both.

LAY-OFF AND RETRENCHMENT
(Chapters V-A and V-B, Sections 25-A to 25-S)

The provisions as to 'lay-off' and 'rentrechment' are contained in :

(a) Chapter V-A (Section 25-A to 25-J) and

(b) Chapter V-B (which contains special provisions relating to lay-off, retrenchment and closure in certain establishments) (Sections 25-K to 25-S).

1. Application of Sections 25-C to 25-E (Section 25-A)

The provisions as to lay-off and retrenchment of workmen as embodied in Sections 25-C to 25-E shall apply only to industrial establishments in which 50 or more workmen on an average per working day have been employed in the preceding calendar month. These provisions shall not apply to industrial establishment :

(i) to which Chapter V-B applies, or

(ii) in which less than 50 workmen on an average per working day have been employed in the preceding calender month; or

(ii) which are of a seasonal character or in which work is performed only intermittently [Section 25-A (1)].

If a question arises whether an industrial establishment is of a seasonal character or whether work is performed therein only intermittently, the decision of the appropriate Government thereon shall be final (Section 25-A (2)].

In Sections 25-A, 25-C, 25-D and 25-E, 'industrial establishment' means :

(i) a factory as defined in Section 2 (m) of the Factories Act 1948; or

(ii) a mine as defined In Section 2 (1)(f) of the Mines Act. 1952; or

(iii) a plantation as defined in Section 2 (f) of the Plantations Labour Act, 1951 (Explanation to Section 25-A).

2. Definition of Continuous service (Section 25-B)

A workman shall be said to be in continuous service for a period if he is, for that period, in uninterrupted service, including service which may be interrupted on account of :

(i) sickness, or

(ii) authorised leave, or

(iii) an accident, or

(iv) a strike which is not illegal, or

(v) a lock-out or a cessation of work which is not due to any fault on the part of the workmen [Section 25-B (1)].

Where a workman is not in continuous service for a period of 1 year, he shall be deemed to be in continuous service under an employer for a period of 1 year, if he has, during a period of 12 calendar months preceding the date with reference to which calculation is to be made, actually worked under the employer for not less than :

(i) 190 days in the came of a workman employed below ground in a mine and

(ii) 240 days, in any other case.

A workman who has actually worked for not less than 240 days during a period of 12 months shall be deemed to have been in continuous service for a period of 1 year whether or not he has in fact been in such continuous service for a period of 1 year [The Co-op. Textile Mill Ltd. *Vs*. Labour Court, Ghaziabad, (1988) Lab. I.C. 425 (All.)]. It is enough that he has worked for 240 days in a period of 12 months. It is not necessary that he should have been in the service of the employer for one whole year [Surendra Kumar Verma *Vs*. Central Govt. Industrial Tribunal-cum-Labour Court, New Delhi, (1980) Lab. I.C. 1292].

Likewise, a workman shall be deemed to be in continuous service for a period of 6 months, if he has, during a period of 6 calendar months preceding the date with reference to which calculation is to be made, actually worked under the employer for not less than :

(i) 95 days, in the case of a workman employed below ground in a mine and

(ii) 120 days, in any other case [Section 25-B (2)].

3. Calculation of Working Days. The number of days in which a workman has actually worked under an employer shall include the days on which he has been :

(i) laid-off under an agreement or as permitted by standing orders made under the Industrial Employment (Standing Orders) Act, 1946, or under this Act or under any other law applicable to the industrial establishment;

(ii) on leave with full wages, earned in the previous year;

(iii) absent due to temporary disablement caused by accident arising out of and in the course of his employment and

(iv) on maternity leave in the case of a female, so however, that the total period of such maternity leave does not exceed 12 weeks (Explanation to Section 25-B).

LAY-OFF

1. Right of Workmen laid-off for Compensation (Section 25-C)

The right of a workman to lay-off compensation is designed to relieve the hardship caused by unemployment due to no fault of the workman. It is based on grounds of humane public policy.

The requisites regarding payment of compensation to a workman, who is laid-off, are contained in Section 25-C and are summarised as follows :

(i) The workman must not be a *badli* workman or a casual workman if he is to be entitled to compensation.

(ii) His name must be borne on the muster rolls of the industrial establishment.

(iii) He must have completed not less than 1 year of continuous service. Where a workman is employed for 11 months before lay-off, he is not entitled to lay-off compensation [Sur Enamel & Stamping Works *Vs*. Thetr Workmen, (1963) 1 L.L.J. 29].

(iv) If the above conditions are fulfilled, the workman whether laid-off continuously or intermittently shall be paid compensation by the employer for all days during which he is laid-off, except for such weekly holidays as may intervene.

(v) The rate of compensation shall be equal to 50 per cent of the total of basic wages and dearness allowance that would have been payable to him had he not been laid-off (Section 25-C).

(vi) If during any period of 12 months, a workman is so laid-off for more than 45 days, no such compensation shall be payable to the workman during any period of 12 months after the expiry of the first 45 days if there is an agreement to that effect between the workman and the employer (Proviso 1 Section 25-C).

(vii) Where a workman is laid-off for a period of more than 45 days during a period of 12 months, the employer can lawfully retrench him in accordance with the provisions contained in Section 25-F at any time after the expiry of the first 45 days of lay-off. When the employer does so, any compensation paid to the workman for having been laid-off during the preceding 12 months may be set off against the compensation payable for retrenchment (Proviso 2 to Section 25-C).

Where the employer decides to retrench a workman under Proviso 2 to Section 25-C. he must comply with the conditions precedent to retrenchment as laid down in Section 25-F.

Who is a badli workman? A 'badli workman' means a workman who is employed in an industrial establishment in the place of another workman whose name is borne on the muster rolls of the establishment. But if he has completed 1 year of continuous service in the establishment, he shall cease to be a badli workman for the purposes of Section 25-C [Explanation to Section 25-C).

2. Duty of an Employer to maintain Muster Rolls of Workmen (Section 25-D)

Section 25-D enjoins upon the employer a duty to maintain a muster roll of workmen notwithstanding that they have been laid-off. He shall also provide for the making of entries in the muster roll by workmen who may present themselves for work at the establishment at the appointed time during normal working hours. If a workman does not so present himself and sign the muster roll, he shall not be entitled to claim lay-off compensation.

3. Workmen not entitled to Compensation in Certain Cases (Section 25-E)

No compensation is payable to a workman who has been laid-off in the following cases :

(i) If he refuses to accept any alternative employment in the same establishment from which he has been laid-off, or in any other establishment belonging to the same employer. The establishment must, however, be situated in the same town or village or situated in a radius of 5 miles (8 kilometres) from the establishment to which he belongs. The alternative employment should not call for any special skill or previous experience and should be such as can be done by the workman. The wages which would normally have been paid to the workman should be offered for the alternative employment also.

(ii) If he does not present himself for work at the establishment at the appointed time during normal working hours at least once a day.

(iii) if such laying-off is due to a strike or slowing down of production on the part of workmen in another part of the establishment. The management will be quite justified in refusing to give work to the workmen in one part of the establishment if there is a strike by workmen in another part of the establishment [Lone Tree Estate *Vs.* Industrial Tribunal, (1962) 2 L.L.J. 319].

RETRENCHMENT

1. Conditions precedent to Retrenchment of Workmen (Section 25-F)

No workman employed in any industry who has been in continuous service for not less than 1 year under an employer shall be retrenched by that employer until :

(i) the workman has been given 1 month's notice in writing. The notice must indicate the reason for retrenchment. Further the workman cannot be retrenched until the period of notice has expired, or the workman has been paid in lieu of such notice wages for the period of the notice [Section 25-F (a)]. This condition is mandatory and non-compliance with it will render retrenchment illegal [National Iron & Steel Co. *Vs.* The State of West Bengal, (1967) 2 L.LJ. 23 (S.C.)]

(ii) the workman has been paid, at the time of retrenchment, compensation which is equivalent to 15 days' average pay for every completed year of continuous service or any part thereof in excess of 6 months [Section 25-F (b)];

(iii) notice in the prescribed manner is served on the appropriate Government or such authority as may be specified by the appropriate Government by notification in the Official Gazette (Section 25-F (c)].

2. Procedure for Retrenchment (Section 25-G)

Where any workman in an industrial establishment, who is a citizen of India, is to be retrenched and he belongs to a particular category of workmen in that establishment, in the absence of any agreement between the employer and the workman in this behalf, the employer shall ordinarily retrench the workman who was the last person to be employed in that category, unless for reasons to be recorded, the employer retrenches any other workman.

Principle of 'last come, first go'. Section 25-G of the Act applies the rule of 'last come, first go' to retrenchment.

3. Re-employment of Retrenched Workmen (Section 25-H)

Where any workmen are retrenched, and the employer proposes to take into his employ any persons, he shall give an opportunity to the retrenched workmen who are citizens of India to offer themselves for re-employment. The retrenched workmen who offer themselves for re-employment shall have preference over other persons. The offer shall be notice in such manner as may be prescribed.

TRANSFER AND CLOSING DOWN OF UNDERTAKINGS

1. Compensation to Workmen in Case of Transfer of Undertakings (Section 25- FF)

Sometimes the ownership or management of an undertaking is transferred, whether by agreement or by operation of law, from the employer in relation to that undertaking to a new employer. In such a case, every workman who has been in continuous service for not less than 1 year in that undertaking immediately before such transfer shall be entitled to notice and compensation in accordance with the provisions of Section 25-F. as If the workman had been retrenched (Section 25-FF).

A workman shall not be entitled to notice and compensation where there has been a change of employers by reason of the transfer, if :

(i) the service of the workman has not been interrupted by such transfer;

(ii) the terms and conditions of service applicable to the workman after such transfer are not in any way less favourable to the workman than those applicable to him immediately before the transfer and

(iii) the new employer is under the terms of such transfer or otherwise, legally liable to pay to the workman, in the event of his retrenchment, compensation on the basis that his service has been continuous and has not been interrupted by the transfer (Proviso to Section 25-FF).

2. 60 days' Notice to be given of Intention to close down any Undertaking (Section 25-FFA)

(i) *Notice* : An employer who intends to close down an undertaking shall serve at least 60 clays before the date on which the intended closure is to become effective, a notice on the appropriate Government. The notice shall be served in the prescribed manner and shall state clearly the reasons for the intended closure of the undertaking [Section 25-FFA (1)]. This Section shall not apply to :

(a) an undertaking in which (1) less than 50 workmen are employed, or (ii) less than 50 workmen were employed on an average per working day in the preceding 12 months,

(b) an undertaking set up for the construction of buildings, bridges, roads, canals, dams or for other construction work or project [Proviso to Section 25-FFA (1)].

The appropriate Government may, if it is satisfied that owing to some exceptional circumstances, it is necessary so to do, by order, direct that provisions of Section 25-FFA (1) shall not apply in relation to an undertaking for such period as may be specified in the order. The exceptional circumstances in the undertaking may be (a) accident in the undertaking, or (b) death of the employer or the like [Section 25-FFA (2)].

(ii) *Penalty* : According to Section 30 undertaking without comparing with the provisions of Section 25-FFA. shall be punishable with imprisonment for a term which may extend to 6 months or with fine which may extend to Rs. 5,000 or with both.

3. Compensation to workmen in Case of closing down of Undertakings (Section 25 FFF)

(i) *Notice and Compensation* : Where an undertaking is closed for any reason whatsoever, every workman who has been in continuous service for not" less than 1 year in that undertaking immediately before such closure shall be entitled to notice and compensation (in accordance with the provisions of Section 25-F) as if the workman had been retrenched. This is, however, subject to the provisions of Section 25-FFF (2). But where the undertaking is closed down on account of unavoidable circumstances beyond the control of the employer, the compensation to be paid to the workmen shall not exceed his average pay for 3 months [Section 25-FFF(1)].

An undertaking which is closed down by reason merely of :

(a) financial difficulties (including financial losses), or

(b) accumulation of indisposed of stocks, or

(c) the expiry of the period of the lease or the lien granted to it, or

(d) in a case where the undertaking is engaged in mining operations, exhaustion of the minerals in the area in which such operations are carried on, shall not be deemed to have been closed down on account of unavoidable circumstances beyond the control of the employer within the meaning of the Proviso to Section 25-FFF (1) [Explanation to Section 25-FFF(1)].

(ii) *Closing down of an Undertaking Set up for Construction of Buildings, Bridges, Canals, Roads, Dams* : Where any undertaking set up for the construction of buildings, bridges, roads, canals, dams or other construction work is closed down on account of the completion of the work within 2 years from the date on which the undertaking had been set up, no workman employed therein shall be entitled to any compensation. But if the construction work is not so completed within 2 years, he shall be entitled to notice and compensation for every completed year of continuous service or any part thereof in excess of 6 months [Section 25-FFF (2)].

SPECIAL PROVISIONS RELATING TO LAY-OFF, RETRENCHMENT AND CLOSER (Chapter V-B, Sections 25-K to 25-S)

The Industrial Disputes (Amendment) Act, 1976 brought about the following two important changes in the Act :

(1) The provisions of Section 25-C to 25-E shall not apply to industrial establishments to which Chapter V-B applies [Section 25-A (1)].

(2) A new Chapter V-B (containing Sections 25-K to 25-S) dealing with special provisions relating to prohibition of lay-off. Conditions precedent to retrenchment of workmen and closure in certain establishments employing 100 or more than 100 workmen (prior to the Amendment of the Act in 1982, this number was 300), restarting of undertakings closed prior to the commencement of the industrial Disputes (Amendment) Act, 1976, penalty for lay-off and retrenchment without prior permission and penalty for closure, has been introduced.

1. Application of Chapter V-B (Section 25-K)

The previsions of Chapter V-B (Sections 25-K to 25-S) shall apply to an industrial establishment in which not less than 100 workmen were employed on an average per working day for the preceding 12 months. These provisions shall not apply to an establishment :

(a) of a seasonal character, or

(b) in which work is performed only intermittently [Section 25 K (1)].

If a question arises whether an industrial establishment is of a seasonal character or whether work is performed therein only intermittently. The decision of the appropriate Government thereon shall be final [Section 25-K (2)].

2. Definitions (Section 25-L)

The term 'industrial establishment' has been defined for the purposes of Chapter V-B as :

(i) a factory as defined in Section 2 (m) of the Factories Act 1948;

(ii) a mine as defined in Section 2(1)(j) of the Mines Act, 1952; or

(iii) a plantation as defined in Section 2(f) of the Plantations Labour Act, 1951 [Section 25-L(a)].

The Central Government shall be the appropriate Government (for the purposes of Chapter V-B) :

(i) in relation to any company in which not less than 51 per cent of the paid-up share capital is held by the Central Government, or

(ii) in relation to any corporation [not being a corporation referred to in Section 2 (a) (i)] established by or under any law made by Parliament (Section 25-L(b)].

3. Prohibition of Lay-off (Section 25-M)

(i) *Lay-off to be with Permission from Appropriate Government or Specified Authority* : No workman (other than a *badli* workman or a casual workman) whose name is borne on the muster rolls of an industrial establishment to which Chapter V-B applies shall be laid off by his employer except with, the prior permission of the appropriate Government or such authority as may be specified by that Government by notification in the Official Gazette (hereafter in this Section referred to as the specified authority). The permission shall be obtained on an application made in this behalf. If such lay-off is due to shortage of power or to natural calamity, and in the case of a mine, such lay-off is due to fire, flood, excess of inflammable gas or explosion, no such permission shall be required [Section 25-M (1)].

(ii) *Application to be made by the Employer for Permission* : An application for permission under Section 25-M (1) shall be made by the employer in the prescribed manner stating clearly the reasons for the intended lay-off. A copy of such application shall also be served simultaneously on the workmen concerned in the prescribed manner [Section 25-M (2)].

(iii) *Application for Permission to continue Lay-off in a Mine* : Where the workmen (other than *badli* workmen or casual workmen) of an industrial establishment, being a mine, have been laid-off under

Section 25-M (1) for reasons of fire, flood or excess of inflammable gas or explosion, the employer shall apply in the prescribed manner to the appropriate Government or the specified authority for permission to continue the lay-off. The application shall be made within a period of 30 days from the date of commencement of such lay-off [Section 25-M (3)).

(iv) *Order granting or refusing Permission for Lay-off to be communicated to Employer and Workmen* : Where an application for permission under Section 25-M (1) or (3) has been made, the appropriate Government or the specified authority may by order and for reasons to be recorded in writing grant or refuse to grant such permission. A copy of such order shall be communicated to the employer and the workmen. The appropriate Government or the specified authority shall however pass the order after making such inquiry as it thinks fit and after giving a reasonable opportunity of being heard to the employer, the workmen concerned and the persons interested in such lay-off. It shall also have regard to the genuineness and adequacy of the reasons for such lay-off, the interests of the workmen and all other relevant factors [Section 25-M (4)].

(v) *Presumption of Permission if no Order communicated Within 60 Days* : Where an application for permission under Section 25-M (1) or (3) has been made and the appropriate Government or the specified authority does not communicate the order granting or refusing to grant permission to the employer within a period of 60 days from the date on which such application is made, the permission applied for shall be deemed to have been granted on the expiration of the said period of 60 days [Section 25-M (5)]

(vi) *Order binding on All Parties for 1 Year* : An order of the appropriate Government or the specified authority granting or refusing to grant permission shall be final and binding on all the parties concerned and remain in force for 1 year from the date of such order. This is however subject to the provisions of Section 25-M (7) [Section 25-M (6)].

(vii) *Review of Order* : The appropriate Government or the specified authority may, either on its own motion or on the application made by the employer or any workman. Review its order granting or refusing to grant permission under Section 25-M (4) or refer the matter or, as the case may be, cause it to be referred, to an Industrial Tribunal for adjudication [Section 25-M (7)]. Where a reference has been made to a Tribunal, the Tribunal shall pass an award within a period of 30 days from the date of such reference [Proviso to Section 25-M (7)].

(viii) *Lay-off Illegal in Certain Cases* : A lay-off shall be deemed to be illegal from the date on which the workmen had been laid-off :

(a) where no application for permission under Section 25-M (1) is made, or

(b) where no application for permission under Section 25-M (3) is made, within the period specified therein, or

(c) where the permission for any lay-off has been refused.

The workmen in the above cases shall be entitled to all the benefits under any law for the time being in force as if they had not been laid-off [Section 25-M (8)].

(ix) *Exemption* : If the appropriate Government is satisfied that owing to such exceptional circumstances as accident in the establishment or death of the employer or the like, it is necessary so to do, it may, by order, direct that the provisions of Section 25-M (1), or, as the case may be, Section 25- M (3) shall not apply in relation to such establishment for such period as may be specified in the order [Section 25-M (9)].

(x) *Section 25-C to apply* : Where a workman is laid-off lawfully under Section 25-M, the provisions of Section 25-C (other than the second Proviso thereto) shall apply [Section 25-M (10)].

A. No Laying-off if Alternative Employment is offered : Sometimes a workman may be offered an alternative employment (which in the opinion of the employer does not call for any special skill or previous experience and can be done by the workman) by the employer :

(a) in the same establishment from which he has been laid-off, or

(b) in any other establishment belonging to the same employer situated (i) in the same town or village, or (ii) within such distance that it will not cause undue hardship to the workman.

In such a case the workman will not be deemed to be Laid-off provided the wages offered for the alternative employment are the same which would normally have been paid to the workman (Explanation to Section 25-M)

B. Penalty for Illegal Lay-off : The penalty for illegal lay-off is imprisonment up to 1 month or fine up to Rs. 1,000 or both (Section 25-Q).

4. Conditions precedent to Retrenchment of Workmen (Section 25-N)

(i) *3 Months' Notice and Prior Permission of the Appropriate*

Government or the Specified Authority required before Retrenchment : No workman employed in an establishment (to which Chapter V-B applies) who has been in continuous service for not less than 1 year under an employer shall be retrenched by that employer until :

(a) the workman has been given 3 months' notice in writing indicating the reasons for retrenchment and the period of notice has expired, or the workman has been paid in lieu of such notice, wages for the period of the notice and

(b) the prior permission of the appropriate Government or 'such authority as may be specified by that Government by notification in the Official Gazette (hereafter in this Section referred to as the specified authority) has been obtained on an application made in this behalf (Section 25-N (1)].

(ii) *Application to be made for Permission* : An application for permission under Section 25-N (1) shall be made by the employer in the prescribed manner stating clearly the reasons for the intended retrenchment. A copy of such application shall also be served simultaneously on the workmen concerned in the prescribed manner [Section 25-N (2)].

(iii) *Order granting or refusing Permission for Retrenchment to be communicated to Employer and Workmen* : Where an application for permission under Section 25-N (1) has been made, the appropriate Government or the specified authority may, having regard to the genuineness and adequacy of the reasons stated by the employer, the interests of the workmen and all other relevant factors, by order, for reasons to be recorded in writing, grant or refuse to grant such permission. A copy of such order shall be communicated to the employer and the workmen. The appropriate Government or the specified authority shall pass such order after making such inquiry as it thinks fit and after giving a reasonable opportunity of being heard to the employer, the workmen concerned and the persons interested in such retrenchment [Section 25-N (3)].

(iv) *Presumption of Permission if no Order communicated Within 60 Days* : Where an application for permission has been made under Section 25- N (1) and the appropriate Government or the specified authority does not communicate the order granting or refusing to grant permission to the employer within a period of 60 days from the date on which such application is made, the permission applied for shall be deemed to have been granted on the expiration of the said period of 60 days [Section 25-N (4)].

(v) *Order binding on all Parties for 1 Year* : An order of the appropriate 'Government or the specified authority granting or refusing to grant permission shall be final and binding on all the parties concerned and shall remain in force for 1 year from the date of such order. This shall however be subject to the provisions of Section 25-N (6) [Section 25-N (5)].

(vi) *Review of Order* : The appropriate Government or the specified authority may, either on its own motion or on the application made by the employer or any workman, review its order granting or refusing to grant permission under Section 25-N (3) or refer the matter or, as the case may be, cause it to be referred, to a Tribunal for adjudication [Section 25-N (6)]. Where however a reference has been made to an Industrial Tribunal under Section 25-N (6), the Tribunal shall pass an award within a period of 30 days from the date of such reference [Proviso to Section 25-N (6)]. Expiry of period of 30 days does not render the Tribunal *functus officio* nor does the reference lapse in such a case [Association of Engg. Workers *Vs.* Indian Hume Pipe Co. Ltd. (1986) Lab. I.C. 749].

(vii) *Consequences of Illegal Retrenchment* : Where no application for permission under Section 25-N (1) is made, or where the permission for any retrenchment has been refused, the retrenchment shall be deemed to be illegal from the date on which the notice of retrenchment was given to the workman, the workman in such a cast shall be entitled to all the benefits under any law for the time being in force as if no notice had been given to him [Section 25-N (7)].

(viii) *Exemption* : If the appropriate Government is satisfied that owing, to such exceptional circumstances as accident in the establishment or death of the employer or like, it is necessary so to do, it may, by order, direct that the provisions of Section 25-N shall not apply in relation to such establishment for such period as may be specified in the order [Section 25-N(8)].

(ix) *Compensation in Case of Permission for Retrenchment — 15 Days Wages for Every Completed Year of Service* : Where permission for retrenchment has been granted under Section 25-N (3) or where permission for retrenchment is deemed to be granted under Section 25-N (4), every workman who is employed in that establishment immediately before the date of application for permission under Section 25-N shall be entitled to receive, at the time of retrenchment, compensation. The compensation shall be equivalent to 15 days' average pay for every completed year of continuous service or any part thereof in excess of 6 months [Section 25-N (9)].

(x) *Penalty for Illegal Retrenchment* : The penalty for illegal retrenchment is imprisonment up to 1 month or fine up to Rs. 1,000, or both (Section 25-Q).

5. Procedure for closing down an Undertaking

(i) *Application for Permission to close to be made at least 90 Days before the Intended Date of Closure* : An employer who intends to close down an undertaking of an industrial establishment to which Chapter V, B applies shall apply to the appropriate Government for prior permission at least 90 days before the date on which the intended secure is to become effective. The application shall be in the prescribed manner. It shall state clearly the reasons for the intended closure of the undertaking. A copy of' such application shall also be served simultaneously on the representatives of the workmen in the prescribed manner [Section 25-O(1)]. Section 25-O shall not, however, apply to an undertaking set up for the construction of buildings, bridges, roads, canals, dams or for other construction work (Proviso to Section 25-O(1)].

(ii) *Order granting or refusing Permission to be communicated to Employer and Workman* : The appropriate Government may, after making such inquiry as it thinks fit and after giving a reasonable opportunity of being heard to the employer, the workmen and the persons interested in such closure, by order grant or refuse to grant such permission. But before, making any such order, it shall have regard to :

(a) the genuineness and adequacy of the reasons, stated by the employer;

(b) the Interests of the general public and

(c) all other relevant factors.

It shall also record its reasons in writing and communicate a copy of it to the employer and the workmen [Section 25-O(2)].

Where an undertaking is permitted, to be closed down, every workmen who is employed in that undertaking immediately before the date of application for permission under Section 25-O shall be entitled to receive compensation. The compensation shall be equivalent to 15 days' average pay for every completed year of continuous service or any part thereof in excess of 6 months [Section 25-O (8)].

(iii) *Presumption of Permission if no order communicated within 60 Days* : Where the appropriate Government does not communicate the order granting or refusing to grant permission to the employer within a period of 60 days from the date on which the application is made, the permission applied for shall be deemed to have been granted on the expiration of the said period of 60 days [Section 25-O(3)]. In such a case also, compensation shall be payable to the workmen as under Section 25-O(2) [Section 25-O(4)].

(iv) *Order granting or refusing Permission Final and Binding on All Parties for 1 Year* : The order of the appropriate Government granting or refusing to grant permission shall be final and binding on all the parties. Further, it shall remain in force for 1 year from the date of such order [Section 25-O(4)].

(v) *Review of Order* : The appropriate Government may, either on its own motion or on the application made by the employer or any workman :

(a) review its order granting or refusing to grant permission, or

(b) refer the matter to an Industrial Tribunal for adjudication [Section 25-O(5)], in which case, the Tribunal shall pass an award within a period 30 days from the date of such reference [Proviso Section 25-O(5)].

(vi) *Consequences of Illegal Closure* : Where no application for .permission under Section 25-O(1) is made within the specified period or where the permission for closure has been refused, the closure of the undertaking shall be deemed to be illegal from the date of closure. In such a case the workmen shall be entitled to all the benefits under any law for the time being in force as if the undertaking had not been closed down [Section 25-O(6)].

(vii) *Exemption* : Where the appropriate Government is satisfied that owing to such exceptional circumstances as accident in the undertaking or death of the employer or the like, it may, by order, direct that the provisions of Section 25-O(1) shall not apply in relation to such undertaking for such period as may be specified in the order [Section 25-O(7)].

Penalty for Closure (Section 25-R)

Any employer who closes down an undertaking without complying with the provisions of Section 25-O(1) shall be punishable with imprisonment for a term which may extend to 6 months, or with fine which may extend to Rs. 500, or with both [Section 25-R(1)].

Any employer, who contravenes an order refusing to grant permission to close down an undertaking under Section 25-O(2) or a direction given under Section 25-P, shall be punishable with imprisonment for a term which may extend to 1 year, or with fine which may extend to Rs. 5,000 or with both. Where the contravention is a continuing one, the employer shall be punishable with a further fine which extend to Rs. 2,000 for every day during which the contravention continues after the conviction [Section 25-R (2)].

UNFAIR LABOUR PRACTICES
(Chapter V-C, Sections 25-T and 25-U)

The Amendment Act of 1982 has introduced a new Chapter V-C containing two Sections 25-T and 25-U, by which certain unfair labour practices on the part of employers and their unions, and on the part of workmen and their unions have been prohibited and made punishable.

The Fifth Schedule (introduced by the Amendment Act of 1982) to the Act deals with these unfair labour practices. The definition of the term 'unfair labour practice' and the Fifth Schedule have been given in the earlier part of this Chapter.

1. Prohibition of Unfair Tabour Practice (Section 25-T). No employer or workman or a Trade Union, whether registered under the Trade Unions Act, 1926 or not, shall commit any unfair labour practice.

2. Penalty for committing Unfair Labour Practice (Section 25-U). Any person who commits any unfair labour practice shall be punishable with imprisonment for a term which may extend to 6 months or with fine which may extend to Rs. 1,000 or with both.

PENALTIES
(Chapter VI, Sections 26 to 31)

1. Penalties. Sections 26 to 31 deal with penalties for various offences. Penalties provided for in Sections 26 to 30, 30-A. 31 (1) have been dealt with at appropriate places. Section 31 (2) deals with penalty for general offences.

2. Penalty for General Offences [Section 31(2)]. Whoever contravenes any of the provisions of the Act or any rule made thereunder shall, if no other penalty is elsewhere provided by or under the Act for such contravention, be punishable with fine which may extend to Rs. 100.

MISCELLANEOUS
(Chapter VII. Sections 32 to 40)

1. Offences by Companies etc. (Section 32)

Where a person committing an offence under this Act is a company or other body corporate or an association of persons (whether incorporated or not), every director, manager, secretary, agent or other officer or person concerned with the management thereof shall be deemed to be guilty of such offence. But any such person may escape liability if he proves that the offence was committed without his knowledge or consent.

2. Conditions of Service to remain Unchanged during Pendency of Proceedings (Section 33)

(i) *Employer not to alter Conditions of Service or punish for Misconduct during Pendency of Proceedings* [Section 33 (1)] : During the pendency of any conciliation proceeding before a Conciliation Officer or a Board of Conciliation or of any proceeding before an arbitrator or a Labour Court or Industrial Tribunal or National Tribunal in respect of an industrial dispute, no employer shall :

(a) in regard to any matter connected with the dispute, alter, to the prejudice of the workmen concerned in such dispute, the conditions of service applicable to them immediately before the commencement of such proceeding 33 (1) (a)), or

(b) for any misconduct connected with the dispute, discharge of punish, whether by dismissal or otherwise any workmen concerned in such dispute [Section 33 (1) (b)].

(ii) *Standing Orders* : Employer may alter conditions of service or punishment or misconduct in accordance with standing orders or contract for any matter not connected with the dispute [Section 33 (2)]. During the pendency of any proceeding in respect of an industrial dispute referred to in Section 33(1), the employer may, in accordance with the standing orders applicable to a workman concerned in such dispute or, where there are no such standing orders, in accordance with the terms of the contract, whether express or implied, between him and the workman :

(a) alter, in regard to any matter not connected with the dispute, the conditions of service applicable to that workman immediately before the commencement of such proceeding; or

(b) for any misconduct not connected with the dispute, discharge or punish, whether by dismissal or otherwise, that workman.

But no such workman shall be discharged or dismissed, unless he has been paid wages for 1 month and an application has been made by the employer to the authority before which the proceeding is pending for approval of the action taken by the employer.

(iii) *Protection to protected Workman* : No employer shall, during the pendency of any such proceeding in respect of an Industrial dispute, take an action against any protected workman concerned in such dispute :

(a) by altering, to the prejudice of such protected workman, the conditions of service applicable to him Immediately before the commencement of such proceedings; or

(b) by discharging or punishing, whether by dismissal or otherwise, such protected workman.

An employer may do so with the express permission in writing of the authority before which the proceeding is pending [Section 33 (3)].

(iv) Who is a protected workman? A 'protected workman' in relation to an establishment means a workman who, being a member of the executive or other office-bearer of a registered Trade Union connected with the establishment, is recognised as such in accordance with rules made in this behalf [Explanation to Section 33 (3)].

(v) *Number of protected Workmen* : In every establishment, the number of workmen to be recognised as protected workmen shall be 1 per cent of the total number of workmen employed therein subject to a minimum number of 5 protected workmen and a maximum number of 100 protected workmen. For the aforesaid purpose, the appropriate Government may make rules providing for the distribution of such protected workmen among various Trade Unions, If any, connected with the establishment and the manner in which the workmen may be chosen and recognised as protected workmen [Section 33 (4)]

3. Penalty for Contravention of Provisions of Section 33 [Section 31 (1)]. Any employer who contravenes the provisions of Section 33 shall be punishable with imprisonment for a term which may extend to 6 months, or with fine which may extend to Rs. 100 or with both.

4. Recovery of Money Due from an Employer (Section 33-C). (i) Section 33-C(1). Where any money is due to a workman from an employer under a settlement or an award or under the provisions of Chapter V-A (relating to lay-off and retrenchment) or Chapter V-B (dealing with special provisions relating to lay-off, retrenchment and closure in certain establishments), the workman may make an application to the appropriate Government for the recovery of the money due to him. The application for the purpose may also be made by any other person authorised by the workman in writing in this behalf, or, in the case of the death of the workman, his assigns or heirs. Even a discharged or dismissed workman may make an application [Tiruchi Srirangam Transport Co. *Vs*. Labour Court, (1961) 1 L.L.J. 729] for it is not necessary that the workman making application should be in service on the date of his application, but he must have been in service during the period in respect of which a claim is made [M. Manicka Mudaliar *Vs*. Labour Court, (1961) 1 LLJ. 592]. In Abhinash Chandra Gautam through his Legal Representatives *Vs*. Union Territory of Tripura, (1983) Lab. I.C. 1738 (S.C.), the deceased appellant was discharged from service. The discharge was held to be invalid and illegal and he was held to be continuously in service by all Courts and this entitled him to back-wages. The appellant obtained another employment as teacher. The Supreme Court held that he was entitled to back-wages as if his service was uninterrupted. However amount earned in employment of teacher was decreed to be deducted from the total amount of back-wages. If the appropriate Government is satisfied that any money is so due, it shall issue a certificate for that amount to the Collector who shall proceed to recover the same in the same manner as an arrear of land revenue [Section 33-C (1)].

Every application for recovery of money shall be made within 1 year from the date on which the money became due to the workman from the employer proviso 1 to Section 33-C (1)]. Any such application may be entertained after the expiry of the said period of 1 year, if the appropriate Government is satisfied that the applicant had sufficient cause for not making the application within the said period [Proviso 2 to Section 33-C (1)].

(ii) Section 33-C (2). (a) *Provisions* : Where any workman is entitled to receive from the employer any money or any benefit which is capable of being computed in terms of money, a question may sometimes arise as to the amount of money due or as to the amount at which such benefit should be computed. Such a question may, subject to any rules that may be made under this Act, be decided by such Labour Court as may be specified in this behalf by the appropriate Government within a period not exceeding 3 months [Section 33-C (2)]. Where however the presiding officer of the Labour Court considers it necessary or expedient to do, he may, for reasons to be recorded in writing. Extend this period of 3 months by such further period as he may think fit [Proviso to Section 33-C (2)].

(b) *Procedure* [Section 33-C(3) and (4)] : For the purposes of computing the money value of a benefit, the Labour Court may, if it so thinks fit, appoint a Commissioner who shall, after taking such evidence as any be necessary, submit a report to the Labour Court. The Labour Court shall then determine the amount after considering the report of the Commissioner and other circumstances of the case [Section 33-C (3)]. The Labour Court shall forward its decision to the appropriate Government and any amount found due by the Labour Court may be recovered in the same name as an arrear of land revenue [Section 33-C (4)].

(c) *Single Application on Behalf of Workmen* [Section 33-C(5)] : Where workmen employed under the same employer are entitled to receive from him any money or any benefit capable of being computed in terms of money, then a single application for the recovery of the amount due may be made on behalf of or in respect of any number of such workmen [Section 33-C(5). This will, however, be subject to such rules as may be made in this behalf.

Section 33-C. 'Labour Court' includes any Court constituted under any law relating to investigation and settlement of industrial disputes in force in any State [Explanation to Section 33-C].

5. Cognizance of Offences (Section 34)

(i) No Court shall take cognizance of any offence punishable under this Act or of the abetment of any such offence, save on a complaint made by or under the authority of the appropriate Government. [Section 34 (1)].

(ii) No Court inferior to that of a Metropolitan Magistrate or a Judicial Magistrate of the First Class shall try any offence punishable under this Act [Section 34 (2)].

6. Protection of Persons (Section 35)

(i) No person refusing to take part or to continue to take part in any strike or lock-out which is illegal under the Act shall by reason of such refusal or by reason of any action taken by him under this Section, be subject to :

(a) explosion from any Trade Union or society; or

(b) any fine or penalty; or

(c) deprivation of any right or benefit to which he or his legal representatives would otherwise be entitled; or

(d) any disability either directly or indirectly or any disadvantage as compared with other members of the union or society [Section 35 (1)].

(ii) In any such proceeding the Civil Court may, in lieu of ordering a (person who has been expelled from membership of a Trade Union or society to be restored to membership, order that he be paid out of the funds of the Trade Union or society such sum by way of compensation or damages as that Court thinks just. Further the rules of a Trade Union or society requiring the settlement of disputes in any manner shall not apply to any proceeding for enforcing any right or exemption secured by Section 35 [Section 35 (2)].

7. Representation of Parties (Section 36)

(i) *Representation of Workmen* : A workman who is a party to a dispute shall be entitled to be represented in any proceeding under the Act by :

(a) any member of the executive or other office-bearer of a registered Trade Union of which he is a member;

(b) any member of the executive or other office-bearer of a federation of Trade Unions to which the Trade Union referred to in Clause (a) is affiliated;

(c) where the worker is not a member of any Trade Union, by any member of the executive or other office-hearer of any Trade Union connected with, or by any other workman employed in, the industry in which the worker is employed and authorised in such manner as may be prescribed [Section 36 (1)).

(ii) *Representation of Employers* : An employer who is a party to a dispute shall be entitled to be represented in any proceeding under the Act by :

(a) an officer of an association of employers of which he is a member;

(b) an officer of a federation of associations of employers to which the association referred to in Clause (a) is affiliated;

(c) where the employer is not a member of any association of employers, by an officer of any association of employers connected with, or by any other employer engaged in the industry in which the employer is engaged and aulhorised in such manner as may be prescribed [Section 36 (2)].

(iii) *Representation by Legal Practitioners* : No party to a dispute shall be entitled to be represented by a legal practitioner in any conciliation proceedings under this Act or in any proceedings before a Court of Inquiry [Section 36 (3)]. But in any proceeding before a Labour Court, Industrial Tribunal or National Tribunal, a party to a dispute may be represented by a legal practitioner :

(a) with the consent of the other parties to the proceeding and

(b) with the leave of the Labour Court. Industrial Tribunal or National Tribunal, as the case may be [Section 36 (4)1.

Section 36 is not violative of Article 14 of the Constitution or principles of natural justice [Co-op. Store Ltd. *Vs.* Industrial Tribunal, (1987) Lab. I.C. 1557].

8. Power to remove Difficulties (Section 36-A)

If, in the opinion of the appropriate Government, any difficulty or doubt arises as to the interpretation of any provision of an award or settlement. It may refer the question to such Labour Court, Industrial Tribunal or National Tribunal as it may think fit [Section 36-A (1)]. the Labour Court, Industrial Tribunal or National Tribunal to which such question is referred shall, after giving the parties an opportunity of being heard, decide such question and its decision shall be final and binding on all such parties [Section 36-A (2)].

9. Power to exempt (Section 36-B)

Where the appropriate Government is satisfied in relation to any industrial establishment or undertaking or any class of industrial establishments or undertakings carried on by a department of that Government that adequate provisions exist for the investigation and settlement of industrial disputes in respect of workmen employed in such establishment or undertaking or class of establishments or undertakings, it may, by notification in the Official Gazette, exempt such establishment or undertaking or class of establishments or undertakings from all or any of the provisions of this Act. The exemption may be conditional or unconditional.

10. Protection of Action taken under the Act (Section 37)

No suit, prosecution or other legal proceedings shall lie against any person for anything which is in good faith done or intended to be done in persuance of this Act or any rules made thereunder.

11. Power to make Rules (Section 38)

(i) The appropriate Government may, subject to the condition of previous publication, make rules for the purpose of giving effect to the provisions of this Act [Section 38 (1)].

(ii) Rules made under Section 38 may provide that a contravention thereof shall be punishable with fine not exceeding Rs. 50 [Section 38 (3)].

(iii) *Rules to be laid before State Legislature or Parliament* : All rules made under Section 38 shall, as soon as possible after they are made, be laid before the State Legislature, or where the appropriate Government is the Central Government, before both Houses of Parliament [Section 38 (4)].

(iv) Every rule made by the Central Government under this Section shall be laid, as soon as may be after it is made, before each House of Parliament while it is in session for a total period of 30 days. This period of 30 days may be in comprised in one session or in 2 or more suggestive sessions. If both the Houses agree in making any modification in the rule, the rule shall thereafter have effect only in such modified form. If both the Houses agree that the rule should not be made, the rule shall thereafter be of no effect. But any such modification or annulment shall be without, prejudice to the validity of anything previously done under that rule (Section 38 (5)].

QUESTIONS FOR EXERCISE

1. Define the following terms as used in the Industrial Disputes Act, 1947 :

(a) Lay-off, (b) Lock-out, (c) Retrenchment, (d) Strike, (e) Wages, (f) Industrial dispute, (g) Average pay, (h) Continuous service, (i) Public utility service, (f) Award, (k) Workman, (l) Industry.

2. Explain the machinery that exists under the Industrial Disputes Act, 1947 for the settlement of industrial disputes.
3. What authorities have been set up under the Industrial Disputes Act, 1947 for investigation and settlement of industrial disputes?
4. What are the various methods for the settlement of industrial disputes under the Industrial Disputes Act, 1947?
5. What are the duties and powers of Conciliation Officers, Works Committees, and Boards of Conciliation in settlement of industrial disputes? How are they appointed?
6. What are the provisions of the Industrial Disputes Act, 1947 relating to notice for changing the conditions of service? What are the matters in respect of which notice of change is prescribed in the Industrial Disputes Act, 1947?
7. Define 'award' and 'settlement'. When and under what circumstances does an award made under the Industrial Disputes Act, 1947 commence to be enforceable?
8. (a) Who are the persons on whom settlements and awards are binding?

   (b) When do the conciliation proceedings commence and conclude?
9. State the provisions of the Industrial Disputes Act, 1947 relating to :

   (a) commencement of an award;

   (b) persons on whom settlements and awards are binding and

   (c) the period of operation of settlements and awards.
10. Define the terms 'strike' and 'lock-out' as used in the Industrial Disputes Act, 1947. When does a strike or lock-out become illegal?